The Personal Cybersecurity Bible

Jerri L. Ledford

D1519148

THOMSON
————— ✴ —————
™
COURSE TECHNOLOGY
Professional ■ Technical ■ Reference

ISBN: 1-59200-949-2

Library of Congress Catalog Card Number: 2005929808

Printed in the United States of America
06 07 08 09 10 PH 10 9 8 7 6 5 4 3 2 1

THOMSON

COURSE TECHNOLOGY

Professional ■ Technical ■ Reference

Thomson Course Technology PTR, a division of Thomson Course Technology
25 Thomson Place
Boston, MA 02210
http://www.courseptr.com

Publisher and General Manager, Thomson Course Technology PTR:
Stacy L. Hiquet

Associate Director of Marketing:
Sarah O'Donnell

Manager of Editorial Services:
Heather Talbot

Marketing Manager:
Cathleen Snyder

Acquisitions Editor:
Mitzi Koontz

Marketing Coordinator:
Jordan Casey

Project Editor:
Jenny Davidson

Technical Reviewer:
Arlie Hartman

PTR Editorial Services Coordinator:
Elizabeth Furbish

Interior Layout Tech:
Digital Publishing Solutions

Cover Designer:
Mike Tanamachi

Indexer:
Kevin Broccoli

Proofreader:
Anne Smith

For Jennifer Whittington, because you're a cheering section all to yourself.
I love you, girl! You're the best friend anyone could have.
Thanks for being there for me.

} Acknowledgments

The people behind producing a book of any type are always too numerous to count. Book publishing is a team effort, and for their efforts I owe Mitzi Koontz, Jenny Davidson, Arlie Hartman, Elizabeth Furbish, and the rest of the publishing team at Thomson a thank you for their assistance and expertise while putting this book together. Without your efforts, and the freedom that you've given me, there wouldn't be a book. You're a great team to work with, and I'll never be able to tell you how grateful I am for all of your efforts.

Thanks, too, to Lynn at StudioB for keeping me on my toes. I also owe a great debt of gratitude to all of the sources that have helped me over time, sharing their time and knowledge with me. Patrick Gray, Shawn Eldridge, and the rest of you security guys have helped me more than you'll ever know.

I'm most grateful to Sean, Jennifer, and Curtis for understanding and supporting me during the great times and the less-than-great times. Your support makes it easy for me.

A huge **Thank You** also goes out to anyone I've missed. There's always someone, but it's not because I don't appreciate you. It's because I have a brain made of Swiss cheese.

Finally, multitudes of thanks go out to you, the reader. A book is nothing more than paper until someone reads it—only then does it become useful information. Thanks for reading, and I truly hope you find the information here to be useful.

Thank you!

Jerri

About the Author

Jerri L. Ledford is a freelance business technology writer of more than 700 articles, profiles, news stories, and reports appearing online and in print. Her publishing credits include *Intelligent Enterprise*, *Network World*, *Information Security Magazine*, *DCM Magazine*, *CRM Magazine*, *IT Manager's Journal*, *Outsourcing Venture*, and many others. Ledford also develops and teaches technology training courses for both consumer and business users. She has developed courses on security, customer service, career skills, and technology for companies such as Sage Online, Writers' Village University, You Don't Say, LLC., Hewlett-Packard, Gateway, Sony, eMachines, and CNET. The author of *Cut the Cord! The Consumer's Guide to VoIP*, Ledford has published several other books on topics such as Web services, eBooks, and preventing identity theft.

TABLE OF *{* Contents

} Introduction

If you've picked up this book, you probably have some concerns about your personal security while you're using the Internet. Good for you. If you're not concerned about cybersecurity and you only picked up the book because the cover caught your eye, don't put it down! Take the time to read the book, and before you've finished the first half, you'll understand just how at risk you are when you're online. Then you'll be ready to protect yourself.

I speak with people daily who find themselves victimized by all types of cybercrimes, from identity theft to cyber harassment. If you're not protected, you could become a victim, too. And once you've been victimized, protecting yourself becomes so much harder. It's best to reduce your risk as you use the Internet to protect yourself before you become a victim.

The first step in protecting yourself is to understand that you're at risk. After that, getting protected is easy. This book is designed to help you first understand the different threats that you'll face while you're using the Internet. Those threats are numerous, and to help you understand them, the book is comprised of three parts.

The first part of the book covers everything from cyberstalking and cyber harassment to phishing, malware, and other major threats to your privacy and security. In each chapter of Part I, you'll find a detailed explanation of the threat, how it happens, and how you can protect yourself.

Part II outlines the various technologies that you can use to protect yourself. Those technologies include antivirus programs, anti-spyware programs, and firewalls. Each chapter gives you a description of the technology and some guidelines for selecting, installing, and configuring the technology to protect you without making you crazy.

Part III is a section of quick takes on what you should and shouldn't do, as well as checklists and worksheets to help you work your way through the various ways to protect yourself, including using technology. Ultimately, you should come away from the last part of this book with a complete plan for your personal cybersecurity, and if you haven't already put the technologies you need to be protected into place, then you should be prepared to do just that.

In the appendices, you'll find a Jargon Buster! It helps you quickly locate some of the words that you might find unfamiliar. There are also several worksheets and checklists to help you get protected, as well as a comprehensive list of Web sites that you can turn to for additional resources. This list is divided into several topics so that you can quickly locate the resources that you need.

The last appendix is a quick guide you can use to ensure that you're protected from any threats you might face while you're online. This section is divided by topic so you can quickly find the information you need, and is drawn from the chapter on that topic, so that you can quickly find the guidelines each chapter lays out.

In addition to these resources, you'll find several special elements in this book to help you quickly learn about a threat or protection technology. Look for Insider Lingo sections to find the definitions of new terms.

Security Breach sections present personal stories about people who have experienced some type of cybersecurity breach. These stories are from the real world, and serve to illustrate how you can be victimized by cybercrime. You'll also find various tips and notes that highlight important points, offset from the rest of the text.

As we've learned repeatedly over the last few years, cybersecurity is a serious concern for anyone who uses the Internet for any reason. If you use the Internet for financial transactions, you should be even more concerned. It takes hackers or criminals only minutes to gather enough information about you to do serious damage to your good name, financial health, and computer resources. It's your responsibility to be as protected as you can possibly be.

The Personal Cybersecurity Bible is your tool for understanding and meeting that responsibility. I hope that you find the book useful, and if you have questions, suggestions, or feedback, please don't hesitate to e-mail me at JerriLynn@gmail.com. I'd love to hear from you.

Understanding Personal Cybersecurity

You've probably heard the term a hundred times or more—*cybersecurity*—and there's no question that it refers to the security of information in cyberspace. But what exactly is cybersecurity, and how has it become personal?

Personal cybersecurity refers to your security in the digital world. These days computers affect every aspect of your daily life. Your personal use of a computer to communicate, shop, and explore is just one way that computers affect you. Other people also use computers in ways that affect you. For example, when you visit your doctor for an annual checkup, are your records computerized? How many times have you made a purchase from a local store where the clerk who checks you out uses a computer to tally the purchase and then asks for your phone number so the company can send you coupons? How often do you call your bank's information hotline to check your bank account balance?

The proliferation of computers and Internet-based services and e-commerce has changed the way you live and the world that you live in. Today, computers are so ubiquitous they go virtually unnoticed in your daily routine. Unfortunately, these changes are built on fertile ground for a new class of crimes—*cybercrimes.*

Cybercrimes are crimes that are made possible by the digital world. Criminals take advantage of your daily exposure to and use of computers and digital information by capturing that information and using it to commit crimes. Defending against those cybercrimes is cybersecurity. Without it, you might as well be sitting in the middle of a prison full of con artists and thieves wearing a sign that reads, "I'm a sucker."

The problem with cybersecurity is that in most cases it's taken for granted because consumers think that it's someone else's responsibility to keep their information safe. After all, it should be safe to operate your computer and live your daily life without a second thought as to your security and safety. But it's not, and people are quickly beginning to understand how vulnerable computers make their lives.

Your best weapon against cybercrime is a thorough understanding of the threats that you face. Cybersecurity is a vast issue that encompasses many threats. This book is designed to help you understand and combat those threats.

Part I helps build that understanding by introducing you to cybersecurity. Chapters in this section of the book explain what is acceptable in cybersecurity and what's not, and outline what responsibility falls on whose shoulders. So, let's get started, shall we?

1 } What's Acceptable Cybersecurity?

Acceptable cybersecurity. There's a term for you. Many experts say there is no such thing as acceptable cybersecurity. It's either good or it's bad; there's no middle ground. But cybersecurity isn't that black and white—you're either protected or you're not. In between those two points, there are lots of factors that determine how protected or vulnerable you are.

It seems that in the past cybersecurity was taken for granted because cybercrimes only happened to "someone else." Now, however, barely a day goes by without a major news story about a criminal that did this or that online. And the threats to you are overwhelming:

* Your personal information can be captured and sold to anyone in the world without your knowledge or consent, and it could take years for you to realize that you've been victimized.

* Your life savings can disappear in minutes and you might never even know a threat exists. By the time you realize your future has been stolen, it's too late. Chances are the criminal will never be found, much less prosecuted.

* Your trust in retailers can be destroyed in a single transaction and the damage done in that transaction could be astronomical.

There's an endless list of the ways in which cybercrimes can affect you. And there's no exact statistic that points to how much cybercrimes could cost you, though there are statistics for some crimes, like identity theft. Just as an example of how damaging cybercrimes can be, identity theft is said to happen to about one in ten people, and it costs an average of $10,000 per victim.

Think about that. If you know ten people, chances are that at least one of them will be affected by identity theft, and it will cost them about $10,000 from the actual crime to complete recovery. Now, imagine that incidence and cost across all of the ways that a criminal can take advantage of you in the digital world. It's astronomical to even think about, and that's before you take into consideration the loss of privacy and trust that go along with cybercrime.

When you think in these terms it's a little easier to see why cybersecurity is essential. Cybersecurity has so many different levels, and threats are coming at you from so many different directions that it seems nearly impossible to keep up with them all. Every advance in technology leads to a new way that criminals can exploit you. The only way to protect yourself is to be vigilant about cybersecurity.

That leads to acceptable cybersecurity. If you're protected from the current threats and are prepared to react quickly to future threats, then you have achieved acceptable cybersecurity. And regardless of what experts believe about acceptable cybersecurity, if it's enough to keep you protected, that's all that really matters.

The Current State of Security

Ten years ago you didn't hear anything about cybersecurity. Even five years ago there were rumbles about it, but cybersecurity wasn't an issue that garnered a lot of attention. Today might as well be another world or another dimension, because cybersecurity is mentioned on almost every newscast or in every newspaper, and the term has come to have real meaning in almost every computer user's daily life. The terrorist bombings of 9/11 combined with the increasing reliance on technology have brought cybersecurity to the front of every American's mind. Am I protected? Or more accurately, are you protecting me?

The answer is probably not. There are companies out there that are working hard to protect you and your personal information, but the vast majority of them don't work hard enough. It's not that they don't try; it's just that there's too much to keep up with. What's more, you probably make their jobs harder with your behavior on the Internet.

For example, music sharing has become one of the most popular American pastimes. Services like KaZaA and Gnutella offer the ability to share digital music files with anyone, anywhere in the world. In short, it's music for free. The ramifications of that aside, there are serious threats when using these types of services.

One little known fact is that about half of the *peer-to-peer* (P2P) files that are shared through these file sharing sites are corrupted with malicious code such as viruses, Trojans, and spyware. In other words, it's highly likely that if you download two files, one of them could put you at risk.

Many of the companies that control these file sharing services have put virus scans and other types of security in place; however, it's not at all unusual for a malicious hacker to get past these types of security technologies. It's really no problem for an experienced hacker to break through these protections to plant their malicious code within the files that are being shared between hundreds of thousands of users.

An alternative is for the hacker to upload a file that already contains the malicious code. Usually, the hacker will make the file appear to be a song or other piece of media that you're looking for. So, you download the file, unknowingly downloading a virus or something worse, and then when you click on the file to open it the virus or Trojan or whatever *malware* it might be is activated and your machine becomes infected.

INSIDER LINGO Malware: This term literally translates to "malicious software," and defines a piece of software or an application that is specifically designed to complete some malicious task, from stealing usernames and passwords to logging all of your Internet activity.

So, it's your behavior that puts you at risk, and though companies try to protect you, if you are knowingly downloading files from unknown sources, you're eventually going to become the victim of some cybercrime. It's these types of behaviors that the organizations you do business with can't protect you from.

Another example is in your password protection. Most Internet services require that you register with a username and password. Unfortunately, that usually results in one of two behaviors. Either the user creates a password that's not only easy to guess but also the only password they use for every service they subscribe to or they use an ambiguous password but then write it down and post it on a sticky note on the computer.

Either behavior is understandable. After all, the average Internet user is subscribed to sometimes dozens of services or even shopping sites that require a username and password. Keeping up with all of those passwords is tough, so it only makes sense to use a password that you know you'll remember or to write the password down so that you don't forget it. That makes it easy for hackers to get at your personal information.

What all of this leads to is the current state of cybersecurity, and the truth is, it's pretty close to abysmal. There are threats at every turn, and just about every user puts himself in harm's way on a daily basis. One of the strategies that's helped to reduce this problem to some small degree is education, but even education will only go so far. Most users don't want to worry about cyber-security until it's a problem. By then, it's too late and your personal information or even your computer system has become compromised.

Once compromised, your options are limited. You can acquire new e-mail addresses, change Internet service providers, have your PC repaired, or work (sometimes for years to no avail) to have your good name cleared, but these are all activities that take place after you've been victimized to some degree. Your best option is to learn what threats you face before those threats become attacks. Only through this knowledge can you then begin to protect yourself.

Don't be fooled, however. Even the most sophisticated computer users occasionally fall victim to the cleverest of hackers. For example, an experienced computer user who subscribes to online banking services can be tricked by e-mails that appear to come from her bank. Or online auction users can be tricked by e-mail announcements that seem to come from auction sites.

Unfortunately, these schemes are often so sophisticated that you have few options for distinguishing the fraudulent e-mails from real e-mails.

Once such confusion happened during 2004 when PayPal sent out notices to its users that a class-action lawsuit had been filed against the company. Within the e-mail, there was a link which users were supposed to click through to reach a Web site where they could register to become part of the lawsuit.

Many users mistakenly thought that e-mail was a fraud, and contacted PayPal for verification. It was a legitimate e-mail, but users were so convinced that that type of behavior could only be expected from hackers that they identified the e-mail as a scam. On the other hand, many PayPal users get e-mails each day stating they need to update their accounts, with links to a site that looks like the PayPal log in screen. These actually are scams, but many users don't identify them as such and they click through the link and inadvertently give away their personal information.

It's a confusing game of figuring out what's legitimate and what's not. Unfortunately, there's no sure solution for that game. That's due, in part, to the way that organizations have handled transactions such as these in the past. When the threats on the Internet were few, it wasn't at all unusual for a company to request personal information through the mail. And even as threats have become more numerous, some companies have held on to this old way of doing business.

Still other companies aren't consistent in the way they handle these types of situations. For example, one department might have a policy against requesting personal information from users while another department does not and frequently requests that information. It creates a state of confusion for the consumer so that at times you just don't know what the right answer is.

The current state of cybersecurity isn't just based on behaviors. Other factors, such as the speed at which technology changes, also play a role in how you are affected by cybersecurity threats. For example, if you use a Microsoft Windows operating system, you know that there are frequently patches that need to be downloaded and installed for the software. The reason this happens is that in an effort to keep up with demand, operating systems, software applications, and other types of technology are often released before they've been properly tested for security flaws and other bugs.

What's more, your systems aren't the only ones that need to be patched. For example, if you're doing business with an online retailer, they have some *technological backbone* that makes it possible for them to provide an online store. Regardless of the operating system or applications that the retailer uses to provide its services to you, it's likely that there are patches that must be applied to that *infrastructure*.

Unfortunately, what often happens is that downloading and installing those patches is put off by the IT managers in the organization because they are spending all of their time on seemingly more important tasks. It's not at all unusual for an organization to reach a point where they need to install hundreds or even thousands of patches.

What this means is that their systems are vulnerable to hackers who might target those organizations and you, the customer, for an attack of some kind. The missing patches make it possible for the hacker to gain access to these vulnerable systems to misuse resources, gain access to your personal or financial information, or to take the systems over completely to use for larger, more insidious schemes.

It all boils down to one thing. You're at risk. Every time you sign on to the Internet; every time you take part in some transaction on the Internet; even every time you read and respond to an e-mail, you're at risk. And while it would seem that the companies you do business with would be responsible for keeping you safe, in truth, the burden of that responsibility falls squarely on your shoulders.

It's not all bad news and scare tactics, though. With a little information and some solid techniques for creating the right kind of personal security, you can protect yourself from hackers and other criminals that would take advantage of you while you're using the Internet. And it all begins with understanding what risks you really are facing.

Today's Risks

You've heard the doom and gloom theory, now take a look at what you're really up against. The average hacker today is not the pasty-faced young kid looking to create mischief or gain access to free services. A more realistic picture would be that of someone of high intelligence, probably well-adjusted and a useful member of society. These people might even hold down jobs that pay well and are in well-respected professions. It just happens that they've learned that there's an easier way to gain the information and resources that they need than putting in long, hard hours in corporate America.

Another picture that could be equally accurate is that of a member of a high-tech crime ring, run in some third-world country—an international gangster of sorts. Either of these pictures would be accurate, because both descriptions are possibilities. Today's hackers are much more sophisticated than they have ever been in the past. And they're harder to track down.

That makes the risks from these hackers much more dangerous than they ever have been in the past. For example, because of the connectedness of the world today, it's possible that some hacker in New Jersey could steal your credit card number from a Web site as you make a purchase. This hacker might be a moonlighting doctor who needs some extra cash to pay off his student loans from medical school.

Now, he doesn't really view himself as a criminal, so rather than using your credit card number himself, he sells the number to some other—"real"—criminal, who might sell it, trade it, or otherwise pass it on to another criminal. Eventually, the credit card number ends up in Russia or Bosnia where it's used repeatedly until it's maxed out.

Here's the difficult part. The crime, although it originated in the US, has passed into international jurisdiction, and the criminals involved may or may not ever be discovered. Even if they are, it's a pretty good bet that they will never be prosecuted for their crime, because the laws surrounding this type of crime are difficult to navigate. You're out the money and there's no justice in your future.

This is just one scenario. There are so many more that there's no way to go into all of them in this book. What you will learn about are the most frequently used attack methods:

* Cyberstalking
* Cyber Harassment
* Spoofing
* Phishing
* Spam
* Pharming
* E-mail Scams
* Identity Theft
* Credit Card Fraud
* Investment Fraud
* Phreaking
* Hacking
* Auction Fraud
* Viruses
* Trojans
* Spyware
* Worms

It's a long list, and some threats are more prevalent than others. But all are threats that you face every time you use the Internet. Some can be pretty sophisticated, too. In fact, with time, security threats continue to get more and more sophisticated, to the point that sometimes even the experts have a hard time distinguishing the threat.

The good news is that for every threat you face, there is a technology or even just an action that mitigates the threat. It may take a change in your behavior, or you may have to purchase and install an application or piece of hardware, but you can protect yourself. You don't have to give in and allow yourself to be victimized.

Available Protections

Security is one of the largest markets in technology today. There's a simple reason for it, too. You're at risk and you want protection. It's available. There is, however, some discussion as to whether the protection that's available is good enough or not, but that's a topic best addressed in a later chapter.

Protection is available. For example, if you worry about spyware or spam, there are applications designed specifically to prevent spyware or spam from being an issue. If you worry about identity theft, there are several programs that might help, but you need a good dose of precaution to go along with those programs.

Some of the protections that are available to you include

* Firewalls
* Antivirus Software
* Spyware Protection
* Updates and Patches
* Authentication Applications

In addition to these technologies, you need to have a personal security strategy in place. Your personal security strategy is based on your personal security needs. For example, if you use e-mail, but you don't shop online, then most of your security strategy will be focused on how you use e-mail, but there will likely be little that addresses how you shop online. You'll learn more about the personal security strategy in later chapters, but it's important to know that technology alone won't keep you safe. Safety requires action and thought on your part. Your skepticism is probably one of the best security tools that you have.

You have a responsibility to yourself and to others on the Internet to take the steps necessary to protect yourself. Security applications provide some protection, but your behavior as you use the Internet is perhaps the biggest factor in how well you are protected. If you engage in risky habits while using the Internet, you're more likely to become a victim of a cybercrime.

Protecting yourself is usually as simple as understanding the threats that you face. In some cases, you can't know what those threats are. For example, you may know that you're faced with e-mail viruses today, but what will tomorrow bring? You can't predict the future—what you can do is prepare to be as responsive to new threats as possible. And that includes understanding what elements are missing from your personal cybersecurity today.

What's Missing?

One of the topics that has yet to be addressed is the legislation surrounding cybersecurity. In the past, there was little legislation and existing laws had no teeth when the Internet and cybersecurity were factors. No one knew how to handle criminals that used the Internet as their medium of choice.

Thankfully, that's changing. Proper legislation that outlines penalties for malicious behavior using the Internet is currently being debated and passed as quickly as our political system will allow, but until recently this legislation wasn't sufficient to provide the protection that Internet users deserved. It was one of the links that was missing in cybersecurity.

New legislations is being passed, however, that offers you some protection, even if it's still not completely there. For example, in the past a virus writer was greeted with a slap on the wrist if he was caught. Today, virus writers, such as those that scripted the MyDoom virus, are facing stronger penalties, both monetary penalties in the form of restitution, and jail time if they are caught. One recent case of a hacker who gained access to an organization's customer files resulted in the hacker being fined several thousand dollars and put in jail for 12 months.

It's not punishment on the scale of murder or larceny, but it is a step in the right direction. When you consider that it's more than there ever has been in the past, the future doesn't look quite so bleak. There's still a long way to go. Many of the issues that surround cybersecurity, like the global nature of some security threats, still have a long way to go before a resolution is found. However, there is at least movement in the right direction.

Another missing element in cybersecurity is the proper technology. We have some protection technologies in the mix. Firewalls, authentication, and authorization are just a few of them. However, there are some areas where improvements would make all the difference in how at-risk you are.

For example, encryption seems to be a big sticking point for many users. We want to be safe, but we also want to have our freedoms. Therefore, strategies like multi-layer encryption and technologies like *smart cards* are not looked at with much interest in the US. We should learn from our European counterparts and embrace these strategies and technologies with open arms.

For example, identity theft is a huge concern in the US. In Europe, however, it's hardly a concern at all. This is due in part to the differences in the financial services industries of the US and Europe. In the US, we tend to want access to everything very easily and in real time. In Europe, users tend to understand that security comes at a cost, and even if that cost is inconvenience, they are willing to pay it to remain secure.

Only time and insistence from the user community can change issues like these. To date, many of the capabilities that other countries use to protect their citizens go unused in the US because we refuse to allow them to be put in place for fear that we will lose control of our privacy or because we fear giving too much control to someone else.

As time passes, however, this is bound to change. You'll become more comfortable with the concepts that other countries have adopted so readily, and when that happens you'll see security improve to some degree. It's hard to say how much that improvement will amount to, however, because it's hard to see where security will be in the future.

Escalating Threats: A Look into the Future

To be able to see into the future would be one of the greatest gifts that any person or group of people could have. Unfortunately, it's not an ability that we have, so we're left guessing at what the future holds. Security is no exception to that rule.

The threats that you face today are not the same as the threats that you faced yesterday. And they won't be the same threats that you'll face tomorrow. Technology changes, matures, and becomes more sophisticated with time. It's reasonable to expect that security threats will follow the same pattern, and in fact, there's evidence that supports that assumption.

Look, for example, at the e-mail viruses that we faced a few years ago. Most of those viruses were an annoyance capable of eating system resources and creating massive amounts of spam, but not too much more. In contrast, the e-mail viruses of today are much more malicious.

An e-mail virus today can not only use up your system resources replicating itself, but it can also specifically target machines, a group of people, and even a specific segment of a network in an attempt to disable its target completely. It's much more dangerous and costly than in the past.

So the question becomes, what will the virus of the future look like? Perhaps it will install itself on your computer and use only a small portion of your resources for a long period of time. If this is the case, you might not ever know that you've been infected by a virus, meaning that the virus could work for an indefinite amount of time without detection.

Another possibility for the future is viruses that do more than just create havoc on a machine. What if a hacker puts together a virus that not only creates havoc but also burrows through your machine, gathering personal and sensitive information which it sends back to its creator without you ever knowing you've been compromised?

It can happen. It does happen, and as the future unfolds in front of you, you'll likely see many other threats to your personal security develop. This is due in part to advances in technology. The Internet has been one of the best tools that an aspiring hacker can hope to find. There are hundreds of Web sites that tell aspiring hackers how they can gain access to your machine or to another machine with which yours may communicate.

These instructions are easy to read and follow, and in many cases, they're not all that hard to find, either. Of course, law enforcement agencies take these hacker information sites down as soon as they find them, but in many cases, that's just too late. And even if they do find and shut down the site in a reasonable amount of time, the hackers will just create another site that performs the same functions.

There's just no way to know with absolute certainty what the futures holds where security threats and solutions are concerned. The only sure bet is that there will be changes in both, and the best way to protect yourself is to establish a security plan and update it frequently to ensure that you're keeping up with technology. There's more information on creating a cybersecurity plan in Chapter 18.

The threats to you as an Internet user are varied. The solutions are varied. In fact, the only real constant is that you will face security threats. It's best to prepare yourself for every eventuality and hope that you never get to that point. However, if you do, at least you'll know you're protected.

2 } Whose Responsibility Is It, Anyway?

Responsibility is a word that you probably hear far more often than you care to. It seems that we have more responsibilities than we have time to manage, but add cybersecurity to that list anyway, because it should be one of those responsibilities that you pay plenty of attention to.

"Wait a minute!" I can hear you say it. "Am I really responsible for cybersecurity, too?" You better believe you are. If you don't take responsibility for it, it won't be long before some hacker or criminal has you at his mercy. Of course, you won't bear the responsibility all alone, but you *will* bear more of the responsibility than you realize.

Security vendors, application developers, and computer and equipment manufacturers will all do their part in keeping you safe. The problem is, no matter how much they do, how secure you are as you surf the Web and use e-mail programs is a matter of your habits and behaviors. As the famous duo Dan Seals and John Ford Coley put it, "It's all up to you."

Understanding Responsibility

Think about the areas in your life where you are responsible for your own security. Your car or truck is a good example. The manufacturer that designed and manufactured the vehicle that you drive took some steps to ensure your safety. They put locks on your doors and installed gauges and lights to let you know when a problem exists with the car. They probably even included specific safety features like airbags and crumple zones that are designed to keep you safe in the event you're involved in an accident while driving the car. However, those capabilities don't inherently make you safe.

❋ A young lady in Nashville, TN, bought a brand new car. It was her first new car, and she financed it without any help from family members or friends. It was an accomplishment that she was proud of.

During the first week she drove the car, she pulled into a gas station to run in and pick up a soda on her way to work. It was cold outside and she knew that she'd only be in the store for two or three minutes, so she left the engine running. Unfortunately, when she came out of the store, the car was gone. The police found it a few days later, badly wrecked and abandoned.

Is there any facet of that scenario that would lead you to believe that the manufacturer of the car was responsible for it being stolen? They provided the appropriate security capabilities. The car owner simply didn't take advantage of them. All too often, that's how it is with cybersecurity.

Computer manufacturers, operating system designers, application designers, even service providers make security features available to their users. Very often, however, users find those security features to be inconvenient and hard to use, so they just don't. And that's where hackers get you.

The concept of hacking started as a means to gain access to someone else's computer, just to prove that it could be done. Many hackers got their start breaking into university or government computers, because they could. However, the adoption of the Internet for every form of business has created a whole new reason, and a new target, for hackers to do what they do best—gain access.

Today, however, the access is a lot more insidious than it was in the past. Today, access is about gaining access to a person or organization's private information, whether it be financial information, trade secrets, or anything else that might be of value. Hackers and criminals now are using every vulnerability to get to *you* instead of to an organizational machine. If you haven't taken advantage of the security capabilities made possible by manufacturers, programmers, and designers, then *you* put yourself at risk.

So, there's more than enough responsibility to go around. The government has the responsibility to hold criminals and hackers responsible for their actions; the manufacturers, designers, and programmers hold the responsibility for making security available to you; and you hold the responsibility for understanding and mitigating the risk in your behaviors. There's more on each of these responsibilities in the rest of this chapter.

Government Responsibility

Technology in general and the Internet in particular are still young in comparison to a lot of other capabilities that we have in the US. For example, the public school system is still struggling for definition and balance, even though public school has been government-mandated since the

1940s. Before that, public schools were voluntary. They made sense, because the US was making the move into the Industrial Age, but before 1940, the government took a hands-off approach to regulating schools and school systems.

When it became apparent that government involvement might be helpful, the government jumped in. The quality of the results are a matter of opinion, but one thing is sure: The government's involvement in schooling has led to some changes that were pretty positive. Technology is likely to take the same course.

The government tends to take a sit-and-wait approach to technology. This is due in part to the belief that technologies of any type will take their own course without government involvement, and in part to the fact that the government needs to assess the situation before it becomes involved.

Where technology is concerned, the government has waited and now is getting involved in all aspects of technology. Security is no exception. The problem is that government involvement in technology security, specifically as it applies to the Internet, took too long in coming. And that delay leaves us in the spot where we are today—with security a major concern that's become a raging battle in which everyone, the government included, is fighting to keep up with the criminals.

For example, viruses have been a problem on the Internet since shortly after the first virus was released into the wild by Rich Skrenta in 1982. Skrenta's virus was attached to the Apple DOS 3.3 operating system and spread by floppy disk. Since that time, the number of viruses that affect users has grown to more than 100,000. Yet it wasn't until the past few years that the government stepped up and began to create legislation that defines criminal hacking, and creates and enforces penalties for that activity.

Even now, the government is struggling to keep up with hackers and other criminals who use technology and the Internet to victimize consumers like you. For example, the Department of Homeland Security (DHS), which was formed shortly after the terrorist attacks of 2001, is still struggling to reach an acceptable level of security for the US and the people who live in it.

In 2003, DHS formed the National Cyber Security Division (NCSD) to focus on addressing cybersecurity and coordinating the implementation of cybersecurity efforts both in the government and in the private sector. Some of the tasks the NCSD took on include.

❋ Developing a national plan for critical infrastructure protection, including cybersecurity.

❋ Developing partnerships and coordinating with other federal agencies, state and local governments, and the private sector to provide cybersecurity and cybersecurity legislation.

❋ Improving and enhancing public/private information sharing involving cyber attacks, threats, and vulnerabilities.

❋ Developing and enhancing national cybersecurity analysis and warning capabilities.

❋ Providing and coordinating incident response and recovery planning efforts.

- ❋ Identifying and assessing cybersecurity threats and vulnerabilities.

- ❋ Promoting and supporting research and development efforts to strengthen cybersecurity.

- ❋ Fostering training and certification in cybersecurity.

- ❋ Enhancing federal, state, and local governments' cybersecurity.

- ❋ Strengthening international cybersecurity.

- ❋ Integrating cybersecurity with national security.

All of these points are good steps for the government to take; however, it has encountered many setbacks in implementing each of those guidelines. For example, the government has had a most difficult time finding organizations to partner with to improve cybersecurity for the nation, businesses, and consumers.

Nor has the government yet developed a national threat and vulnerabilities assessment. There is also no government or industry contingency recovery plan in development or in place in the event there is a large-scale cybersecurity attack. In short, the government is struggling for every inch of ground that it gains over cybercriminals and hackers.

All of this comes down to the responsibilities that the government has for keeping you safe. As those 11 points, which were outlined by the NCSD, clearly point out, the government has a responsibility for cybersecurity on a national level. Additionally, however, the government has the responsibility of ensuring that proper legislation protects you, and that research into and development of protection technologies continue. At the same time, the government also has a responsibility to mandate certain guidelines or standards that apply to cybersecurity.

There have been some steps taken in this direction. The Sarbanes-Oxley Act is one example of legislation that the government has put in place to protect you. Sarbanes-Oxley outlines for corporations how certain types of personal and confidential data should be handled by the organization, including who has access to it and how it is to be used, stored, and disposed of. Other legislation that mandates cybersecurity protection includes.

- ❋ **Graham-Leach-Bliley Act:** Requires financial institutions to protect the privacy of their customers, including non-public and personal information. Although the legislation refers to financial institutions, many organizations (such as universities and retailers) fall under the definition of financial institutions.

- ❋ **The USA Patriot Act:** Although this legislation refers specifically to terrorism, it does hold some weight in the cybersecurity industry, as it allows for electronic surveillance (including e-mail and other Internet communications), and it allows for some financial surveillance, as well.

- ❋ **Government Information Security Reform Act:** This legislation outlines management controls for how information is handled and secured.

- ✻ **Corporate Information Security Accountability Act:** Outlines certain security policies and procedures that are required of corporations, in addition to mandating security audits for some organizations.
- ✻ **Health Insurance Portability and Accountability Act:** Targeted specifically to the insurance and medical industries, this piece of legislation provides certain security and privacy regulations that pertain to electronic dissemination of your personal information.
- ✻ **CANSPAM Act:** Defines guidelines for organizations that send out marketing materials via e-mail. This act includes guidelines for how you can opt not to have these marketing messages sent to you.

Despite the efforts that the government is making, there's still a long way to go. The hands-off approach that the government has taken to technology and the Internet in the past has left those agencies trailing in the dust of hackers and criminals who have found the Internet to be fertile ground for their schemes. Government agencies are scrambling, but it's going to take them some time to catch up, and that means that effective security needs to be championed by other industries and consumers.

Their Responsibility

When it comes to deciding who has more to lose from cyber attacks, it's a toss up between the corporation and the consumer. According to a survey done by the Computer Security Institute, the average cybersecurity breach costs corporations about $204,000, a figure that has been steadily declining since 2001.

It's possible, however, that those numbers aren't entirely accurate. Many corporations don't share information about cybersecurity breaches because it could reduce public trust in their organizations. That lack of communication is one of the toughest challenges to cybersecurity because it makes it difficult for authorities to know what crimes have been committed and against whom.

High-profile cases of corporate cyber attacks are responsible for some of the increase in security in the corporate world. For example, a security breach at the data brokerage ChoicePoint in 2004/2005 resulted in about 700 people having their identities stolen. When the breach occurred, the company didn't immediately report the incident. Instead, it mailed letters to only the people that had been affected who live in California.

California has a law that requires that type of information be disclosed to its residents. However, there were some 35,000 or more vulnerable records, and the majority of the victims didn't live in California at the time. ChoicePoint says its reason for not sharing news of the breach more publicly in the beginning was that it seemed the breach was related only to people who lived in California. However, it's more likely that the company feared the fallout that would result from public knowledge of the security breach.

There was plenty to worry about. ChoicePoint aggregates information about people that includes social security numbers, credit histories, medical histories, motor vehicle registrations, job applications, law suits, criminal files, professional licenses, and other personal (and often confidential) information. In all, the company aggregates more than 19 billion pieces of information that you might prefer that no one else knew.

That's a lot of power for any single company to weld, and in today's marketplace where customer information is the Holy Grail, many companies have records like these on file for customers and potential customers. For example, think of the number of pre-approved credit card applications that arrive in your mailbox in any given month. Each of the companies that sends you something like that probably has records stored in its corporate computer systems that include your name, phone number, address, and credit history, or portions of your credit history.

That puts a lot of responsibility on the corporation's shoulders. Even those corporations that don't deal in your personal information—application designers, computer manufacturers, and programmers—have a responsibility to supply the tools or applications that help keep you secure when you're using your computer or are on the Internet.

All of those organizations bear some of the security responsibility. For service or application providers, like merchants, online financial institutions, and other service providers, there is the responsibility to put security policies and procedures in place that keep you safe on their side of the fence. For example, your online bank has a responsibility to ensure not only that their Web site is secure, but also that the employees who handle your information maintain security inside the organization. An online merchant has a responsibility to keep its shopping site, including checkout forms and pages, secure, but it is also responsible for keeping your information secure inside the organization.

These security policies and procedures will differ from organization to organization according to the service or application provided, but there should be some common elements no matter who you do business with.

* The corporation or organization should develop and implement an ongoing security program that is regularly audited, assessed, and updated.

* Top management should be responsible for the policies and procedures that the organization implements.

* Specific security strategies should be developed to combat the threats discovered in the security assessment, whether those threats are current or potential future threats.

* The organization or corporation should have a clear means of communicating security policies and procedures across the organization as well as to the consumer.

- ❋ A minimum level of protection should be established and if that level is not achieved, severe penalties should apply to all responsible parties, including third-party security application vendors.
- ❋ Adherence to all established security policies and procedures should be mandatory, not optional.
- ❋ Staff and consumer or user education concerning security policies and procedures needs to be a priority.

Most corporations and organizations have learned the value of good security policies and procedures, even if it was a lesson hard learned. However, that doesn't mean that those organizations are secure. Too many small details have a tendency to slip through the cracks during the normal course of daily workflow. Security patches are a good example.

Operating system patches and application patches are commonplace. In fact, many of the security breaches that occur via the Internet occur because an operating system or application had a flaw or bug that program developers patched after the release of the program. Unfortunately, IT managers are already overloaded with keeping the network and applications on the network operating efficiently. All too often, patching is the last thing on their minds.

It shouldn't be. Patching should be one of the first things on their minds, because patching is a simple step to creating security. However, it's time consuming, and if an organization has hundreds of servers or machines, it can seem to be an overwhelming task. For example, the Microsoft Windows operating system reportedly contains about 35,000 lines of code. According to security experts, an average of about 20 errors need patches in each 1,000 lines of code. Patching all of those vulnerabilities is a full-time task, and that's before you take into consideration any future versions of the application or program.

It would take several IT people weeks to download and apply all of those patches. Fortunately, there are automated programs that can perform this task without anything more than a person to set it up and monitor that the tasks are performed when scheduled.

Technologies like these are designed to make it easier for an organization to meet its security responsibilities. The rub often comes when the bill arrives. Security technologies are expensive at best. Add in applications and technologies to help with the security tasks that need to be performed, and the price tag is astronomical.

That puts some security responsibility onto your shoulders. You must ensure that the companies you do business with take security very seriously. At the same time, you also need to be very serious about security.

Your Responsibility

People—the human factor—it's the element of many systems that makes that system vulnerable. Where security is concerned, people are perhaps the biggest vulnerability, because we're busy, and most of us are not security or technology gurus who know what needs to be done and when.

In 2003, the Blaster worm, a virus that propagated through e-mail, infected more than 120,000 computers in the first 36 hours after it was released into the wild. The worm then launched attacks against specific Web sites causing some sites (the Maryland Motor Vehicle Administration Web site, for example) to shut down.

Two other major viruses hit in 2003. The BugBear.b virus was programmed to determine whether the person receiving it used any of about 1,300 financial institutions listed in its code. If the victim did, then the virus attempted to capture that person's username and password. The other, the SQL Slammer worm, had no malicious payload; however, it infected more than 90 percent of the vulnerable servers worldwide in less than 10 minutes after its release into the wild.

It wasn't special technology or even magic that made it possible for these viruses to spread so rapidly. It was user behavior. Even though most users know not to download attachments from someone they don't know, that didn't stop the users from doing just that. The results could have been devastating if any of the viruses had been just a bit more sophisticated.

They are getting more sophisticated, too. Viruses were mostly nuisances in the past, but today they are carriers for code that is much more dangerous than it has ever been. With user habits not improving much over the past decade, it's only a matter of time before major damage is achieved with a virus or other malware, and what used to take weeks or months to propagate now takes only minutes, making the risk even greater.

Your behavior is the most important responsibility in personal cybersecurity. How you use the Internet and the technologies that go along with it directly affects how safe you are. If you consistently download files that arrive attached to e-mails from people you don't know or if you download files that you aren't expecting, you put yourself at risk.

Of course, downloadable files are just one aspect of the risky behavior that puts consumers at risk. When was the last time you patched your operating system? Just as patches are essential for organizations, they are also essential for individuals. And the same is true for protection technologies such as spyware prevention and removal, firewalls, encryption technologies, and antivirus programs. If you don't use these technologies, you're putting your computer, and any personal or confidential information you have stored on that computer or that you transmit using that computer, at risk.

Your responsibilities don't end at technology, however. Here are some additional security responsibilities that fall squarely on your shoulders:

- ❋ It's your responsibility to familiarize yourself with the security procedures of the organizations with which you do business—and then follow them!

- ❋ You're responsible for keeping your usernames and passwords safe, for making them hard to guess, and for not sharing your accounts with other users.

- ❋ You should report security problems to the proper administrators as soon as you realize there is a problem.

- ❋ It's your responsibility to avoid hacking the system, whether it's the network at your place of employment or another system to which you have (or would like to have) access.

- ❋ Always use the proper security precautions, including proper password methodologies, security technologies, and physical security.

- ❋ It's your responsibility to use properly supported software, not pirated or borrowed copies.

- ❋ You should pay attention to logical security measures, such as updates and patches.

- ❋ It's your responsibility to become knowledgeable about security requirements and guidelines.

One common myth that many people believe is that the systems that they use are protected, whether by the computer manufacturer, the software developers, or the programmers, but the truth is, they may not be. That means for you to truly be safe and secure when you're using your computer and the Internet, you have to take responsibility for your own safety.

You can't rely on others to protect you any more than you would rely on an automobile manufacturer to keep you safe if you don't follow certain guidelines, like locking your doors and wearing your seatbelt. The problem with cybersecurity is that there aren't many established guidelines. Most of your protection comes down to doing for yourself what you used to expect from others.

The operating system example is a good one. You expect your operating system to be safe automatically. It's not. You need to be aware of that, and then you need to know how to make it safe. The same is true for all aspects of cybersecurity. In future chapters you'll learn more about the risks you're facing and how to protect yourself, but the most important guideline that you should know is that you must protect yourself.

It's not difficult. You may need to add technology solutions to your arsenal, but even that won't help you if you practice risky behavior. Therefore, you also have to practice safe behavior. Listen to the experts when they tell you not to download files from strangers or from people you know if you're not expecting the file. Stay away from sites, like those that feature adult content, that are known to be infected with malicious code. And above all else, treat your Internet connection just as you would treat your home or your car. Be cautious.

II | Understanding Cybersecurity Threats

Cybersecurity might be viewed as a war. There's a constant battle going on between hackers or criminals and you, law enforcement agencies, government agencies, and private corporations. What's at stake is money, computer resources, corporate power, trust, even identities—yours and corporations'.

The battlefield is the Internet, or your computer, or corporate networks. Even government networks are at risk. And the only way to win the war is to understand the threats that you face. They may be threats that you're aware of. They may even be threats of which you have no knowledge or understanding.

Winning takes time, and action. The first step is to understand what you're up against. This part of the book is written to give you that understanding. The following chapters look at the different threats that you'll face and they provide you with quick tips for protecting yourself. More detailed protection methodologies follow in the next section of the book.

Arm yourself. Understand your enemy, and understand their plan of attack. Through that understanding you gain an edge in this battle that's likely to rage on for many years.

3 } Overview of Cybersecurity Threats

Cybersecurity has been a problem since the Internet became a global capability. However, before 2000, threats to the Internet and Internet users were usually committed by individuals who just wanted to prove their ability to gain access to a specific system or information. Since 2000, however, threats and cybercrime have grown consistently year after year.

Some years a specific type of cybersecurity threat might decrease, but in those years another type of threat increases. For example, this year the levels of *spam* are decreasing; however, the spam that is sent is far more malicious than it has ever been, and between January 2005 and June 2005, virus-laden e-mails increased by more than 50 percent.

INSIDER LINGO   Spam: Unsolicited e-mail from marketers or advertisers.

In all, the estimates are that cybercrime costs consumers and businesses combined about $1.6 trillion, annually. Add to that the estimate that about 237 million cybersecurity attacks occurred during the first half of 2005, and all of the media coverage of cybersecurity seems to be validated.

There are dozens of ways in which criminals can use the Internet to cause financial and other types of damage, and today there's good reason for those criminals to do it—money! There's money to be had in cybercrime, and criminals, from thugs that used to hide in shadows waiting to steal your wallet to organized crime rings, are getting into the game.

The best way to protect yourself from cybercriminals is to first understand what threats you're facing. An overview of those threats is provided in this chapter. Later chapters will examine each of the threats in more detail.

What Are the Threats?

There are dozens of types of cybersecurity threats to worry about. Within those broad categories of threats there are also sub-categories and specific threats to worry about. But it doesn't end there, because what is a threat today may not be a threat tomorrow. Instead, something new will threaten your privacy, your safety, or your finances.

Some of the threats that you'll face include

* **Denial of Service (DoS) Attacks:** A denial of service attack is a targeted attack in which a hacker or criminal tries to overwhelm a server, mailbox, or computer with the specific intent of bringing down the service provided by that resource.

* **Distributed Denial of Service (DDoS) Attacks:** This type of denial of service attack is most often conducted using a network of personal computers with broadband connections that have been taken over by hackers using viruses, Trojans, or other types of malware to infect the computers.

* **Logic Bombs:** These types of attacks are similar to viruses or Trojans; however, a logic bomb is set to activate at a specific time. Once activated, the malicious payload can rewrite your hard drive, and delete, alter, or corrupt data on your hard drive.

* **Phishing:** Phishing is the practice of gaining access to personal data, including financial data, for the express purpose of financial gain or identity fraud. Phishing techniques include fraudulent e-mails with corrupt links, and spoofed Web sites that collect your personal information without your knowledge.

* **Pharming:** Pharming is also called DNS Poisoning because information on a DNS server is altered so that when you attempt to access a Web site you're redirected to a fraudulent Web site where personal information such as usernames and passwords or financial account information is collected for use or resale at a later time.

* **Trojans:** These are malicious programs that seem to be harmless. A Trojan is usually delivered via an e-mail or in a download, and once on your system, the program can cause damage to the system or can open doors for other programs to cause harm to your system.

* **Virus:** A virus is a program or piece of code that gets introduced to your computer without your knowledge or consent. Once downloaded to your hard drive, the virus propagates and sends itself to other people by attaching itself to some other program or e-mail. Increasingly, viruses also have the capability to harm your computer or programs on your computer. The ability to propagate itself and attach to other programs is what differentiates a virus from other types of malicious programs.

* **Worms:** Worms are like viruses, but where a virus needs someone to send the attachment to another person in order for the infection to spread, a worm can travel from one

computer to another without any assistance from a person. Worms are also capable of propagating, so a single worm on your system could replicate and soon be dozens of worms, all replicating and moving to other computers.

❋ **Internet Fraud:** Fraud takes many forms, and Internet fraud is no exception. Internet fraud can take the form of bogus sweepstakes, money transfer scams, drug advertisements and sales, work-from-home scams, and any number of other forms that are designed to trick consumers into paying for a product or service that doesn't exist or giving away personal information.

❋ **War Driving:** War driving is a practice in which hackers or other criminals cruise around neighborhoods with high-powered computer equipment in their cars looking for unprotected wireless networks. Once the network is found, the criminal parks on the street, gains access to the network, and then uses the network resources for malicious or criminal activities. War driving is related to war dialing, an older version of the same scam in which hackers or criminals used computer programs to dial random telephone numbers until they found a number that allowed them to access the Internet.

❋ **Port Scanning:** Port scanning is a process that involves using a piece of software to scan for open ports, or access points, on your computer. Hackers and criminals use port scanning to find unprotected access points through which they can gain access to your computer. Unprotected ports are one of the easiest ways for hackers or criminals to get into your computer or network.

❋ **Social Engineering:** Social engineering isn't specifically a computer security risk; however, it's the principle on which many Internet security attacks are based. Social engineering is a practice hackers use to convince others that they are someone that they, in reality, are not. This trickery is often used to gain access to personal and confidential information, especially usernames and passwords or financial account information.

There are many other types of security threats that you may face on any given day. Hackers and other criminals will use whatever means they can devise to gain access to your personal information, to your financial information, or to any other information that might have resale value. It's all about what's in it for the criminal.

What's at Stake?

Criminals don't commit crimes without good reason. And hackers don't hack computers without good reason, even if that reason is nothing more than proving their abilities to other hackers. In each type of cybersecurity attack, there's some specific reward in store for the hacker or criminal who completes the job correctly.

In most cases, the reward is money. There's a lot of money in hacking—more specifically in selling information gained by hacking—and many hackers have partnered with criminals for financial gain. It's called hacking for profit, and more and more computer-literate people are realizing that there's money to be had in personal and financial information.

The financial driver for cybercrimes continues to grow, and as it grows, hackers and criminals find easier, faster ways to get the information that they're looking for. For example, one of the newest threats is *botnets*. A botnet is a network of computers that have been taken over with the express purpose of using those computers to complete malicious tasks. Those tasks range from corporate hostage-taking to distributed denial of service attacks.

 **INSIDER LINGO** Botnet: A botnet is a network of computers that have been illegally taken over with the express purpose of using those computers to complete malicious or illegal tasks.

A botnet can consist of hundreds or thousands of computers that have malicious code planted on them that makes them *zombies*. Once the code is implanted, the hacker or criminal can control the zombie from anywhere in the world. And they do. Usually botnets are used for tailored attacks against specific organizations or individuals, and the return on the time invested into capturing these resources and then targeting a corporation or individual can be millions of dollars.

 **INSIDER LINGO** Zombie: A zombie is a computer that has been taken over by a criminal or hacker for use in malicious or illegal tasks. Zombies can be linked to create a network of zombies that encompasses hundreds or thousands of computers.

Financial gain isn't the only driver for cybercrimes. In some cases, it's your computer resources that the hacker is after, as in the botnet example. But there's also your identity. How much is your identity worth?

To you, it's probably priceless. It's the name that you were given when you were born and have since built into everything that you are today. To others, however, your identity might actually have a monetary value.

There are many ways that a criminal or hacker can use your identity. They can commit *identity fraud*, which is to actually take over your identity and try to pass themselves off as you. In identity fraud, the criminal or hacker might open new financial accounts or utility accounts; they may even try to convince other people that they are you. In some cases, identity fraud is committed when an illegal immigrant uses your name and social security number to secure a job.

Another way that a hacker or criminal may use your identity is to steal what is rightfully yours, like the money in your bank accounts or your financial strength where credit accounts are concerned—they may even open new accounts using your credit rating for the basis of the account. To some extent, this is identity fraud, but only inasmuch as the criminal needs to appear to be you long enough to gain access to your accounts. Once they have access, they drain the accounts quickly and move on to the next victim.

Ultimately, however, many security experts believe that what's really at stake is security on a much larger scale. Just as gangs and crime rings affect our physical security on a larger scale— the terrorist attacks of September 11, 2001, are an example—it's possible that cybercriminals could represent a larger threat to our virtual selves.

For example, in March 2005, a group of criminals and hackers targeted the US utility power grid in an attempt to take over that network and gain control of those utility functions. It was an unsuccessful attack that caused only minor concerns in a few areas, but it's an indicator of what the future might hold. In addition to that, the growth of corporate security threats to include hackers gaining access to corporate networks and holding them for ransom is another example of cybersecurity threats that could have much worse repercussions than simply emptying out your bank account.

If a criminal organization were to target all of the companies within a specific industry at one time, they could effectively cripple that industry. Fortunately, it doesn't seem that there are criminal organizations that have that type of power yet, but there's the possibility that they may have it in the future.

Cybersecurity is a risk to many facets of our normal, daily lives on numerous levels. The risk doesn't stop at the individual, or at the corporation, or even at the government. It encompasses all of these factors all of the time. And that's what makes cybersecurity such an overarching concern for everyone, whether they use a computer or not.

Who Is the Criminal?

So you may be asking yourself who the criminal is. There's really no easy answer to that question. Cybercriminals can be anyone, from your next-door neighbor to the guy in the next cubicle at work to that sweet waitress who served you dinner at your favorite restaurant last night. Your doctor, lawyer, dentist, or daughter's best friend might be a cybercriminal. Even your family isn't exempt from the possibility.

The point is that the criminal could be anyone, but usually they fall into one of three general categories:

* People without technical training or knowledge, but with the opportunity to commit the crime. These people are usually in a desperate situation and see the opportunity as their way out. In some cases, these are one-time criminals.

* People with technical training or the knowledge needed to commit the crime. These criminal are motivated by something, usually financial gain, to use their skills to complete these malicious tasks.

* Members of organized crime groups or organizations. This group of criminals encompasses many different groups of people. For example, a terrorist faction might be the driving organization, or a political faction. In some cases, even a corporation is at the center of a rash of cybercrimes because they are trying to steal competitive secrets or put their competition out of business. There are also the standard group of deviants, gangs, and organized crime rings.

What's striking about these categories is that the majority of hackers or cybercriminals fall into the two categories that comprise people who aren't schooled in technology. That points to two trends in cybercrime. The first is the sheer number of people who are committing these crimes. Cybercrime is growing at an alarming rate. That factor leads into the second trend: There is now a glut of information available online that makes it possible for anyone who can read to commit a cybercrime.

For example, there are Web sites on the Internet that tell anyone who reads through those sites how to conduct phishing attacks, how to write viruses, even how to gain access to a computer through security vulnerabilities. These sites—there are reportedly hundreds of them—are often unmonitored, and although you must look closely to find them, if you want to, you will.

Once someone with criminal intent gains access to the information they need to commit a cybercrime, they can generally be defined by the type of cybercrime they commit. Some of the different classifications of criminals are virus writers, botnet operators, phishers, pharmers, and spammers. Of course there are many others, but what generally defines a criminal hacker is what they do.

It's surprising who the criminal is. The once-held belief that cybercriminals are pasty-faced young kids with nothing but time and an abundance of computer knowledge is a thing of the past. Today, cybercriminals can be anyone, and in fact, the Computer Crime & Security Survey of 2003 found that the majority of hackers were independents who were faced with an opportunity and grabbed it. The following list shows the percentage of respondents affected by each type of cybercriminal. You may notice that the total adds up to more than 100 percent. That's because many of the respondents were affected by more than one type of cybercriminal.

- ✳ 82% Independent Hackers
- ✳ 77% Disgruntled Employees
- ✳ 40% US Competitors
- ✳ 28% Foreign Governments
- ✳ 25% Foreign Corporations

As you can see, the criminal can be anyone and everyone. Protecting yourself from everyone is no easy task. It begins with understanding the threats and having knowledge of how to protect yourself.

The Basics of a Cybersecurity Threat

People often worry that hackers and other criminals will try to destroy the Internet, but that begs the question: Why? Why would a hacker or criminal want to destroy his livelihood? The Internet is the way these unsavory characters make money, and they wouldn't want to put that in jeopardy.

Instead, cybercriminals look for virtual vulnerabilities in the systems that access the Internet and then exploit those vulnerabilities to gain access to information which leads to financial gain. It's ironic that we're traversing our way through the Internet Age, and the greatest threat to this age is the Internet. That's because the Internet itself has opened a whole new world of vulnerability.

For example, you would never dream of leaving your home to go to the movies or even just to the grocery store without locking the doors behind you as you leave. But millions of people on any given day leave their computers completely unprotected and don't think twice about it. That's where cybersecurity threats start—with unprotected systems that allow criminals access to private information.

To find these unprotected systems, criminals and hackers use various technologies that either search for the vulnerability or con you into providing information that you wouldn't otherwise give out. It's as if the Internet is an entirely different world where there's no threat to your personal property or financial stability. Unfortunately, that's not true. The Internet is part of this world, and is subject to many of the same threats that you face in the real world.

Once a criminal or hacker has found a way into your system, he can go through any personal information that's stored on your computer, drain your system resources for use on another malicious project, or place bits of code and programs that collect your username and password or account information as you log in to services on the Internet. Once that information is gathered, it's sent to a collection site where the hacker or criminal picks it up periodically and then sells it to the highest bidder, or in some cases to multiple bidders.

It all sounds absurdly easy, but it's not. Carrying out these types of attacks requires some skill and understanding of how the Internet and computer programs work. The criminals or hackers also need to understand how people think. Fortunately for the criminal—and unfortunately for you—user behavior makes a hacker or criminal's job much easier to accomplish.

The Need for Cybersecurity

By now it should be apparent that there's an extreme need for cybersecurity. Organizations attempt to keep you safe to some degree, and there are programs and technologies that you'll learn more about in future chapters that make the job easier, but ultimately it comes down to one thing—your behavior when you're online.

Your habits as you surf the Web and use e-mail programs are your front line to defense. If you download attachments from people you don't know, if you surf the Internet without proper security technologies in place, or if you click through links in e-mails from people you don't know, you're putting yourself and your computer at risk, and that risk could lead to the loss of money or even damage to your computer.

To protect yourself you need to learn how to use the Internet responsibly, and you need to know what to expect from the companies with which you do business online. Then you need to demand that those companies meet their responsibilities in keeping you safe.

Without these strategies, you might as well be walking around with a sign taped to your back that says "Steal my personal information, please."

Cyberstalking and Cyber Harassment

Cyberstalking and harassment are often overlooked as benign crimes that don't contain any real threat, but nothing could be further from the truth. What makes these crimes really dangerous is that law enforcement agencies have just as hard a time with these types of crimes as they do with stalking and harassment in the real world.

Kathryn Howard is a freelancer. In 2003, she had to turn down a potential job because of health issues she was experiencing. It's bad enough to have to turn down a job, but what followed for Kathryn was much worse.

The potential client that Kathryn had to turn away has stalked and harassed her online ever since she turned down the job. The client hounds her constantly with unwanted e-mails, and he even stalks her by following her into online communities. Kathryn has tried numerous times to get this person to stop, to no avail.

What Is Cyberstalking?

Stalking in the real world usually consists of a person following someone despite the fact that the person being followed has made it clear that they don't want the attention of the stalker. The stalker might follow the victim into shopping centers, restaurants, her home, or any other place the victim frequents. *Cyberstalking* consists of the same behavior; it's just carried out in a different environment.

INSIDER LINGO Cyberstalking: The act of stalking a person using the Internet or other electronic capabilities.

Cyberstalkers find targets in a variety of ways. It's estimated that more than 1 million women are being cyberstalked at any given time. It's possible that they simply said something that the stalker found offensive or threatening. In other cases, cyberstalkers choose victims deliberately because of their online affiliations, gender, race, employer, or political affiliations.

The following list describes some characteristics of cyberstalking:

* Cyberstalkers are motivated by a desire to control their victims.
* The majority of cyberstalkers are men.
* The majority of cyberstalking victims are women.
* Victims of cyberstalking can either be strangers or they may be acquaintances of the cyberstalker.
* Cyberstalking can be triggered by a simple obsession brought on by any number of factors, or it can be triggered by a love obsession; False Victim Syndrome, which is the situation in which the cyberstalker believes that his victim is stalking him; or because the cyberstalker believes that he's in love with the victim, in which case the cyberstalker is said to be *erotomanic*.
* Cyberstalking is usually characterized by the relentless pursuit of the victim using e-mail, instant messaging programs, or other means of communication made possible by the Internet.

INSIDER LINGO Erotomania: A condition where a criminal commits a crime because he believes that he or she is in love with the victim and that the victim returns those feelings.

The real difference between cyberstalking and stalking in the real world is the geographical boundaries that exist. In the physical world, a stalker is located in the same city, even the same neighborhood as the victim. The Internet makes it possible for someone who lives on the other side of the world to stalk any victim he chooses.

For example, a cyberstalker could reside on the South Pole, but even if you're on the North Pole, the cyberstalker can make your life miserable. And cyberstalking is easy to do. As long as the cyberstalker has an Internet connection and a little time, he can terrorize you from anywhere he happens to be.

The Internet also makes it possible for a cyberstalker to bring other people unknowingly into the crime. For example, if a cyberstalker has targeted you as his victim, he can use your name in chat rooms and other Internet forums to falsely post inflammatory messages designed to create problems.

The first case of cyberstalking ever prosecuted involved a 50-year-old former security guard. The guard, who had been rejected by a woman, posted false messages on Internet message boards that the victim had rape fantasies. He included the victim's home address and telephone number with the posts, and as a result, the woman was raped.

The security guard story is an extreme case of cyberstalking, but it's proof that it can and does happen—and that the threat from cyberstalking is not as benign as many law enforcement agencies would have you believe.

In most cases, law enforcement agencies treat cyberstalking just as they would any other stalking case. The de facto standard is that nothing can be done about the crime until physical violence actually takes place. It's this very standard that has made it possible for Kathryn Howard's potential client to continue stalking her two years after she turned down the job that he offered.

The other issue that many law enforcement agencies face is a lack of understanding of the crime and how to deal with it. It's hard to prosecute someone who lives in another state or even another country. That combined with confusion in law enforcement agencies about how cyberstalking should be investigated and prosecuted often leaves victims with little recourse.

Another complication is the ability of the Internet to support anonymity. That very anonymity gives cyberstalkers an advantage because with the right knowledge, a cyberstalker (or anyone else, for that matter) can keep his identity hidden from all but the most talented computer experts or hackers.

Cyberstalking is a serious crime, and though it may not have the same repercussions as stalking in the physical world, it's just as dangerous. Cyberstalking often is the precursor to more threatening danger, even physical violence.

What Is Cyber Harassment?

Cyber harassment, like cyberstalking, has its roots in the physical world. Just as you can be harassed in the real world, you can also be harassed using the Internet. Unfortunately, the Internet makes it possible for the harasser to be on the other side of the world, which can make prosecuting this kind of crime very difficult.

 Cyber Harassment: Cyber harassment is the criminal act of harassing or threatening a person with malicious intent using the Internet or Internet technologies.

Cyber harassment and cyberstalking often go hand-in-hand. What starts as cyber harassment can often lead to cyberstalking, or is a part of the process that a criminal uses when cyberstalking his or her victim.

The first cyber harassment case was successfully prosecuted in 2004. In the case, James Robert Murphy of South Carolina was sentenced to 5 years probation, 500 hours of community service, and more than $12,000 in restitution when he was convicted of harassing an employee of the City of Seattle.

The allegations against Murphy included that he sent threatening e-mails to the employee and her co-workers; he formed an anti-fan club against the woman, from which she received hate e-mails and threats; and he used the woman's name to send hate mail and pornographic e-mails to her co-workers.

There's more to the story. Murphy, who had an on-again, off-again relationship with the woman he harassed, also sent false information about the woman's background to her employers trying to get her fired.

There are hundreds of other cases detailed on the Internet, and only about 18 percent of all cyber harassment cases are ever reported to the authorities. In some cases, that's because victims don't know that they should report the crime or they don't think the police or other law enforcement agencies can help them.

In truth, those agencies may not be able to help. Many states have begun to enact cyberstalking and cyber harassment laws, but they are similar to the laws for stalking or harassment in the real world—unless there is some form of physical contact or violence, there isn't much more that law enforcement agencies can do than log a complaint.

That dearth of action makes cyber harassment all the more dangerous because in many instances, cyber harassment is just the first step in the escalation to harassment, even harm, in the real world.

Another issue that makes cyber harassment difficult to deal with is that there are numerous triggers that might set a harasser off. For example, if you are a regular member of an e-mail list or a chat room, anything you say can be misconstrued by a harasser. Even if what you said is taken as it was meant, if you don't agree with the harasser, he may find that reason enough to target you for his malicious behavior. Some of the ways in which these criminals harass people using the Internet include.

* Sending unwanted or threatening e-mails directly. These e-mails may be disguised as coming from a different sender.

- ✵ Sending e-mails that appear to be from you to other people. These e-mails might contain inflammatory statements, or they could possibly contain viruses, pornography, or other unwanted materials. The purpose of this activity is to make it appear that you are being malicious.

- ✵ Signing you up for lists that you don't want to be signed up for. For example, a harasser who has your e-mail address may sign you up for pornography mailing lists, spam mailing lists, or any of a number of other lists or services that flood your e-mail box with unwanted e-mail.

- ✵ Sending you text messages or instant messages that are threatening or demanding. Cyber harassment isn't limited just to the Internet. *Short messaging services* (SMSs) such as text messages or instant messages are a favored tool of cyber harassers, and it's easy for them to find your username or telephone number if they have your full name.

INSIDER LINGO Short Messaging Service (SMS): A service that is available for most cellular telephones that allows short messages to be sent directly to the phone. SMS messages are usually referred to as text messages.

- ✵ Electronic sabotage. The harasser can send you thousands of e-mail or text messages (using an automated messaging program that has the capability to send thousands of messages per minute) in an attempt to shut down your e-mail or cellular phone service.

There are two factors that make cyber harassment truly frightening. The first is that cyber harassment usually takes place in your home or workplace—two places where you feel safe and protected. The other factor is that cyber harassment is often the precursor to a more threatening crime such as stalking or harassment, or even assault, in the physical world.

On a final note, cyber harassment takes on an even more difficult slant when the harasser gets other people involved in the harassment. In some cases, the harasser will post false statements from you in online forums with the express purpose of creating *flame wars*. In other cases, the harasser may gain access to your home address or telephone number—it's easy to do if they have your full name—and post that information along with false or inflammatory statements in online forums. In those cases, other people will call or even come visit you because they disagree with the statements they believe you made.

The Internet offers all manner of ways for a harasser to become someone else, even you. That anonymity creates entirely new problems for law enforcement agencies as they try to track and apprehend criminals that make the Internet and Internet technologies their medium of choice.

What's the Real Threat?

As you've seen, it's a short step from the virtual world of the Internet to the real world, and any criminal who uses the Internet as his playground understands what is required to take that step or to convince others to take that step. That makes these crimes potentially deadly in a real-world setting.

Add to that the confusion that many law enforcement agencies face as they try to track and apprehend cyberstalkers or cyber harassers, and you have a mess just waiting to happen. Realistically, most police departments and law enforcement agencies don't have the manpower or the expertise needed to handle this type of crime.

To you that means that the criminal faces little, if any, repercussion from his actions. And since many law enforcement agencies take the stance that it's not a crime until physical harm is done, then you're left fending for yourself in cyberspace. By the time the crime escalates to the real world, it's already too late for you.

Don't let the picture get too grim, however. In many cases, cyberstalking and cyber harassment are simply nuisances that go away after you change your e-mail address or phone number. It's only the extreme cases where these threats translate to physical threats to you.

That doesn't diminish the impact of the threat, however. It's emotionally draining and very frightening to know that when you open your e-mail box or log on to your favorite chat room there might be some psychotic user who's going to give you a hard time or persuade others to give you a hard time. And in the event that the harassment or stalking does escalate, getting help in the real world could be frustrating.

Ultimately that means that the real threat to you is considerable. Cyberstalking and cyber harassment might be fairly benign crimes, but only until they become serious.

What's in It for the Criminal?

Cyberstalking and cyber harassment are less crimes of monetary gain and more crimes of power. A cyberstalker or cyber harasser has little money to gain from his activities. However, these criminals are not usually motivated by money. Instead, their primary motivation is emotionally grounded.

Cyberstalkers or cyber harassers may commit their crimes:

* Because they believe they are in love with the victim.
* Because they believe the victim is in love with them.

- ❋ Because they believe the victim deserves the harassment because they have angered or wronged the criminal in some way.
- ❋ Because they believe that the victim wants or needs their attention.

The criminal's thinking may not make sense to you. It may not make sense to anyone who doesn't have a degree in criminal psychology. They believe they are justified in their actions and that you deserve, for whatever reason, the attention they are focusing on you.

For the criminals who commit the crimes of cyberstalking or cyber harassment, the payoff is emotional. It's usually centered around having the power to affect you in some way, and what's most likely to stop the crime is to take that gratification or power away from them.

Anatomy of a Cyberstalking or Cyber Harassment Threat

The reason that a cyberstalking or cyber harassment case gets started isn't always the same. It's possible that you said something that the criminal doesn't agree with. Or perhaps you had a relationship with the person in the past that didn't work out. It may even be that you are affiliated with an organization or religious group that the criminal finds offensive.

Regardless of what the reason is, something sets the cyberstalker or cyber harasser off, and he feels the need to contact you repeatedly to share his disapproval. Depending on your response, the criminal may become more and more obsessed with you and contact you more often and in more ways.

If you respond to the e-mails, instant messages, or text messages—especially if you respond with annoyance or anger—you risk alienating the criminal further, which serves only to fuel his desire to contact you. In all cases, cyber harassment and cyberstalking are about power. The criminal needs to feel in control. He needs to feel as if he is the center of your life, and he will take whatever steps are necessary to make it so.

If over time you don't respond to the criminal, he may move on to another victim. However, in some cases that serves only to create an intense need or desire for that person to hear from you, so he may escalate his intimidating behavior by conning other people into harassing you as well. The criminal may even convince someone to take the threats to the next level and approach or harass you in the real world.

In either case, only two things stop the harassment. The criminal either focuses on another victim, which usually happens when he feels you have gotten what you deserve, or you make yourself completely unavailable for him to harass or stalk. That's a difficult task to do, especially if the criminal has your full name.

A quick Web search and a small amount of cash yields more information about you than you would ever knowingly release to someone. This is because there are *information aggregators* who collect, organize, and store public information about you which they turn around and resell to anyone who has the money.

INSIDER LINGO

Information Aggregators: Individuals or corporations that collect public information about you, organize it in a manner that's accessible by other people, and then resell that information to anyone who can afford the price they are asking. Information aggregation is a legal practice, and many organizations, such as creditors or employers, purchase this information during background checks and pre-employment screenings.

It's surprisingly inexpensive and very easy for anyone interested to purchase a file that has information such as your last known address, previous address, credit accounts, even medical information and contact information. Many Web companies, like Intellus or ChoicePoint, are built on this practice of aggregating and selling personal information.

If the cyberstalker or cyber harasser doesn't find another victim to focus on, it's entirely possible that he will eventually escalate the threat into the physical world, at which point he could show up on your doorstep and possibly begin stalking or harassing you.

One young woman, Amy Boyer, was being cyberstalked by an emotionally unstable criminal. He obtained her social security number over the Internet and used that number to find out her license plate number and place of employment. He then detailed his plans to kill Amy on a Web site he posted under her name. Within minutes of the criminal's last entry to the Web site, Amy was murdered as she got into her car at work.

The incident that resulted in Amy Boyer's death eventually led to a piece of legislation called Amy Boyer's Law, which prohibits the sale or display of a person's social security number to the public, including over the Internet, without the person's permission. The law also outlines penalties for anyone who is convicted of the crime. Unfortunately, the legislation was too late to help Amy Boyer.

It's frightening how easy it is for someone with an unhealthy obsession or abnormal interest in you to begin haunting your every move. Your best protection, under these circumstances, is to know who you are in contact with and to ensure that the people you communicate with are who they say they are.

Tell-Tale Signs

Cyberstalking and cyber harassment aren't difficult to discern. Your first clue will probably be the hateful or threatening e-mails that you receive from your stalker or harasser. Of course, threatening or hateful e-mails by themselves don't constitute cyberstalking or cyber harassment, but it's one sign that something might be amiss.

If you receive repeated hateful or threatening e-mails, instant messages, or text messages, then you probably are being stalked or harassed. Another sign that someone has targeted you for cyber harassment or cyberstalking is if you block an annoying person from one type of communication and he begins to contact you through another type of communication.

For example, if you block someone that has been sending you threatening e-mails and he suddenly starts harassing you in chat rooms, you're being cyberstalked. If he starts sending you threatening instant messages, then you're being harassed.

Cyberstalking and cyber harassment can take many forms. In one case, a woman complained to the US Attorney General's office that a man had been cyberstalking and cyber harassing her 9-year-old daughter. The criminal had been posting messages on online forums stating that the child was available for sexual encounters and giving the family's telephone number.

Local police were unable to help the family stop the problem. Their solution was to tell the victims to change their phone number. Eventually, the FBI was called in to investigate the crime, but not before the emotional damage had already been done to the girl and her family.

One final clue that someone is targeting you for cyberstalking or cyber harassment is if you suddenly start receiving e-mails for lists that you did not join. The same is true if you start receiving e-mails from people who are upset by a comment that you supposedly made, but you did not actually make it. It's not uncommon for a cyberstalker or a cyber harasser to post inflammatory messages with your name attached to them. This is the criminal's way of indirectly giving you a hard time.

There are no hard and fast rules that state, "If this happens you're being cyberstalked," or "If this happens you're being cyber harassed." Instead, it takes some interpretation. If you are repeatedly bombarded with unwanted messages or hateful or threatening e-mails, it's best to err on the side of caution and assume that you *are* a victim of these crimes.

Cyberstalking and cyber harassment are serious crimes. If the crime isn't handled, it can eventually escalate to physical violence. Even without the physical violence, the trauma of the crime is enough to keep an individual fearful of her every move for years to come.

SECURITY BREACH

Another case of cyberstalking and cyber harassment involved a woman who had met a man through the Internet. They chatted online for a while before the relationship took a frightening turn. Suddenly, the man was everywhere that the woman went. He sent hundreds of threatening e-mails. He bought the woman's social security number, home address, and telephone number online and called her house and spoke with her children.

He even called her co-workers and spoke with them. The woman tried every avenue she knew to get help with extracting this stalker from her life, but no one seemed to know how to help her. Time and again she was told that without some physical threat or harm, there was nothing that could be done to stop the harassment and stalking.

Fortunately, the stalker was eventually caught in another state for harassing and stalking another woman. He was eventually put in jail and prosecuted for the crime, though the sentence that he received amounted to a slap on the wrist for bad behavior.

To prevent a cybercriminal from stalking or harassing you, you should learn how to protect yourself. There are a few steps that you can take to avoid the unwanted attention of unstable individuals.

Protect Yourself

Even if you don't have any worries that a cybercriminal might try to stalk or harass you, you should take some precautions to prevent the crime from ever happening. Most of the precautions are common sense, and though they may be a little inconvenient at times, your safety is worth it.

Here's what you can do to protect yourself from cyberstalking and cyber harassment:

* Use gender neutral and age neutral usernames and e-mail addresses.

* Avoid giving out your personal information for forum and e-mail registrations.

* Check your *Internet Service Provider's (ISP's)* policies about harassment, cyberstalking, and other abusive behavior to be sure that you have recourse if someone starts exhibiting abusive behaviors.

* Use caution with e-mail signatures. Use signatures for business communications, but turn them off when you're posting to online forums or answering e-mails that aren't business related.

* Request that your name be removed from information aggregators or location services such as 411.com, Switchboard.com, and WhoWhere.com.

> ❋ Getting your name removed from one of the information aggregators should be easy. Some companies have a form included on their Web site that lets you request removal; others may require a print letter or a telephone call. The aggregator's Web site should have a page that lists directions for getting your name removed, though you may have to spend a few minutes searching for the information, because the site owners won't make it easy for you to find.

❋ Use automated filtering programs, such as those included in Microsoft Outlook and Outlook Express, to block unwanted messages or messages from unknown sources.

Despite your best efforts, it's possible that you could still become the target of a cyber harasser or a cyberstalker. If you do, you don't have to deal with the abuse. There are steps that you can take to stop the abuse as soon as you realize that it's becoming a problem.

If you suspect that someone is harassing or stalking you online, here's what you can do:

❋ The very first thing to do is begin collecting the communications from the person who is harassing or stalking you. If it's e-mails, print them off and keep them all together in a file. If it's instant messages, log and print them. For text messages, save the messages to your phone. These records are important should it ever become necessary for you to turn to law enforcement agencies.

❋ Avoid contact with the stalker or harasser. If you must, and you know who the abuser is, send a single, clear request to the stalker or harasser to cease all communications in all forms. Once that message is sent, resist the urge to respond to any messages in the future, no matter how much you might want to state your own thoughts and feelings on the matter.

❋ Report the abuse to your ISP as soon as it begins. If the ISP can't or won't do anything to help, continue reporting the abuse at regular intervals, and keep copies of all the requests that you send.

❋ Contact the police and file a report. When you contact the police, be very clear in your explanation of what's happening and be sure to let the officer taking the report know that you have supporting evidence of what's happening to you. However, don't be surprised if you don't get a lot of cooperation from your local law enforcement agencies. Most don't have the personnel or expertise to put much time or effort into cybercrimes that don't involve monetary losses.

❋ Visit SpamCop (http://www.spamcop.net) to have the e-mails that are sent from the criminal analyzed and to have the criminal's ISP contacted about the unwanted messages. SpamCop requires a free registration, but the reporting service is also free.

❋ Report the cyberstalking or cyber harassment through the WiredSafety Web site (https://www.wiredsafety.org/forms/stalking.html). You must report the abuse first to local law enforcement agencies and then on the WiredSafety Web site. Once you report it, site volunteers will work to help you resolve the issue.

Cyberstalking and cyber harassment are serious crimes. Take personal responsibility for protecting yourself, but understand that no matter how you try, it's possible that someone could target you anyway. If that's the case, know how to stop the abuse before it turns into something more than threats and harassment.

5 } Spoofing, Phishing, and Other E-mail Scams

Spoofing, phishing (pronounced "fishing"), and other types of e-mail scams are the most frequently occurring security attacks on the Web. They also represent among the costliest risks to Internet users, both in the amount of money that these scams squeeze from unsuspecting Internet users and in the fact that these scams are often a preamble to identity theft. Unfortunately, more than 30 percent of Internet users don't know how to recognize these scams.

However, none of these scams are new. What is new is the technology. Spoofing and phishing have roots in old paper scams that affected hundreds of thousands of people before computers ever came into being. Hoaxes have been around since the beginning of time, and spam is what used to be called junk mail. Today's technology just makes it easier for hackers, thieves, and other malicious characters to reach thousands more people in a fraction of the time. And so it becomes a numbers game, with hackers and thieves counting on even a small response to these kinds of scams.

Before we go into a more detailed explanation of what spoofing and phishing are and what some of the other e-mails scams might be, let's run some hypothetical numbers. Say, for example, that a hacker or thief wants to see how much money he can steal from unsuspecting Internet users. This malicious person then sends out an e-mail to 100,000 people, pretending to be from the account management department of a well-known bank. The e-mail warns that an account is about to be deleted, and it is requesting that you verify your account by providing personal information that will allow the attacker to have access to your bank account or credit card. This doesn't take long using an automated e-mail system and software that configures potential e-mail addresses. And who cares if some of the e-mails bounce back, right? The attacker isn't in this for perfection; he's in it for quick cash.

So, the e-mails go out. Assume that about five percent of those e-mails bounce back as undeliverable. That means that 95,000 e-mails actually landed in real people's e-mail boxes.

Now, assume that only five percent of the people who received the e-mail actually respond to it and provide account information as well as a username and password. In total the attacker will receive access to 4,750 accounts. And he'll gain that access in a matter of hours.

If we are true to the national average, only about 40 percent of those accounts will have a balance the hacker can access. That puts him at a total of 1,900 viable accounts. Conservatively, assume that he manages to grab an average of $200 from each account. In reality, the amount he receives will vary by account simply because some victims will have more money available than others. But for this example the average is about $200 per viable account.

That means the attacker or thief has access to $380,000. Ridiculous, isn't it? Here's the truly scary part: This hypothetical attacker has accomplished this in a span of less than 24 hours and it was very inexpensive, if it cost him anything at all. It will take each of the victims anywhere from four weeks to about two years to clear up the bogus charges or withdrawals, and it could cost them thousands of dollars.

Spoofing and phishing attacks alone are increasing at a rate of nearly 100 percent per month. There are upwards of 2,000 bogus e-mails circulating at any time, trying to con users out of sensitive information. More than 57 million consumers received bogus e-mails requesting account information in 2003. And it costs them more than $2.4 billion each year.

What Is Spoofing?

Spoofing is a type of social engineering. Someone attempts to steal personal, private information by tricking a person into believing they are communicating with a legitimate person or entity, when in fact, they are actually communicating with a criminal who wants nothing more than to steal their information. It's a con game where the con artist uses technology to accomplish the con. Spoofing on the Internet usually takes the form of an e-mail or Web site that purports to be from someone or some entity that it is not.

A spoofing attack usually starts with an e-mail that appears to be from a business entity with which you may or may not do business. eBay and PayPal are two companies that are often targeted as the corporate victims of spoofing attacks. In the case of eBay or PayPal, a user receives an e-mail that claims something has changed and users are asked to re-register or update their account. Typically, a direct link to the Web site is included.

When the users click on the link within the e-mail, they are taken to a site that looks and acts like the site they are expecting, but in truth, it's a "shadow copy" of the site—a false world. Behind the scenes, access to the site is actually funneled through the attacker's computer so that he can monitor all of the victim's activity and collect any information he wants.

If the user clicks through the e-mail to the Web site, then the attacker can cause false or misleading information, such as log-in prompts, to be sent to the user. Information such as username and password requests are controlled by the attacker, and when the user enters this information, the attacker records it for future use.

Spoofing isn't always about stealing your personal information, however. Although that's usually why a hacker or criminal will employ spoofing tactics, sometimes it's just about fooling you. Some hackers only want to see what they can accomplish with their computer skills, and spoofing is one way to fool you into believing something that isn't true. Using spoofing skills, those hackers will gather only the information needed to gain access to your system without doing any actual harm to your computer or your finances.

Conning Strategies

There are two triggers in spoofing attacks that work well for getting users to divulge sensitive information. The first is the tone of the message. It is usually written in a manner that creates excitement in the recipient. For example, Figure 5.1 is a spoofed e-mail that was sent to users, trying to get them to provide "banking details" to keep their account from being deactivated.

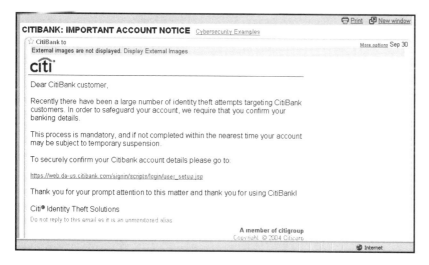

Figure 5.1

This is a spoofed e-mail that appears to come from Citibank.

As you can see, the e-mail attempts to elicit a sense of urgency in the recipient. Attackers count on you being very excitable when it comes to financial accounts, because when we're upset or have a sense of urgency, we don't always stop to think about the validity of such an e-mail. The thought process is, "It looks official, and the company says I need to do something now, so I must need to do it."

In truth, most companies, including financial institutions, would never ask you to divulge sensitive information via the Web or through e-mail any more than they would call you out of the blue and ask you to give them that information over the phone. Even if they did, you have no way of knowing that it's really the bank on the other end of the line, so you would probably not give them the information.

Instead, when a bank or other financial institution has a problem, the most likely course of action that company would take would be to send you a letter, in the mail, requesting that you call them. In that case, you know you're connecting with an authentic bank employee, because you've called them using a phone number you can verify with the branch office.

Only when you've connected to the bank on your terms would they request your personal or sensitive information.

The second trigger that often draws doubtful users into a spoofing attack is the context of the attack. The context—pictures, text, appearance, and timing of events—will often elicit a response to a spoofing attack.

One way to think of contextual clues is as being like road signs. Experienced drivers respond to road signs without much thought because they've seen these signs so many times. Contextual clues on Web sites work much the same way. Interface designers spend their time designing Web site elements that elicit specific behavior from Web users. Attackers simply borrow those elements.

For example, you receive an e-mail that isn't quite right. You have some level of doubt, but you click through a link included in the e-mail and it takes you to a Web site that has the correct company logo and the correct "feel" of the site you're expecting. You immediately feel more secure. After all, it looks like the official site.

That's often where many people get taken, however. Using a piece of software that can be obtained on the Internet for free, a hacker can build a Web site that pulls objects such as logos, graphics, text, and navigation bars from other Web sites. For example, the attacker can design a Web site that looks and feels like the Citibank Web site, simply by using a snippet of code that tells the bogus site to retrieve the graphics or other elements from the real site. What you see is a Web site that looks exactly like the Citibank site, even though the address for the site might be something different.

In some cases, the attacker may even use another snippet of code to camouflage the Web site address bar or the status bar, making it look as if you're at the expected Web site, when in fact it's just a small window on top of the attacker's site making the site appear legitimate.

For all of this trouble, spoofing attacks result in users unknowingly providing the attacker with sensitive information. In some cases, the attacker simply sits behind the Web site and watches passively, recording information such as passwords, account numbers, and usernames for later use to access existing accounts or create new accounts.

In more sophisticated versions of spoofing scams, the attackers can even alter information traveling to you or from you to someone else. For example, assume you've entered into a spoofed Web session unknowingly. During the time you're on the Web, you surf several Web sites and then decide to make a purchase at a well-known e-commerce site. During the purchase process, you're asked to submit your shipping address. When you click the "submit" button on the ordering page, the attacker then can alter the shipping address to have the item shipped to some other location. It's also possible for the attacker to change quantities, item numbers, or any other information that will be transmitted electronically.

Even more alarming is the fact that it is possible to spoof the whole Web, just as easily as a single page or Web site can be spoofed. And it uses the same technology, so even when you're on a trusted Web site, you could be at risk. Attackers can plant fake links on any popular Web site without the knowledge of the Web site owner or administrator. They can also trick search engines into indexing parts of fake sites.

It starts with URL rewriting. The attacker uses a piece of software that rewrites all of the Web links on a legitimate Web site to point to the attacker's Web site. So the URL http://www.yoursite.com becomes http://www.attackersite.com/http://www.yoursite.com.

When you click on a link on the legitimate site, you're taken to the attacker's site. You believe you're still on the Web site you intended to be on, because the rewritten URL directs the attacker's Web server to borrow elements or even whole pages from other Web sites. At this point, you're trapped in the attacker's false Web, and the only way to get out is to close out of your browser completely.

What Is a Phishing Attack?

Phishing is a type of spoofing. The same basic definition and principles apply. The only real difference is that the attacker's purpose is always to gain sensitive information, whereas spoofing attacks are sometimes just about misleading the victim, without theft being the object of the attack.

Phishing, which began in 1996 as an attempt by hackers to obtain AOL customers' usernames and passwords, has grown into a multi-million dollar business. And in January 2004, more than 175 unique phishing attacks were reported by the Anti-Phishing Working Group. That's an increase of over 50 percent from December 2003, just one month before.

One recent phishing attack used the FDIC and Department of Homeland Security as a lure to draw people into divulging sensitive information. More frequently, phishing e-mails target financial institutions and e-commerce sites.

 "Phishing is the hottest and most troublesome new scam on the Internet"
—FBI

A phishing attack that affected many people at a critical time was a campaign contribution solicitation sent to John Kerry (and even some George Bush) supporters during the last few weeks of the 2004 election campaign. The e-mail claimed to have come from Kerry's brother and asked people to contribute to the campaign by clicking a link in the e-mail.

When users clicked on the link, they were taken to a Web site that looked like Kerry's campaign Web site. Only the most observant of users realized that the Web site was actually http://www.JohnKerrys.com (John Kerrys, not John Kerry). The e-mail was discovered and one day later the Web site collecting the information was taken down, but the number of people who were potentially victimized by the site was never determined; it could have been in the thousands.

The longest living phishing site on record was up for 31 days before authorities removed it, but the average spoofing or phishing Web site is only active for 6.1 days. During that time, however, thousands of people will hit that site. And what makes phishing more difficult to control is that in many cases, the site owner usually lives in another country, making the site difficult to trace and remove. In fact, two-thirds of attackers are located in countries such as South Korea, China, and Russia (three of the top countries for committing cybercrimes).

Other E-mail Scams

Spoofing and phishing aren't the only game in the scam arena. Simpler e-mail scams and hoaxes are also numerous.

One e-mail hoax that circulates constantly is the wealthy foreigner scam. It's also called the Nigerian money scam, because in many cases, the sender claims to be in Nigeria. And there are several versions of this scam.

One of the most basic is an e-mail that claims to be from a politically persecuted family member whose politician-relative was killed by the government. It goes on to explain that the government has frozen the deceased's financial accounts and won't release the money to family; however, it will release the money to someone from another country and asks the person receiving the e-mail to assist this family member in collecting the money. For your troubles, you're offered a sizable cut of a multi-million dollar fortune.

Ultimately, the e-mail is more of an annoyance than anything, but follow it through, and you could get taken, because at some point you'll be asked to provide your bank account information to have your cut of the money wired into it. This hoax, like most of them, has less threat of serious damage than spoofing or phishing because most people catch on before it reaches that level. It's really more of an irritation, especially after you've received it a few dozen times.

There are dozens of variations on these hoaxes. You may have seen some of them:

- ❄ An offer for a once-in-a-lifetime business opportunity.
- ❄ An offer to work from home for "easy money."
- ❄ A notice that you've won a lottery that you never entered.
- ❄ Unbelievable investment opportunities.
- ❄ An offer for cable descrambler kits.
- ❄ An award of a vacation or an offer of a vacation as a promotion.
- ❄ An announcement of slave reparations.
- ❄ Many charity petitions, especially for children who are ill.
- ❄ Claims that a teacher needs your assistance tracking something through e-mail for a class project.
- ❄ Claims that Bill Gates or another large company will pay you to forward an e-mail.
- ❄ Petitions.
- ❄ "News" about celebrity deaths, especially those that request an action on your part.
- ❄ Warnings of viruses, hoaxes, and potentially dangerous situations.

There are many examples of these types of hoaxes. Here are a few that you might find interesting:

- ❄ **The Britney Spears Hoax:** As you can see in Figure 5.2, this hoax claimed that Britney Spears had tried to commit suicide, when in fact she had made no such attempt. And this was not the first time Britney was the subject of such a hoax. Previously, rumors were circulated that she had been killed in a car accident.

> 12:03 (CNN) NY - Britney Spears, the pop music diva, was rushed to New York Cornell Medical Centre early this morning with symptons of an apparent drug overdose, sources said. Ms. Spears, 22 years old, has been in New York the last week promoting the release of her latest CD, "In The Zone", and was said to be recovering after receiving medical attention. There is no timetable for her release, say those close to the situation.

Figure 5.2
The Britney Spears suicide hoax.

- ❄ **Phone Number Hoax:** Telephone hoaxes have been around as long as the telephone. The Internet simply provides a much wider audience that can be reached much faster. The method of this scam is usually an e-mail that claims that your e-mail address has been placed on a list of people that want to receive bulk e-mails. To have your name removed from the list, a phone number is listed for you to call. The problem is that the phone number is usually a premium number, and the cost of calling that number can be anywhere from $2 to $6 per minute.

❋ **Plug-In Fragrance Hoax:** Plug-in fragrances are one of the hottest home care items on the market. Dozens of companies offer them and millions of people use them. If you're one of those users, an e-mail that looks legitimate and warns that they cause a fire hazard gets your attention. It's a hoax. Figure 5.3 shows one version of the e-mail.

Figure 5.3

The plug-in fragrance hoax.

Friends,
My brother and his wife learned a hard lesson this last week. Their house burned down...nothing left but ashes. They have good insurance, so the home will be replaced and most of the contents. That is the good news. However, they were sick when they found out the cause of the fire.

The insurance investigator sifted through the ashes for several hours. He had the cause of the fire traced to the master bathroom. He asked my sister-in-law what she had plugged in in the bathroom. She listed the normal things. ...curling iron,blow dryer. He kept saying to her, "No, this would be something that would disintegrate at high temperatures." Then, my sister-in-law remembered she had a Glade Plug-in in the bathroom. The investigator had one of those "Aha" moments. He said that was the cause of the fire. He said he has seen more home fires started with the plug in type room fresheners than anything else. He said the plastic they are made from is a THIN plastic. He said in every case there was nothing left to prove that it even existed. When the investigator looked in the wall plug, the two prongs left from the plug-in were still in there.

My sister-in-law had one of the plug-ins that had a small night light built in it. She said she had noticed that the light would dim....and then finally go out. She would walk in a few hours later, and the light would be back on again. The investigator said that the unit was getting too hot, and would dim and go out rather than just blow the light bulb. Once it cooled down, it would come back on. That is a warning sign.

The investigator said he personally wouldn't have any type of plug in fragrance device anywhere in his house. He has seen too many burned down homes.

Thought I would warn you all. I had several of them plugged in my house. I immediately took them all down.

The list and number of hoaxes that circulate on the Internet are endless. Every organization can be named, and no one with an e-mail address is immune to them. Though usually these types of hoaxes are nothing more than an annoyance, some can be costly. And unfortunately, recovering the money you lose in any e-mail scam could take months or years, if it happens at all. In many cases, the originator of the scam used a bogus e-mail address, or worse, a valid e-mail address stolen from a person who is completely unaware of what's happening. In either case, the e-mail address may be traceable, but the person who sent the e-mail is not.

Protecting Yourself
The best thing you can do to protect yourself from any kind of e-mail scam is to look at every e-mail with a high dose of skepticism—even e-mails that seem to come from someone you know. Although you may recognize the e-mail address, there is no way to be certain that the address hasn't been stolen or borrowed with malicious intent.

Be Skeptical

View all e-mails with skepticism, and never provide personal, private information through e-mail. Unless you have a security program installed that directly addresses the security of e-mail, you can't know who is viewing that mail as it makes its way to its final destination. For that matter, you don't know who has viewed, and possibly altered, e-mail that you receive. E-mail is not a secure means of communication, so don't send anything through e-mail that you wouldn't pass around to everyone you know.

It's also important to stay calm when you're dealing with information that comes to you through the Web. For example, if you get an e-mail from a financial company with which you do business, and you're told that your account has been deactivated, take a deep breath before you respond to the e-mail. Better yet, don't respond at all. Instead, take the time to call the company to handle the issue. Yes, it will require a few minutes more than if you were to do it online, but the ultimate result of that extra time could mean the difference between your financial security and years spent trying to clear up an identity theft case.

This is especially true of any e-mail that asks you to provide a username, password, or account number. Legitimate companies don't ask for that kind of information through e-mail. When in doubt, call the company.

Fortunately, there are some common clues that might alert you to a spoofing or phishing attack. Figure 5.4 is a phishing e-mail with some of the most common clues labeled. In many cases, you have to be very attentive to find these clues.

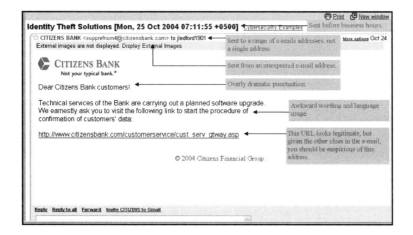

Figure 5.4
Some of the most common errors that can be found in phishing e-mails.

In addition to the clues labeled in Figure 5.4, you may also see:

✿ **Unexpected Return Address**: A return address from some domain other than the site the e-mail purports to come from.

⁂ **A Strange Web Link**: One character you may see in the Web address is the "@" symbol. Typically, Web site addresses don't contain that character. So, if you see a Web site address that looks like this: http://www.companysite.com/@www.anotheraddress.com, be suspicious!

⁂ **Grammatical Errors**: Although criminals are catching on, many attackers still seem to be English language challenged. The result is stilted word usage, misspellings, incorrect punctuations and capitalization, or missing words. A professional within a real organization would not make these mistakes.

Avoid Click-Through Links

One element that many spoofing or phishing e-mails have in common is a click-through link that takes you to a Web page that is supposed to belong to a legitimate company. In fact, many times the Web page does belong to a legitimate company, and the attacker has simply laid bogus elements over valid elements of the page in order to steal your sensitive information.

Don't click onto the Web through an e-mail. Instead, open a new browser window and type the company's main Web site address into the address bar of the new browser. From the front page of the site, you can then navigate to wherever you need to go. And if there's a problem with the site, there will usually be an announcement on the front page of the site.

> ⁂ Don't type or cut and paste the same Web site address that appears in the e-mail you receive into your browser window. This is probably a bogus Web site, or at best it is the legitimate site with fake overlays that an attacker is monitoring. If you go to the company's front page (i.e. http://www.yourbank.com), then you can navigate through the site safely.

Don't Fill Out E-mail Forms

Some scam e-mails will look like a form, and you'll be asked to fill the form out and return it to the return-to address that is automatically generated when you reply to the e-mail. Don't fill that form out. Instead, call the company to find out if they really need the information for which you've been asked.

Check E-mail Headers

When in doubt about the validity of an e-mail, you can always check the header to see if it comes from who it seems to come from. Some of the things to look for, as illustrated in Figure 5.5:

⁂ Origin

⁂ Relay

⁂ Final destination

❊ IP address

❊ Domain name

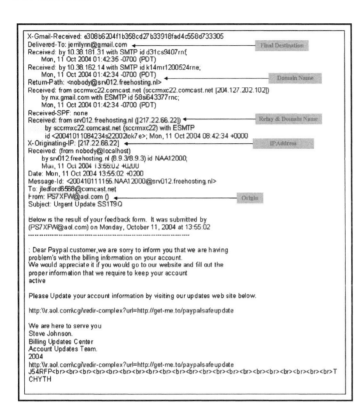

Figure 5.5
The header of this spoofed e-mail about a problem with a PayPal account is labeled with the elements to look for when determining the validity of an e-mail.

Check Web Site Security

Secure Web sites have a designation in the address bar that lets you know they are secure. For example, a regular Web site address looks like this:

http://www.yourbank.com

A secure Web site address looks like this:

https://www.yourbank.com

The https indicates that the site is secure. It literally means Hyper Text Transfer Protocol Secure. And usually there is a small icon that looks like a lock in the lower right-hand corner of the browser screen.

❄ **INSIDER LINGO** Hyper Text Transfer Protocol Secure: The secure version of the communication protocol used on the Web; this protocol provides limited authentication and authorization for commerce sites on the Internet by sending your username and password in an encrypted format rather than as plain text.

❄ The secure indicators are not always foolproof. Although you should always check to be sure that a Web site to which you are providing sensitive information is secure, these indicators can be spoofed by savvy hackers with a little bit of JavaScript know-how. Always use extreme caution when providing sensitive information, even to trusted Web sites. If the site feels wrong or something seems out of place, call the company instead of using the Web site.

Disable JavaScript

JavaScript is the programming language generally used in building Web sites. Hackers with JavaScript knowledge can mimic or imitate any element of a Web site in a manner that makes it virtually invisible to the site's users. JavaScript, ActiveX, and Java all tend to facilitate spoofing, phishing, and other cyber attacks.

Disable these capabilities if you're planning to spend a lot of time on the Internet. You will lose some functionality, but the extra protection is worth it. And if you really need to have one of these applications running, you can selectively enable them, as needed.

To enable or disable JavaScript:

NAVIGATOR 3.x

1. From the main menu, go to Options | Network Preferences.
2. Click on the Languages tab.
3. To enable, check the Enable JavaScript box.
4. To disable, uncheck the Enable JavaScript box.
5. Restart the browser.

COMMUNICATOR 4.x

1. From the main menu, go to Edit | Preferences.
2. Select Advanced panel.
3. To enable, check Enable JavaScript box.

4. To disable, uncheck Enable JavaScript box.

5. Restart the browser.

EXPLORER 3.x

1. From the main menu, go to View | Options.

2. Click the Security tab.

3. To enable, check the Run ActiveX scripts box.

4. To disable, uncheck the Run ActiveX scripts box.

5. Restart the browser.

EXPLORER 4.x

1. From the main menu, go to View | Internet Options.

2. Click on the Security tab.

3. Select Custom and click on Settings.

4. To enable, select Enable under Active scripting.

5. To disable, select Disable under Active scripting.

6. Restart the browser.

Stay Vigilant

Protecting yourself from attackers who use spoofing, phishing, and other types of e-mail scams isn't easy. These scams get more and more sophisticated every day, and even cybersecurity professionals are amazed at how quickly hackers can adapt to avoid being stopped by or even to use new technologies to their advantage.

Vigilance is the best protection. Stay wary of all Internet communications, and view everything with a critical eye. Add those elements to your security plan, and you'll be far safer.

Report Suspicious E-mails and Web Sites

There are many organizations working to keep you safe online. However, if users don't let them know when a spoofing or phishing attack occurs, or that there is a hoax e-mail circulating, these organizations can't help.

If you receive an e-mail that you think is suspicious, report it to the agencies listed next. Be sure to include the entire message with all header information intact, but don't forward the message because that causes some information to be lost. Some organizations even have specific guide-lines for reporting spoofing or phishing on their Web sites.

❋ **Anti-Phishing Working Group:** http://www.antiphishing.com

❋ **Internet Fraud Complaint Center of the FBI:** http://www.ifccfbi.gov

❋ **Your ISP**

❋ **The company targeted by the attack**

Reporting an attack can be a lot of work. It will probably take you from 15 minutes to about an hour, depending on how long it takes to track down the abuse e-mail addresses for your ISP and the target company. But the sooner these companies are alerted to scams, the sooner they can shut them down. And even if you didn't fall for this scam, one may come along in the future that will affect you. These organizations can help keep that from happening.

6 } Identity Theft

Here's a riddle: What are you given at birth, work to build throughout your life, and might continue to be known as after you die?

The answer: Your name. It's the one thing that truly belongs to you throughout your entire life. Your personality develops around your name, people know you by your name, and in many cases, you acquire "stuff" with monetary value based on your name.

So what would happen if someone stole your name to use as his or her own? It happens all the time. In fact, it's happened as many as 27.3 million times to Americans in the past five years. It's called identity theft, and it's one of the fastest growing crimes in the US.

What Is Identity Theft?

Identity theft has become so much of a problem that suddenly you hear about it every day. There are stories about identity theft on your nightly news channel, on the Internet, and in the newspaper, and people might even pass stories they've heard on to you at work or at social functions.

 **INSIDER LINGO** — Identity Theft: The stealing of personal information such as social security numbers and credit card numbers with the specific intent to use that information fraudulently to obtain access to personal and financial resources.

It's not that identity theft is new. It's not. As long as people have been around, there have been a few bad souls who pretend they are someone they are not for the purpose of obtaining something that the person they are impersonating has or has access to. What's different now is that the Internet makes it much easier—and much faster—to steal a person's identity.

SECURITY BREACH

Organizations such as the Red Cross and the Internal Revenue Service (IRS) can be used to draw people into an identity theft scam. For example, one scam involves a donation request from the Red Cross. The request comes to your e-mail box with a file attached that seems to be a donation request form. When you click to download the file, the form is downloaded, but an executable file is also opened and installed on your computer. The executable file uploads the completed donation request form to a Web site that does not belong to the Red Cross.

Another scam was an e-mail that claimed to be from the IRS. The e-mail contained an attached executable form and instructions that the form must be filled out to avoid penalties or other repercussions. Like the Red Cross scam, the form, when completed, was uploaded to a Web site that did not belong to the IRS.

In both of these scams, the identity thief sent the messages and then collected the forms once they were uploaded to the bogus Web site. The forms all contained private information such as social security numbers, which the thief could sell or use for other financial gain.

Identity theft is so much a problem now that more than 246,000 people in the US alone fell victim to identity theft in 2004. It's estimated that worldwide around 10 million people each year are victimized by identity theft. In fact, identity theft is so prevalent that it happens almost twice as much as any other type of fraud. Some estimates are that 13 people every hour have their identity stolen.

Today's technology makes stealing someone's identity easy to do. In the past, it was necessary to have a person's social security number to steal his identity. Today, all a criminal needs is your name and address. In most cases, the criminal can find any other information he needs by using search engines and information aggregation companies on the Internet.

Technology even enables thieves to steal your identity without having your full name and address. For example, with an account name or username and password, a criminal can gain access to and clear your checking account in a matter of minutes. If the criminal is looking for a long-term haul, then all he or she needs to do is change the address on your credit accounts and request new cards.

It's frightening how prevalent—and how easy—it is for someone with malicious intent to gain access to your identity and all the power that it holds. You've worked for years to build your name and reputation, and a thief can undo all of that in a matter of hours.

How Does Identity Theft Affect You?

There are two broad types of identity theft: financial identity theft and personal identity theft. Within those two categories there are dozens of subcategories or different types of identity theft.

For example, a criminal can commit financial identity theft by stealing enough information about you to open new credit accounts in your name. That type of identity theft is financial identity theft, but it's also personal, because the criminal is pretending to be you to some extent. It's called *identity fraud*.

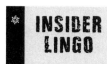 **INSIDER LINGO** — Identity Fraud: A type of identity theft where the criminal not only steals your personal information but also pretends to be you. Identity fraud usually contains elements of social engineering.

In financial identity theft the criminal is specifically trying to gain access to your personal financial information. To gain access to this information, the criminal might use any number of different tricks or scams. For example, a hacker or criminal might send an e-mail like the one shown in Figure 6.1. This e-mail is designed to excite the recipient with the threat of account termination. True to many e-mails of this type, there's a click-through link that the person receiving the e-mail is supposed to follow to provide information that will keep his account from being suspended.

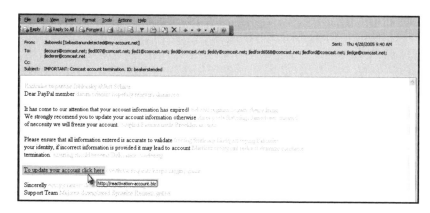

Figure 6.1

An e-mail from a hacker or criminal that's meant to mislead the person receiving the e-mail into providing personal, confidential information.

One thing that's notable about the e-mail in Figure 6.1 is that the click-through link actually leads to a different Web site than you would think. In this case, the link leads to the site http://www.reactivation-account.biz, rather than to a PayPal or Comcast account Web page. It's not entirely unbelievable that the Web site URL would lead to the address that appears when you hold the cursor over the URL for a few seconds, but it's unlikely, and the fact that the URL ends in the .biz extension is certainly a red flag since both PayPal and Comcast have .com domains.

❄ The URL: http://www.reactivation-account.biz was determined to be a phishing site by Digital PhishNet, a joint effort by Industry and Law Enforcement. To protect users who might go to that site now, the page that was there when the phishing e-mail was sent has been replaced by an alert page to let you know that the original site was bogus. In some cases where phishing is discovered, this is the type of protection you can expect.

Finally, this particular e-mail is obviously sent by someone who is a novice at attempting to steal personal information. The first clue that it's a bogus e-mail is the contradiction between the subject of the e-mail, which says a Comcast account is being terminated, and the body of the e-mail, which says a PayPal account has expired. As if that's not enough, the "To:" field contains multiple e-mail address, all very similar. This is a sure sign that someone is attempting to score your username and password or account information.

Personal identity theft is targeted at your personal life rather than your financial life. For example, a criminal may decide that you have unfairly attained a certain status or place in life. On the Internet, perhaps you're a well-respected member of a mailing list that this criminal also belongs to. Because the criminal believes that you don't deserve the status that you have, he will work to discredit you by pretending to be you.

In this example, the criminal or hacker might send inflammatory e-mails that seem to come from you, or he may find a way to gain access to your username and password so that he can send or post messages from your account. You're the only person who knows that they aren't real, and you can't prove it because the identity thief has access to your account.

In the physical world, personal identity theft consists of someone taking your name as his or her own. For example, a criminal can obtain your name, address, and social security number using the Internet and then use that information to start new cell phone, telephone, and utility accounts. There are even reports of illegal immigrants stealing names and social security numbers online so that they can work here in the US without being deported. The criminal in a case like this is usually only caught when the IRS realizes that too little taxes are being paid on the income that's generated by a single social security number.

Both types of identity theft lead to one thing—damage to your name and reputation. Sometimes it takes years for this damage to be realized, but it happens. In addition to this damage, however, there is often financial damage that occurs. Depending on whose estimate you believe, the average amount of money that identity theft costs its victims is between $600 and $2,000. That amount can be considerably more or considerably less, according to how quickly you catch the crime and how much purchasing power you have.

In some cases, financial companies will absorb a portion of these costs, on a voluntary basis. You can be responsible for a certain dollar figure; usually $50 if theft is reported within a specified amount of time. And if you don't discover the crime within that time frame, you can be held responsible for the entire amount that is stolen from you.

The crime of identity theft is most often committed to gain access to your personal identity or your financial identity, but the effects of the crime don't stop there. It's not at all unusual for an identity theft victim to suffer from the same mental anguish that other crime victims suffer from. Add to that shame and embarrassment, and there's so much more at stake from identity thieves that just the loss of your name or your money.

What's in It for the Criminal?

Identity theft is a lucrative gig for most criminals. For example, assuming that an identity thief is using *phishing* as a tool to steal identities, he can expect about a 5 percent return on the number of e-mails sent to potential victims. So, if the identity thief sends out 100,000 e-mails with the express intent of gathering credit card numbers, he can expect a response from about 5 percent of those e-mails. That's 5,000 responses to those e-mails.

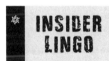 **INSIDER LINGO** Phishing: A cybercrime that involves trying to gain access to private or personal information using fraudulent claims or false identities and accessing Internet resources to convince victims to give up this sensitive information.

Now, given that the national average is that only about 40 percent of people have an available balance on their credit card, then only about 2,000 of those credit card numbers will have any value. Taking a final, conservative step, assuming that the criminal gets $200 from each of those 2,000 credit card numbers, the total money available to the criminal will be about $400,000. And the criminal can score that amount of money in a few hours. It's not bad for a day's work.

It's also possible that the criminal is simply collecting credit card numbers to sell to another criminal. If that's the case, the identity thief will probably be paid a set amount per card number, whether or not there is any purchasing power available to that number. When the card numbers are sold like this, the identity thief might make slightly less money, but there's far less work involved, and he or she gets paid whether there is an available balance on the card or not.

In the case of personal identity theft, there are several payoffs for the thief. The first is your identity, which is especially valuable to a person whose identity is worthless to them. For example, if you have a black-sheep cousin who has never amounted to anything, chances are his identity is worthless. He can't get credit; he can't open a checking account; he can't even open utility accounts because the deposits are too high.

Your identity solves that problem. By stealing and using your identity, suddenly that worthless cousin is capable of opening utility accounts, opening bank accounts, maybe even buying a car or a house. And it's a pretty good bet that you'll never know what's happened until you try to purchase your own home or car, or when you start receiving collection notices or foreclosure notices in the mail. It's happened to thousands of people in the US.

Another payoff for a personal identity thief is your accomplishments. In some cases of identity theft, the primary motivator is jealousy. The thief believes that your life should have been his or that you don't deserve the life you have, so he sets out to take over your life. Remember the movie *Single White Female*? It was the story of two female roommates, one normal and one psychotic. The psychotic roommate tried to take over the normal roommate's life. It happens outside of the movies, too, though usually not with such drastic consequences.

There is a lot to gain from stealing identities, and until recently, the penalties for identity theft were lacking. It's no wonder that many individual criminals and crime rings have turned to identity theft as a means of financing their operations. There's money to be made in addition to other types of gains.

Anatomy of an Identity Theft

There are dozens of ways in which identity theft can take place. The most common way that identity theft starts is through non-technological channels. However, the rapid adoption of the Internet and e-mail has brought an entirely new facet to identity theft. What used to take weeks or months to accomplish can now be accomplished in minutes or hours.

Yet another example of an identity theft scam that involves a government agency is a letter circulating to military families. The families are asked to click a link in the e-mail that is supposed to take them to a Web site where they register for a special tax refund that is available online to military service members. The link in the e-mail leads to a fraudulent Web site and when the victim clicks through the link and fills in his personal information, it's collected and sold by an identity thief.

Typically, when the crime of identity theft is committed using the Internet and the capabilities it allows, the crime starts with an e-mail containing a false claim that an account that belongs to you is in jeopardy of being shut down because it's out of date or because of some other type of violation. The e-mail usually has a link in it which you are supposed to click through to a Web site where you're asked for your username and password or account number.

When you enter your username and password or account number (and in some cases, you'll be asked for all three) and click to submit that information, there's most often a short delay and then an error page appears, or you're redirected to a page that looks just like the one you were on and asked to resubmit the same information.

The first time you submitted the information, it was collected by a *keylogger* or other pieces of code and stored on a server somewhere until the criminal downloads and access or sells the information. At that point identity theft is just beginning. It's the first and most critical step to gaining control of your identity.

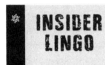

INSIDER LINGO Keylogger: An application used to capture and record keystrokes. Originally, keyloggers were used as diagnostic tools in software development, but today many hackers and criminals use them to collect usernames and passwords or other sensitive information as you type it into your computer.

The second time you are prompted to enter the information, it's because you have been returned to the legitimate Web site, where you haven't actually entered your username and password yet because you entered it for the benefit of the hacker the first time.

This is just one scenario, however. It's possible for hackers or criminals to steal your identity without you doing anything other than what you would normally do. For example, a blank e-mail might contain a keylogger that is installed on your computer without your knowledge. Then every keystroke that you enter is logged, and each time you access the Internet, that information is downloaded to the hacker's server or storage site.

You never know what's going on until weeks, months, or years later when you discover that you've become a victim of identity theft, and even then you may not know how, or even when, your identity was originally stolen. Some victims have been able to track the theft back ten years or more. Others never figure out when the identity was actually stolen, only that it was and tens of thousands of dollars in damage have been done.

One often-overlooked risk for identity theft is a dishonest employee in an organization with which you do business. One case of identity theft involved an employee stealing the credit card information of customers that made purchases through the company's online channel. Once the order was submitted, the employee printed off copies of the order, including credit card information that she later used to purchase goods using the Internet herself. This thief collected more than $200,000 in goods bought with stolen credit card numbers before she was caught.

SECURITY BREACH

Finally, there's the ChoicePoint fiasco that took place in early 2005. ChoicePoint is an information aggregator that collects information about people that is a matter of public record (and in some cases, private record). The company collects and organizes the information for the purposes of pre-employment and background checks. Unfortunately, ChoicePoint wasn't able to control who had access to those records.

A criminal used social engineering techniques to con his way into ChoicePoint as a client purchasing background checks on its employees. Once the criminal had access to ChoicePoint's system, he accessed hundreds of thousands of records which he then used for illegal purposes. It's still unclear how many of the people whose records were accessed actually fell victim to identity theft, and it could be years before the whole story is told.

Tell-Tale Signs

Identity theft can be hard to spot, and the reason that your identity was stolen could make it that much more difficult to uncover. However, there are a few signs of identity theft. Some of them are obvious, whereas others are less obvious, but if you know what you're looking for, you can spot them.

* Watch your postal mailbox. Identity thieves often change the billing address on your accounts to have the bills redirected to another location in hopes that you won't notice the theft. If you suddenly stop receiving credit card bills, call your credit card company to find out why.

* Examine your credit card statements closely. The cleverest of identity thieves don't max out your credit cards immediately. Instead they find ways to drain the money slowly, in small increments that are less likely to be noticed. If you find charges that you haven't made, immediately contact your credit card company to dispute the charges.

* Watch your e-mail box closely. If you begin receiving notifications about new accounts or if the volume of spam that you ordinarily receive becomes greater, it's possible that someone has stolen your identity and is using it to open new accounts or sign up for new services.

* Check your credit report regularly. Experts recommend that you check the report at least one time each year, but it makes more sense to check your credit report quarterly. Examine the report closely and look for accounts for which you have no records or for activity on accounts that you don't use. These are signs that someone may be using your name and credit rating to establish new accounts or re-activate old ones.

> ※ As of September 2005, everyone in the US is entitled to one free credit report each year from each of the three major credit reporting agencies—Experian, Equifax, and TransUnion. To get your free credit report, go to http://www.annualcreditreport.com.

- ※ Watch your checking accounts, especially if you use them to shop online. Sign up for Internet banking, and check your account balances and transactions regularly. Additionally, if your bank offers an electronic alert service, set up alerts to let you know if your account drops below a specific balance or if there are changes made to your account. Finally, watch your mailbox for checks that you didn't order or for paper bank statements that do not arrive when they should.

- ※ Don't throw away that social security statement before you examine it closely. Illegal immigrants may steal your name and social security number so that they can get a job. That income will be credited to your social security earnings and will be reflected on your benefit statement. Check the statement closely when it arrives and compare your earnings to the earnings listed on the statement.

If it's cleverly executed, identity theft can be hard to spot. In some cases, it's blatantly obvious that your identity has been stolen, but the remaining cases can go on for years because the victims don't monitor their financial status and reputation. Don't let the minor details fall by the wayside. Those details might be your first indicators that someone has stolen your identity.

No one is exempt from identity theft. Even people without computers can become victims, but your chances are far greater if you have a computer and use it to access the Internet and exchange e-mail. The simple fact is that identity theft scams abound on the Internet. And no one is exempt from them.

Identity theft is a slippery crime. It's hard to track, harder to stop, and growing at a pace that's astounding. Every e-mail that you receive is suspect. Every Web site that you visit is potentially bogus. The sophistication of identity theft scams increases every day, so your best protection is to be very vigilant and always skeptical. You never know when you might become a target.

Protecting Yourself

Identity theft is one of the fastest growing cybercrimes, because it's one of the most lucrative. What that means for you is that you're always a target, even if you haven't been affected by identity theft yet. Your best option is to learn to protect yourself.

Some of the most effective ways to protect yourself are also the simplest. The following list provides strategies for keeping your identity secure as you surf the Web.

❋ Identity thieves don't care how they get your information, so they'll try anything once. From simple schemes to sophisticated schemes, if the reward is financial or personal information, an identity thief will try it. So, one of the best ways to protect yourself from identity theft is to view everything online with an extreme dose of skepticism, and when in doubt, double-check everything. For example, if you receive an e-mail that seems to be from your bank asking you to provide account information, call the bank and ask if they would send that type of communication, or why they need your information. If the e-mail was legitimate, your local branch will be able to verify it.

❋ Never download attached files from people you don't know. Attached files can be viruses, Trojan, keyloggers, or other types of malicious software. And they don't just come from strangers. Use caution when downloading any file, even from people you know. If you aren't expecting a file, don't open it until you verify that it really was meant for you and that it doesn't contain anything harmful.

❋ If an e-mail includes a link and instructions to click through the link, don't. Instead, type the main URL of the company that the e-mail was supposed to come from into the address bar on your Internet browser. Once you get to the Web site, sign in to your account as you always would, and if there are issues of which you should be aware, there will probably be information about them on the Web site. If you don't find the answers you're looking for, you can always call the company directly.

❋ It seems to go without saying, but never post your username and password in a place where someone snooping around can find it. One of the biggest security risks on the Internet is someone else accessing your account. In today's busy world, keeping up with your username and password is the last thing you want to worry about. But writing your username and password down where other people can find it puts you unnecessarily at risk.

❋ Another username and password issue to avoid is using the same ones for all of the services that you access online. Never use a single username or password for all of your Internet services. Instead, vary your username and passwords, and if possible, never use the same one twice. By varying these, you prevent a thief from having access to more than one of your accounts.

❋ Don't use passwords that are easy to figure out. It sounds like an old song and dance, but the truth is, the majority of people use a password that any experienced hacker could figure out in a matter of minutes. For example, do you use your anniversary or your spouse's birth date as a password? Maybe it's a combination of your children's birthdates. The most effective and safest passwords are made up of random numbers and letters that have no meaning to you at all.

❄ Request that your name, address, e-mail address, and telephone number remain private when doing business with online merchants and service providers. Most merchants now give you the option to opt out of communications from their partners or affiliates. Opt out of those communications so that your personal information isn't shared with other merchants. Also have your information removed from online directory services such as Four11.com and Switchboard.com.

❄ Review the privacy policy of your ISP and any merchants with which you do business. This document is long and boring, but it gives you information about how your personal information is handled. It also lets you know what repercussions you have in the event that you think your privacy has been violated.

Protecting yourself from identity theft is a full-time job. There's an entire side of identity theft that doesn't even touch cyberspace. The threats from this crime exist both in the real world and in cyberspace. Protecting yourself in cyberspace requires vigilance and an understanding of how you're at risk. And even the most protected people sometimes fall victim to identity theft.

If you suspect that you've become a victim of identity theft, swift action is your best recourse. Immediately close any accounts that you think have been affected and then place a fraud alert on your credit report. This can be done by contacting the three major credit-reporting agencies.

It's also essential that you keep detailed records of everything from bills and statements for the affected accounts to communications with those companies. Keep a log of your conversations, too. Write down the date, time, and person you spoke with and notes on the conversation. These records will help you prove your case if it's necessary to go to court over the crime.

Finally, report the identity theft to your local law enforcement agency and to the Federal Trade Commission's (FTC) identity theft unit (http://www.ftc.gov/idtheft/). Your local law enforcement agency will probably take a report, but what they can do beyond that is determined by how much training the agency has. Identity theft is often a multi-national crime, meaning that it crosses many country boundaries. For example, the person who ends up using your identity for financial gain could possibly be in Siberia, even if your identity was stolen in the US. This makes tracking and prosecuting identity thieves very complicated.

The FTC, on the other hand, compiles a database of identity theft cases that many law enforcement agencies access as they are investigating and prosecuting identity theft cases. This resource makes it possible that eventually the identity thief will be caught and prosecuted, and because organizations such as the FBI access the database, it's more likely that some justice will eventually be served.

Keeping your identity safe is complicated, and there's no single strategy that will keep you safe. But using a good dose of caution will go a long way.

7} Credit Card Fraud

One of the most frequently mentioned cybercrimes is *credit card fraud*. Millions of people every year have their credit card numbers stolen online. In 2004, fraudulent credit card purchases totaled more than $788 million in the US alone. The worldwide figure for Internet purchases made with stolen credit card numbers is in the billions.

INSIDER LINGO
Credit Card Fraud: A crime that happens when a criminal obtains your credit card account number through illegal means and uses it to make fraudulent purchases of goods and services.

There are many ways that your credit card can be obtained for fraudulent use: It can be stolen, you can lose the card, or a merchant that you do business with might not handle the card in the most secure manner.

SECURITY BREACH
In June 2005 it was announced that 40 million credit cards, including Visa, Master-Card, and American Express, were compromised when hackers gained access to CardSystems, a credit transaction clearinghouse.

In the ensuing investigation, CardSystems admitted that they should not have had transaction information that included names and card numbers stored on the premises. However, they did, and hackers gained access to names, account numbers, and verification codes. Visa downplayed the instance, citing research conducted by Visa that found that only about two percent of the numbers gathered in such an incident are ever used.

Do the math. Two percent of 40 million is still 800,000 card numbers that were put at risk. Remember, statistics report that nationwide, the number of credit cards that have an available balance is about 40 percent, which means the hacker potentially captured 320,000 credit card numbers; that would equate to about $64 million in available funds if you use the relatively conservative figure of $200 per card. It's not a bad haul for a few days' work.

Credit card fraud is a real problem, even as industry experts claim that credit card fraud is on the decline. About 23 percent of all credit card transactions are what's called *card not present* (CNP), meaning they are transactions that are accepted without actually seeing the credit card. It's most often schemes that involve CNP transactions that are fraudulent.

INSIDER LINGO Card Not Present: Concerning credit card transactions, there are two types: card present and card not present. Card not present transactions are the type of transactions that typically occur when a consumer is shopping online or over the phone.

While the threat of credit card fraud seems to be declining, it's still a very serious threat. The losses to credit card fraud each year, combined with the number of times that it happens and the ease with which most fraudulent credit card transactions are conducted, make it more than a passing concern.

What Is Credit Card Fraud?

You hear about it almost every day on the news or in the papers. Credit card fraud is one of the most frustrating crimes in our society, mostly because it's easy for a criminal to grab a credit card number, max out the card, and disappear into cyberspace, leaving little trail to follow. In the event that there is a trail, it usually leads to another country where it's virtually impossible to find the cooperation needed to apprehend the criminal.

What makes it especially difficult is that the credit card doesn't specifically have to be available to the criminal for him or her to access it. There are three ways that criminals can use your credit card:

* **By presenting the physical credit card to a merchant.** Criminals usually get hold of your credit cards if you lose your wallet or if it's stolen. It's even possible that you could misplace your card, only for someone to pick it up and use it and then return it without you ever knowing that it was used.

* **By presenting the credit card number and verification information such as the CVV number off the back of the card.** These types of transactions usually happen online or over the phone, and criminals can gain access to your card number in any number of ways—by tricking you

into providing the number, by stealing it when you are engaged in a legitimate transaction, even by stealing the number from a merchant that is keeping it on file for future purchases.

✳ **By presenting a cloned card to a merchant.** Cloned credit cards are the dirty little secret of the Internet. It takes seconds for someone to gather enough information about you to clone your credit card. In most cases, it happens when you present your credit card for payment at a physical location. The person you present the card to *skims* the card number and information and sells it to someone who specializes in creating cloned cards. That person then sells the cloned card to someone who uses it just as they would any credit card, either online or in the real world.

INSIDER LINGO   Skimming: This is a process by which criminals capture credit card information that is used to create cloned credit cards. In the real world, the clerk or server you hand your card to swipes it through a card reader twice. The first time is to authorize your charge; the second time is to capture your information. Skimming is much more difficult to accomplish online.

Despite the fact that there are only three ways to use a credit card, there are dozens of ways for criminals to get them. It's not at all unusual to hear about e-mail scams designed to get your credit card number. But there are also scams that are designed to get other information that makes it possible for a criminal to use your credit card number.

For example, if a hacker or criminal manages to get your credit card number, it still might not be usable without the CVV number on the back of the card, or your billing address and zip code. The criminal or hacker might even be trying to gain access to your mother's maiden name for the purpose of changing the billing address on the card.

To accomplish this, it's possible that the criminal could call you requesting that information. The call will seem very official, and the caller will probably tell you that he or she is from your card company's fraud unit. He will tell you that there's a transaction that his company suspects could be fraudulent and will ask you to verify some information.

The information the caller asks you for to use for verification will be things like the CVV number, for security purposes, of course, or the billing address of the card. He might even go so far as to ask you to provide your social security number. All the while, he'll be fabricating a story about the fraudulent charges and by the time you hang up the phone, you'll be grateful to the caller for keeping you safe.

Only, you're not safe. On the contrary, it will probably take less than 15 minutes from the time you hang up the phone for your card to be used fraudulently. And that's just one of the many, very effective scams that criminals use to get your credit card number.

Another way that your credit card number can be compromised is when you're purchasing goods or paying for services online. It's not at all difficult for a hacker or criminal to place a small piece of code on a legitimate Web site that covers up the form in which you type your credit card information. Then, when you enter the information and click send, it's collected and you're shown a time-out error so that you have to re-enter your credit card information to complete the purchase. In some cases, you may not even receive that. The information is simply collected and your purchase is never completed, though it appears that it was.

How Credit Card Fraud Differs from Other Scams

There are a lot of scams that you have to worry about, especially if you're using the Internet to make purchases and do business. Credit card fraud is probably one of the worst—especially if the credit card number that gets stolen happens to be a debit card that draws funds directly from your checking account.

Rebecca used her credit card to make a purchase through an online merchant. About two months later, when Rebecca was reviewing her credit card statement, she found several charges on her credit card statement that she had not authorized.

Rebecca immediately called her credit card company to report the fraudulent charges, and the company agreed to remove the charges from her bill. They didn't even hold her responsible for the first $50 of the fraudulent charges. They did, however, require that she sign a fraud affidavit swearing that she did not authorize the charges and that she had no knowledge of the charges.

Rebecca didn't lose any money because of the fraud, but many times that's not how credit card fraud works. It's a crime that can be expensive for the victims, and it can be very frustrating to repair.

In the case of a criminally misused credit card number, federal law requires that the owner of the credit card be held responsible for no more than $50 as long as the fraud is reported within a specified amount of time (which varies from company to company). However, most credit card companies voluntarily cover even that $50 so that the consumer who has been victimized isn't responsible for any lost money at all.

With a debit card that's attached to a checking account, the damage can be more frustrating. The same federal laws apply, but it could take as many as 90 days before the bank credits the missing funds back to your account. During that time, you have to find a way to manage the missing money. And since banks charge overdraft fees when accounts are overdrawn, the negative balance on your account can become unmanageable very quickly.

SECURITY BREACH

When Mary and her husband first opened their checking account, they were tickled with the debit cards they were issued on the account. The debit cards made it much easier to manage their money, and even made shopping online possible. It wasn't until several months later that they realized that debit cards were subject to the same risks that credit cards are subject to when used online.

Shortly after Mary received her paycheck one week in November, she tried to take money out of her account at the automated teller machine. Much to Mary's surprise, the request was denied. When she spoke to a representative the next day she learned that there had been a $1,800 charge to her account the day before from an adult-oriented Web site.

The charge effectively wiped out the available balance in the account, which resulted in several checks and other charges to the account being refused for insufficient funds, and Mary found herself without any money, fighting to have a charge that she didn't make reversed. Her bank did eventually return the money to her account, and they reversed the overdraft charges that resulted from the fraudulent transaction, but it took more than three weeks, during which time Mary was without that money and without access to her bank account.

Mary's situation is one that happens frequently since debit cards have been so readily adopted. Debit cards work just like credit cards, which means they're subject to the same-threats that credit cards are subject to. The downside is that the money for any "charges" that you make with your debit card comes straight out of your checking account, even if those charges are fraudulent.

At this point it is helpful to note how credit card fraud differs from other types of fraud. Most fraud is committed with an ultimate goal in mind—to gain access to financial resources. The difference with credit card fraud is that it is committed for financial gain, but the financial gain can be either direct or indirect.

Direct financial gain is, quite obviously, the reward for a criminal when he uses the account number himself to acquire cash, goods, or services. Indirect financial gain is the result of selling the credit card number to someone else who may either use it or pass it on to yet another person to use.

The result of indirect financial gain is that your credit card number could end up being used by someone on the other side of the globe. And the person using the number won't be the person who stole it. In some cases, the person using the card might not even know that the number is stolen.

For example, in one case of credit card fraud, credit card numbers were stolen from an American by a criminal in the US. That criminal sold the card numbers to a broker, who sold the card numbers to someone in Romania, where they were used to order hundreds of thousands of dollars' worth of products through the Internet.

All fraud is bad, but credit card fraud is unique in how easy it is to accomplish and how difficult it can be to prosecute. It's one of the problems that have stumped the credit card industry for so long, and it costs credit card companies billions of dollars each year.

A Note about Gray-Market Goods

A growing aspect of credit card fraud is the purchase and resale of goods using the Internet as a buying tool. What happens is that the criminal uses the stolen credit card number to purchase goods over the Internet, then sells the goods to someone else for a profit.

In some cases, these goods are shipped to a location where the secondary buyer picks them up, so that the criminal who is using a stolen credit card to buy the goods never comes in contact with them. In this way, the criminal makes it very difficult for the authorities to catch him.

The goods that are purchased with stolen credit cards are called *gray-market goods* because they are not purchased legally, but they also are not purchased on the black market. And the market for gray-market goods grows every day, because it's a fast, easy way for a criminal to convert your stolen credit card number into cash.

Anatomy of Credit Card Fraud

Most credit card fraud is committed in roughly the same way. Your credit card number gets stolen, and the criminal sells it off to someone else who uses the card to make illegal purchases until one of two things happens—you spot the fraud on your credit card statement or your available balance runs out.

That's not the only way the crime can play out, but it's the most frequent way. A similar scenario that could happen is that your credit card number is stolen, possibly by an employee of some company with which you're doing business, and then the employee either uses the credit card number herself or she shares it with her friends, who don't particularly care that the credit card number is stolen. The friend then uses the card to make purchases.

It's not a far-fetched scenario. It's happened. An employee of one of the top cell phone companies scammed nearly a million dollars from customers using this exact scam. When she was finally caught, the authorities figured out that the employee had been sharing the stolen numbers with her friends, at least one of whom was also charged with a crime.

Another way that credit card fraud happens is when a criminal gains access to your personal information and uses that information to open new credit card accounts with the intention of using the cards and never paying the bill. You won't even know this has happened until some debt collection agency contacts you demanding payment for an account that you never opened.

This is exactly the scenario that many people face. They learn about the theft long after the damage has been done. What is truly difficult about the delayed nature of discovery for this type of credit card fraud is that it's extremely difficult to find the criminal. By the time the crime is even discovered, the criminal is long gone.

All credit card frauds have a few things in common:

❋ The credit card number is stolen.

❋ The credit card number is eventually used in fraudulent transactions.

❋ The crime is discovered, either because you notice the fraudulent charges on your bill or because a collection agency begins hounding you for repayment of a debt you didn't create.

❋ The crime is reported and investigated but the criminal may or may not ever be apprehended.

It all seems pretty simple, but it's really very complicated. Once you discover the crime, an entirely new set of circumstances come into play. You must immediately report the fraud. However, when you discover and report the crime determines how the situation unfolds from that point.

If you catch the fraud quickly, you stand a better chance of stopping the crime before it becomes too costly. You also stand a better chance of having the credit card issuer cooperate with removing the charges from your account.

On the other hand, the longer it takes you to discover the crime, the fewer your options. For example, if someone steals your credit card number and begins charging very small amounts to the card, the crime could go unnoticed for months or even years. When you do finally discover the charges, only charges made within the last 30 to 90 days (depending on your credit card company) will be reversed. Charges that are older than the maximum reporting time that's outlined by the card issuer are your responsibility, and if you've already paid for those charges, you're just out that money.

The scenario that you just read is one that's happening more and more, too. Criminals, especially those outside the US, have discovered that they can capture a credit card number, begin charging small amounts—usually under $15 each month—to the card, and it will go unnoticed more often than not.

It doesn't seem like a whole lot, but think about it. If a criminal is receiving $15 a month from 5,000 credit card numbers, he's making $75,000 a month, and 5,000 card numbers per month is a low estimate. These operations are equipped to capture and access more than 5,000 cards each month.

The income from these fraudulent charges is long-lasting, too. Many credit card holders don't look at their monthly bills closely enough to catch the small dollar charges. And when they do, it's easy for the card holder to assume it's some charge that they accrued as a by-product of doing business with another company. Many times, the card holder won't question the transaction because he's embarrassed that he doesn't remember why he's being charged that monthly fee.

Tell-Tale Signs of Credit Card Fraud

Credit card fraud isn't hard to spot. Once a card has been stolen, it's just a matter of time before the account will be used. In most cases, credit card fraud is discovered because the credit card holder notices charges on her statement that she didn't authorize.

Cheryl used her credit card to pay all of her monthly bills. At the end of each month's billing cycle, Cheryl would pay the entire balance due on the card and start over again.

Most months when Cheryl's credit card statement arrived in the mail she would open it, glance through the charges, and write the check for the full amount due. Cheryl, like many people today, is a busy, career-oriented person who works more than 80 hours a week and travels frequently, so when she did have a few minutes' downtime, she didn't want to spend it examining her credit card bill.

One month, however, a charge caught Cheryl's attention as she glanced through the credit card bill. The charge was labeled with a Web site address and it was $13.86. Cheryl spent a few minutes trying to remember authorizing the charge, but the Web site name was unfamiliar to her, so she called her credit card issuer to ask for details about the charge.

As she investigated, Cheryl discovered that the charge was made to her account every month and had been a recurring payment on the account for more than a year. When she couldn't remember why the charge was there and couldn't find anything in her records that showed she authorized the charge, Cheryl reported it to the credit card company as being fraudulent.

The credit card company agreed to stop the charge and return the money to Cheryl's account. They also credited two months' worth of the fee back to the account, but the remaining ten months were never credited because they fell outside of the company's required time limit for disputing unauthorized charges. In total, Cheryl lost just over $138 in payments that she'd made to the account, but she also lost several hours of her time during the process of trying to straighten it out.

Unauthorized charges are the most obvious sign of credit card fraud. That's why it's critical that you check your bill every month as soon as it arrives. However, it's not always that easy.

In the case where a criminal uses your personal information to create new accounts, you don't have a point of reference to alert you to the fraud. Instead, catching these fraudulent accounts requires that you check your credit report regularly. Most consumers only check their credit report if they have been denied credit, and some not even then.

However, that's where you're most likely to find credit card fraud that involves new accounts. Every debt that is in your name and under your social security number is listed on your credit report, even if it's a fraudulent account.

Another sign that someone might be using your credit cards for fraudulent purchases is if you suddenly stop receiving the bills. Often, a criminal will change the billing address on your account when he gains access to your account for two reasons. The first is to obtain another card for the account. He accomplishes this by calling the credit card company and first reporting a change of address and then a few days later reporting a lost or stolen card. Fortunately, many credit card issuers have begun to verify address changes before they make them.

The other reason is to keep you from seeing the bill. If you don't receive a credit card bill for a month or two, that's plenty of time for the criminal to max out your credit card completely. By the time you get the bill delivery straightened out, the criminal is already abusing someone else's credit cards.

In an effort to keep criminals from pulling this specific trick, many credit card holders sign up for Internet access to their account. It's an excellent concept, but the criminal can change the user-name and password to access the account. If that happens, it could take days or weeks for you to get it straightened out so that you can access your account again.

Protecting Yourself from Credit Card Fraud

Avoiding credit card fraud, like avoiding any crime, requires a dose of common sense and some skepticism. By following a few simple guidelines, you can reduce your risk of credit card fraud drastically.

Here are some steps you can take to protect yourself.

❅ One of the easiest ways to protect yourself from credit card fraud when shopping online is to have a single, low-balance account that you use only for shopping online. This account should be used only for online shopping and it should have a balance that's not over $500. A similar strategy is to have a prepaid credit card that you use for shopping online. Pre-paid MasterCards and Visas work just like credit cards, but you add money to the card before you can make a purchase with it. The downside of this type of card is that you have limited purchasing power. However, in the event that you fall victim to credit card fraud, a prepaid card is an excellent way to limit your risk.

❅ Save every receipt and invoice for every credit card transaction in any given month and compare those receipts to the charges that appear on your monthly statement. If you find a charge to your account that you didn't authorize, immediately contact your credit card issuer to dispute the charge.

❋ Set up Internet billing and account access. One of the easiest ways for a thief to steal your credit card account is to take your bill out of the mailbox or to find a statement in the trash. Electronic account access, statements, and payment methods reduce your risk of credit card fraud so long as you keep your account number, username, and password safe.

❋ Immediately notify your credit card issuer if your bill doesn't arrive on time or if you expect to change your address in the near future. If your bill doesn't arrive on time, contacting the credit card issuer will help to ensure that there have been no changes to your account billing address. If you're changing your address, contact the company as soon as you know what your new address is to ensure that a credit card bill isn't left in the mailbox for the next people to move into the house or apartment that you're leaving behind.

❋ Never provide your credit card account number, username, or password to anyone via e-mail. If you receive an e-mail that requests you fill out a form with personal information and send it back, don't. If you're making a purchase online from a merchant that doesn't have a payment system set up online, don't send your credit card number to them through e-mail. Instead, opt to call the company directly and provide your credit card number that way.

❋ Mistrust any e-mail communication that you receive that states your account is in danger of being frozen or that tells you the credit card issuer suspects fraud and wants you to verify your account number, username, and password. Most companies will not contact you via e-mail for account verification. If you receive an e-mail from the company that you aren't sure is legitimate, either call the number listed on the back of your credit card, or log onto the company's Web site by opening a new browser window and typing the direct Web address of the company into the address bar.

❋ Never enter your credit card information on a Web site that you aren't sure is secure. Secure Web sites usually have a small padlock icon in the bottom-right corner of the Web browser. The URL in the address bar may also have the prefix *HTTPS*, which means that the site was designed using a programming language specifically intended to promote Web security.

INSIDER LINGO HTTPS: Hyper Text Transfer Protocol Secure. A Web programming language that is designed to help build secure Web sites.

Despite your best efforts to protect yourself from credit card fraud, it's possible that you will become the victim of a credit card fraud scheme. If you do, quick action is the best way to limit the amount of damage done by the crime.

Here are some strategies to help you stop the damage from credit card fraud and begin the repair process.

❋ If you suspect that someone has used your credit card account for an unauthorized transaction, immediately contact your credit card issuer and explain the situation to them. The sooner your report the fraud, the more cooperation you will get from the credit card issuer. Fast reporting will also limit the amount of damage that the thief can do to your financial standing.

❋ Immediately close accounts that you believe have been compromised or new accounts in your name that you didn't open.

❋ File a fraud alert with the three major credit reporting agencies—Experian, Equifax, and TransUnion.

❋ Report the credit card fraud to your local law enforcement agency and to the FTC. Neither agency is likely to be much help in recovering from the crime, but the sooner you let the authorities know about the crime, the better chance they will have of finding the criminals.

❋ Starting the day you discover the credit card fraud, maintain a log that includes copies of all your statements, notes on telephone communications with the credit card issuer and law enforcement agencies, and any receipts that might be relevant to the crime. Keep all of this information together in one place as you will likely refer to it often during the clean-up period.

❋ Some credit card issuers offer insurance against credit card fraud and identity theft. This is one of the hottest new insurance products on the market, but be sure you read the fine print before you purchase an insurance policy that promises to protect you against either of these crimes. In most cases, the policies are written in such a manner that they are mostly worthless unless you're facing tens of thousands of dollars in fraudulent charges. And while these policies often promise to limit your liabilities if your credit card number is stolen and used fraudulently, federal law and most credit card issuers' policies already provide that type of protection.

Credit card fraud is a serious crime, and while by all reports it's declining in number of occurrences, it still happens far too often for you to ignore the need to protect yourself. Monitor your financial accounts regularly, and use caution when using your credit card online. At the first sign that there might be trouble, begin drawing on the resources at your disposal.

8 } Investment Fraud

The Internet turned out to be the tool that brought investing to everyone. From the ability to trade online to companies that let you invest in some of the hottest stocks on the market for $5 to $25 per month, suddenly anyone and everyone can get in on the investment game. And people have. In 1980 only about 1 in 18 people owned stock of any type. Today, that number is 1 in 3.

Unfortunately, with the increased number of investors, Internet capabilities also brought an increase in the number of investment frauds that plague those investors. Today, Americans lose nearly $10 billion each year to investment fraud, and there are investment schemes that have grossed more than $1 million a month. That's money taken from working stiffs like you and me, money that's meant to improve our future.

What's scary about these numbers is that they don't seem to be decreasing. According to industry experts, investment fraud, even after the *Dot Com Bust*, seems to be increasing. And it only makes sense that it should, because surveys have found that about 72 percent of people in the US use their computers to conduct sensitive transactions, such as banking transactions, online. To add heat to the fire, 75 percent of people who are hit by investment scams lose money—an average of $625 per person.

INSIDER LINGO Dot Com Bust: The period during 2000–2002 when the inflation that technology brought to the stock market was corrected. Many companies failed and the value of many others was reduced greatly by decreased financial backing and demand for higher profits.

Averages being what they are, that puts investors' losses at anywhere from $1 to $1 million or more if they fall victim to one of these scams. But even these numbers aren't entirely accurate. It's estimated that only about 1 in 10 instances of Internet fraud, including investment fraud, are ever reported. That means there are far more victims out there that just never bothered to report the incident to the police, either because they were embarrassed by the theft or because they didn't feel there was anything that the authorities could do to help. Especially in cases where investment fraud victims lose less than $100, they are more likely to accept the loss and go on about the process of their daily lives.

Regardless of their reasons for not reporting the crime, the fact remains that they don't. And that simply muddies the waters where statistics are concerned. What's perfectly clear is that credit card fraud *is* a problem. It happens too often to new investors, and it erodes confidence in the Internet and in investing. The only way to protect yourself from this type of fraud is to know what it is, how it happens, and what you can do.

What Is Investment Fraud?

The Internet is an excellent tool for investing. Before the Internet, the average person didn't have stocks or other investments. Sure, people had retirement plans—most people worked their entire adult lives for the same company and could count on those retirement plans to support them through their golden years. A few of the wealthier individuals in the nation did make investments, but the majority of people didn't invest in the stock market or other securities because they knew they had a retirement fund to carry them through their golden years.

The Internet changed all of that by changing companies and the way they do business. Suddenly, every organization became very aware of costs versus profit. Even as early as the 1980s, organizations went from maintaining employees for 20 years or more to keeping them only until they could find someone who knew more and would accept less money to do the job. You could no longer plan to be with one company your whole life. At the same time, the Internet made investing accessible to anyone who had the inclination to put his money somewhere other than a low-yield savings account. Unfortunately, it has also added risk to investing—and those risks are more than just that of a failed investment.

It's the risk of investment fraud, and technically, it's not a new risk. It's just a more pronounced risk now that the con artists that used to strike one person at a time can reach millions with the touch of a button.

Investment fraud is a crime that takes place when you are persuaded to make an investment in a company, stock, or other vehicle that's not real. For example, about 52 percent of the investment fraud reported during 2004 was related to the *Nigerian Letter Fraud*. The Nigerian letter fraud involves an e-mail that purports to be from a wealthy businessman or royal family member in Nigeria who is being persecuted by the government of that nation. The letter tells a story of persecution and government restriction on funds that rightfully belong to the person who sent the e-mail. It goes on to explain that the money can be released to someone not related to the family and asks the person receiving the e-mail to please help by providing account information so the money can be transferred into the receiver's account. Once it's there, you are supposed to disburse the money to the free family members.

INSIDER LINGO — Nigerian Letter Fraud: This scam is often referred to as the *419 Scam* because of the code in Nigerian law that it violates. The scam aims to take money from unsuspecting people by convincing them to provide account information in an effort to help the family of a persecuted political or royal family. This scam has been around for decades and originally used postal mail as a means of scamming unsuspecting people.

For their help, the person who receives the e-mail will be given a percentage of the money. Usually, it's an amount that is in the tens of millions, and the percentage is healthy. It's a very attractive scam. All you have to do is provide your banking account information for the money transfer.

However, when you provide your account information, instead of being wired a large amount of money, your account is cleaned out and you're left wondering what the heck happened.

The Nigerian letter scam has many variations, and each variation is a little more clever than the last. It's also not the only scam of which you should beware. Investing in stocks online and other types of *confidence fraud* are just as, or more, dangerous, and some of them are considerably harder to spot.

INSIDER LINGO — Confidence Fraud: Fraud committed when a criminal creates confidence in his or her victims. Elaborate stories are often created with the intent of playing on the target's sympathies. Confidence fraud can include investment fraud, auction fraud, phishing, or any of a number of other types of fraud or criminal attacks.

Who's at Risk?

There are some categories of people that seem to get hit with certain types of fraud more often than others. With investment fraud, seniors are the prime target, especially seniors who are struggling to get their retirement incomes up to the level at which they lived before they retired.

SECURITY BREACH — One retired policeman was sitting in his favorite coffee house trying to decide what to do with his retirement. He wanted to start some type of a business or make some type of investment that he could rely on in his later years to maintain the lifestyle to which he'd become accustomed. But this retired policeman didn't know a whole lot about business. His whole life had been devoted to keeping the people of his city safe, not learning business and investing principals.

So, when he struck up a conversation with a businessman in his favorite haunt, he was enthralled by the investment opportunity that the man eventually began telling him about. During the course of the conversation, the retired policeman learned that the businessman was once a bank manager, and when he heard about the investment opportunity, the retired policeman thought it must be a sure thing.

That's not say he wasn't nervous about the investment. After all, he'd never invested in anything but his retirement plan with the police department. However, he took a chance and gave the businessman $5,000. About a week later, the businessman returned his $5,000 along with $2,500 in interest.

The retired policeman knew a good thing when he saw it, so the next week he gave the businessman $25,000. A month later the businessman returned the $25,000 along with $15,000 interest.

The retired police officer decided it was time to make some serious money, so he took a $200,000 mortgage on his home, gave it to the businessman, and he never saw the money again. He also never heard from the businessman again, and found no record that the man ever even existed. After some research, he discovered that the investment the businessman told him about was a fraud. Nothing of the sort ever existed.

The lesson in the story is that anyone can fall victim to investment fraud. It doesn't matter if you're a police officer, a banker, or a finance manager. There are some very slick scams going on, and you're always a target. It's your knowledge that will keep you from becoming a victim.

That doesn't exempt people who are younger from becoming victims of investment fraud, however. It can, and does, affect anyone, and Internet-based investment fraud is especially dangerous for the younger generation, because that generation tends to use the Internet more than seniors.

Your economic level doesn't exempt you from investment fraud, either. Investment fraud targets every income level. If you have a higher income, you probably have more credit and so can tap into that credit to make investments. If you have a lower income, then you're probably looking for that one thing that will increase that income and improve your lifestyle, so you'll find a way to invest in a program that looks like it could bring a sure return.

Everyone's a target. What makes the difference between a target and a victim is the action that you take when you're hit with this type of scheme. The first step to avoiding investment fraud is to know what form this fraud can take.

Anatomy of Investment Fraud Scams

It seems that when you're using the Internet, there is danger at every turn. But half of protecting yourself is knowing what to look for. Investment fraud is no different.

Already in this chapter you've heard about the Nigerian letter scam, and you've heard about the social engineering types of scams that can happen in the real world, but there are other types of investment fraud as well.

One other investment fraud scheme, for example, is based on investing newsletters. These newsletters are either sent as spam or they are sent to people who sign up on a Web site to receive the newsletter. In the newsletter, there is information about a specific stock that is guaranteed to do very well or an investment opportunity that is sure to have a great return in a very short amount of time, and of course, there's only one brokerage firm that has authority to sell the investment, usually the owner of the Web site where you signed up for the newsletter.

Because the newsletter appears to be reputable and maybe because the Web site associated with the newsletter looks professional, you're more likely to trust that these are safe investments, when in fact, they are just scams. That's not to say that every investment newsletter is a scam, but some of them are, and caution is necessary when investing on the Internet.

Investment fraud often offers such benefits as investing in offshore companies so that the transaction is tax exempt. Any "opportunity" that seems to promise a way around taxes is probably a scam. We don't like paying taxes, but as many people are quick to say, "There are only two things in life you can count on: death and taxes."

If you're investing, you'll have to pay taxes on the money that you earn from those investments. Any investment program that promises that you won't probably isn't legitimate, and you should avoid these investments in favor of more legitimate possibilities.

Most investment scams come to you in terms that make them look extremely attractive. Whether you receive an unsolicited e-mail, a telephone call, a newsletter, or a piece of mail, the hook is generally attractive enough to tempt even the biggest skeptic. Lines like "Guaranteed Return" or "Risk-Free Investment" are used to draw the investor into the scam, or your emotions are triggered by excitement or pity because emotions tend to cloud judgment. Criminals know this and use it to their advantage.

Then, once your attention has been piqued, one of two things can happen. The first is that you invest in whatever the scam artist is offering and you never hear from them again. Or, a trick that's becoming more and more frequent is that you're given the opportunity to invest and make a return and then invest again. This cycle might happen a few times until you're confident enough that you bet the farm on the investment, then suddenly, the person or firm that's handling the investment is gone, and there's no way to track them down.

Thieves make millions of dollars on these schemes each year. The average victim loses about $15,000. And unfortunately, the Internet has made it much easier for these criminals to reach more and more victims.

Tell-Tale Signs

One of the most frustrating things about the Internet and cybercrimes like investment fraud is that they get more and more sophisticated with each new iteration. Scams that were easy to spot a few months ago have already matured to the point that you probably wouldn't recognize them now. And it's sure that the scams you see today will be replaced by even more sophisticated scams tomorrow.

So, how do you know if you're being targeted for an investment fraud? The presence of high-concept promises is one way. "Guaranteed Return" or "Risk-Free Investment" are two such promises. Another is "Tax-Free Investment." If a claim sounds like it's too good to be true, it probably is. Here are some more signs that you can look for.

* Investment opportunities that arrive through unsolicited e-mail from people or companies that you don't know.

* Investment newsletters that seem to focus on one product or investment vehicle, especially if it seems to be the sole focus of the entire newsletter.

* Investments that the "adviser" tells you to keep quiet. Chances are the adviser is just trying to keep you from learning that this investment is a fraud, and playing on the need for secrecy is one way to do that.

* Any investment opportunity that requires you to provide your checking account number to collect the earnings from the investment. Legitimate financial advisors won't need your checking account. All they need from you is payment for the investment in the beginning. At some point, you may need to supply your social security number for tax purposes, but use caution when providing it. Your social security number is the key to your identity.

* Investment opportunities that come from a wealthy foreigner or foreign royalty. Wealthy foreigners don't solicit strangers through e-mails; they already have elaborate, multi-national networks of contacts they can turn to in cases of need.

The trickiest aspect of investment fraud is that it's often cloaked in very legitimate sounding, or legitimate looking, clothing. For example, one of the hardest types of investment fraud to spot is the bogus investing Web site.

These sites look legitimate. They seem to be professionally designed, they appear very attractive, and they use all of the right terms in all of the right places. As you shop for a site through which you plan to make investments, these sites blend right in.

Unfortunately, what happens is that you choose the site and set up your account for investing, but then, after you make the investment, you never receive the paperwork. Or perhaps you invest through the site for a couple of months and then all the sudden it's gone. You probably didn't think to write down the phone number off the site, and even if you did, if you realize the site is gone and try to call the number, you'll probably find it's a completely bogus phone number. It's even hard for law enforcement agencies to track these sites and site owners because very often the registration information for the site is completely bogus or the site has been hijacked from a legitimate owner by a criminal who's there one minute and gone the next.

Small cap stocks also get used in investment scams. Criminals, posing as investors, band together to artificially inflate the price of a stock, and then the criminals sell off, leaving you holding a loss. To accomplish this artificial price inflation, investors create massive spam campaigns that exaggerate the benefits of the stock and often leave off necessary details. As people buy the stocks, the price rises, then the investors who created the artificial price inflation sell off, causing the stock price to drop rapidly. They make a nice profit and you get left holding the bag.

It's hard to spot these schemes. So your best protection is always to be skeptical about any investment opportunity that comes up. Even skepticism isn't enough, though. Investment fraud, as with every other kind of cybercrime, can happen to even the most skeptical and the most cautious among us. It is hard to spot because it takes many different forms. So, the scam of the day today is probably going to be different from the one that you face tomorrow.

Sam heard about a great new Internet company that was supposed to be the next big thing. The company, Interactive Products and Services, seemed as if it might be a good company to get into while it was still young. Internet stocks, after all, are perfect for the get in early type of investing that made many people very rich during the *Dot Com Boom*.

So Sam invested in the company during a direct public offering that was done entirely on the Internet. The offering brought more than $190,000 from 150 people, Sam included. Unfortunately, Sam and 149 other people later learned that it was all a scam. They money he and the others invested was never been used for the business. Instead, company owner Matthew Bowin took the money and used it to buy groceries and stereo equipment. Sam never got his investment back, but Bowin did eventually wind up in jail for 10 years.

Dot Com Boom: That period of time from the late 1990s to the early 2000s when Internet growth and Internet company growth was disproportionately inflated by demand. During that period, the world shifted from the Industrial Age to the Information Age, placing more value on information than on products.

One scam investment opportunity promised investors their money would be doubled in about four months' time. The scammers collected more than $3.5 million offering "prime bank" securities to unwary investors. Prime bank securities aren't even a legitimate investment vehicle, but many people weren't aware of that and invested their hard-earned money into these bogus securities. The money was never returned to them.

There are many schemes that offer up some type of private investment. For example, one scheme involved an eel farm, and the farm owner promised investors a 20 percent return on their investment. With the average return on investment being less than 10 percent these days, that's an attractive return. Unfortunately, it was a bogus scam, and investors lost all their money.

There are other scams. These are just a few examples of what you might face as you invest online, and there's really only one way to protect yourself—know how to *properly* make investments in a manner that ensures you are protected.

Protecting Yourself

Investment fraud happens. Even the most careful investors can fall for a very convincing scam. But it's much harder for criminals to take advantage of you if you know how to protect yourself. Here are some of the things that you should do to keep the scammers at bay.

* **Do your research.** Don't invest in anything that you haven't taken the time to check out. For example, is the investment that you're considering audited by one of the large international accounting firms? Fraud investments are usually not audited at all, and if they are, they are audited by a small financial firm that might as well be the CPA down the street. It's someone you've never heard of, and often a criminal who's in on the fraud. Another sign to look for is whether or not the investment is registered with your state securities commission or the SEC. If it is not, the investment is a fraud, because investments must be registered with these agencies, even offshore investments. If an investment claims to be exempt from the required registration, take your money elsewhere, because it's a scam.

You can use the following resources for information about investments that you're considering: *Securities and Exchange Commission*, 800-732-0330; *North American Securities Administrators Association*, 202-737-0900; *National Futures Association*, 800-621-3570.

❋ **Take your time investing.** Many fraudulent investment schemes push investors to make snap decisions or to invest their money quickly without taking the time to check out the investment. They play on your emotions and try to cloud your judgment. Avoid any investment where you're pressured to make a fast decision. Legitimate investments and legitimate investment advisers won't push you to make a decision before you are ready.

❋ **Know who you're dealing with.** Even a flashy, well-designed Web site doesn't mean you're dealing with a legitimate investment company or adviser. Research the people you plan to invest with and in. It takes very little to create an eye-catching Web site and even less time to take it down once the criminal has your money. Refer back to rule number one: Always do your research *before* you make any investment.

❋ **Be skeptical.** It's an often-heard warning, but that's because it is so very valid. Be skeptical about any investment opportunity that comes to you through e-mail, especially if it's spam. Be skeptical of investments that promise guaranteed returns. Real investments can't guarantee a return. They may have a good chance of making a return, but they can't be guaranteed. Be skeptical of offshore investment opportunities. There are some valid investing opportunities in offshore companies, but those investment opportunities are regulated just like any other investment opportunity. If an investment scheme promises you that it's tax-free because it's an offshore investment or makes similar claims based on the fact that it's an offshore investment, don't risk your money.

❋ **Understand what you're investing in.** Take some time to learn about investing in general before you start looking at specific investments. If you don't know the difference between stocks and bonds or options and futures, you'll make an easy target for a criminal. Learn about the market before you even begin to look at investments.

❋ **Get any and all investment details in writing.** If you can't get the details about your investment in writing, before you make the investment, then don't invest! Getting the details in writing is a way to protect yourself. It's also a way to slow down the investment process so that you aren't taken by some scammer. And if they refuse to send you the details in writing, or if they push you to make the investment without the details, then you should walk away from the investment, no matter how good it seems.

Investment fraud is a serious crime, and the schemes that criminals use to get your money just keep getting more sophisticated. Like other cybercrimes, protecting yourself takes a good dose of skepticism and a few strategies for keeping yourself safe.

 There are some services that might enable you to take your investment losses, especially those that result from fraud, as a deduction on your taxes. Check with companies like JK Harris 165 Services or your tax adviser to find out if you're eligible to take your losses as a deduction if you become the victim of investment fraud.

9 Phreaking and Hacking

Hackers, crackers, phreaks, script kiddies, ankle biters—all are terms used to describe a person who is knowledgeable in computer programming languages and how they work. Each of these people performs a slightly different task when hacking computers, computer programs, and networks.

❋ **Hackers:** A hacker is a person who is proficient in computer programming languages and computers and understands how computers and their programs operate. Because of this understanding, hackers find it easy to manipulate programs and computers.

❋ **Crackers:** Technically, a cracker is a hacker. But crackers are specifically criminal hackers who manipulate computers and programs for financial gain, usually outside of the confines of the law.

❋ **Phreaks:** Hackers who target communications systems, such as telephone networks, with the intent of gaining access to free communications services. Phreaks more recently have turned to other means of hacking, since the public telephone network offers little challenge.

❋ **Script Kiddies:** Script kiddies are hackers who don't have enough skill to write their own cracking programs. These hackers usually use hacking programs that other, more experienced hackers have developed to conduct denial of service attacks and other large scale attacks.

❋ **Ankle Biters:** Ankle biter is another name for a script kiddie. These hackers use existing hacking tools to break into networks through known vulnerabilities.

These aren't the only disciplines in what is generally called hacking, either. Those who count themselves in the hacking community also don't like being lumped together, and some will probably get bent out of shape if you don't use the correct name that defines what they do. However, we'll risk upsetting the different factions of the hacking community in favor of avoiding confusion. For the purpose of this chapter in particular and the book as a whole, we'll refer to anyone who attempts to gain unauthorized access to computers or computer applications and programs as a hacker.

Hacking actually started as what's called *phreaking* back in the 1950s. Back then, hackers used their skills to gain access to the public telephone networks to make free telephone calls. Of course, times change, and when computers became a method of communication, hackers saw them as a "new frontier." In the early days of computer hacking, the game was about gaining access to the computer or network because with that access came a feeling of power.

INSIDER LINGO   Phreaking: A technique used to gain access to the public telephone network. Phreaking is undergoing a shift from telephones to other communication services like e-mail and VoIP. The point of phreaking in the past was to gain access to free communications services. Today, phreaking is more targeted to eavesdropping on electronic communications methods for the purpose of financial gain.

You may remember the movie *War Games* from the 1980s. The movie portrayed a teenager who hacked into government computers and nearly set off World War III. It wasn't long after that movie was released that a real hacker—a college student—hacked into and shut down military and intelligence computers.

Hacking has come a long way since then. What used to attract restless kids now attracts criminals, and what used to take days to accomplish can now be done automatically using snippets of code and automation. In some cases a hack can take less than a minute. Hacking has grown up. It's no longer a kid with a funny sounding name. Hacking today is a multi-million dollar business run by criminals and malcontents, and you're footing the bill.

What Is Phreaking?

Phreaking and hacking are tied together as only family members can be. Phreaking was the infant that grew into hacking, and like all children, as it grew and matured it changed both in scope and content. Today's phreaking is very different from what it was in its humble beginnings.

As mentioned, phreaking was the earliest form of hacking. In those early days, phreaking was all about gaining access to the public telephone networks so that the *phreak* could make free telephone calls. Yet, even then, the methods that phreaks used were very sophisticated. Over time, that sophistication has increased.

It all started with what's called a little *blue box*. It's a device that phreaks programmed with musical tones played at the correct frequency to gain access to the public telephone network. Once access was gained, the phreak used the blue box to dial the number he or she wanted to reach.

INSIDER LINGO — Blue Box: A device, built by phreaks, that plays the correct musical tones at the correct frequencies to allow the hacker to gain access to the public telephone network. It's called a blue box because the first such device was encased in a blue plastic box.

Phreaks even learned how to simulate the tones that were used to signal the amount of money deposited into a public pay phone so they could gain access through those pay phones to long distance and international calls. The devices used for this type of phreaking are called *red boxes*. However, it didn't take long for the phone company to discover these activities and put protections in place.

INSIDER LINGO — Red Box: The red box performs a similar function to the blue box. The difference is that red boxes are specifically designed to play musical tones at frequencies that trick pay phones into believing that money has been deposited into the phone. When these boxes were used frequently, there were some that were sophisticated enough to make both the frequencies required and the sound of the coins dropping into the pay phone.

By the 1980s, phone companies began to move to digital networks and in the process installed filters that served to combat phreaking. It wasn't their main purpose, just a nice side effect of the new technology. The way signaling at public pay phones was handled was also changed, in effect rendering red boxes useless. Some older equipment remained until the 1990s, and phreaking continued to some degree until that time. Then, as the Internet became a real communication tool, phreaking took on a different face.

The use of the Internet as a major means of communication lent new life to phreaking. The Information Age steamed into the picture, bringing with it unexplored territory, and phreaks found they again faced a new challenge.

Today, telephone services aren't as challenging as they were in the past, so phreaks have moved into the new frontier of the Internet with new intentions—electronic eavesdropping. Phreaks now use sophisticated equipment and setups to gain access to computers and computer networks and capture the images displayed on computer screens or information sent over the Internet.

There are also a number of services that phreaks are very interested in gaining access to. For example, caller ID information is very valuable to a phreak who will gain access to a telephone network, capture that information, and then use it in all kinds of social engineering scams. In one such scam, caller ID information is used to *spoof* a credit card issuer when a call comes in. When you answer, the caller tells you he is from your credit card issuer and proceeds to use social engineering to convince you to provide confidential information that he then uses to steal your credit card account or make fraudulent charges against that account.

 Spoofing: This is a technique which hackers use to accurately masquerade as something or someone they are not. In the case of spoofing Web sites, the hacker sets up a bogus Web site that looks convincingly like the real thing. In the case of spoofing a person, the hacker has enough information to accurately portray someone he is not.

Voice over Internet Protocol (VoIP), an Internet-based telephone service that's growing rapidly, is also an attractive target to phreaks because these services transport call information via the Internet. Just as an e-mail is sent across the Internet from one place to another, VoIP calls are transported in the same manner. Unfortunately, that puts these calls at risk in the same way e-mails are at risk. They can be intercepted and redirected or recorded without much difficulty.

 **Voice over Internet Protocol:** This is a means of routing telephone calls or voice communications over the Internet. VoIP makes it possible for people to have low-cost telephone conversations using a broadband connection.

Phreaking started out as a relatively benign hacking activity. Over time, it's grown into a threat to organizations specifically and to the people those organizations service. Typically (at least in the past), a phreaking scam hasn't been targeted at individuals, but at corporations and phone companies. As this criminal activity continues to grow and more malicious people and groups use phreaking techniques to lead into other criminal activities, however, it becomes more of a personal threat.

What Is Hacking?

There are a lot of politics that go into the term hacking. In a very general sense, hacking is the act of gaining access to a network, a computer, or an application. Generalities don't tell the whole story, however. There are different types of hacking that have different results. For example, there are some hackers who do what they do to help organizations understand what their security risks are. There are even organizations that employ these hackers full time to help them understand what they can do to improve their internal (and outside) security.

Then there is the group of hackers who only hack into systems to prove to themselves and other members of the hacking community that they can. It's still wrong, but these people mean no harm and are not malicious. To them it's a game, and they are often referred to as white-hat hackers.

How deep can you go and how fast can you get there? These are the goals of this group of hackers.

The final group is the criminals. These are what are called the black-hat hackers, and they gain access to systems specifically for financial gain, whether that gain is the sale of captured corporate secrets or the theft of your personal information. These hackers are the ones that give them all a bad name.

Hacking as an activity is growing in intensity and frequency because there's more than enough money to go around. Criminal organizations around the world have turned to hacking as a way to fund illegal operations from terrorism to drug trade. And individuals interested in earning a little extra money free of taxes and restrictions like working for eight hours a day have found that hacking is an easy way to boost their income.

It doesn't require any specialized training, either. Anyone with an understanding of computers and the Internet can find all the information they need to perform some hacking activities by simply doing a Web search. For example, Figure 9.1 shows the hacking Web site HNC3K.com.

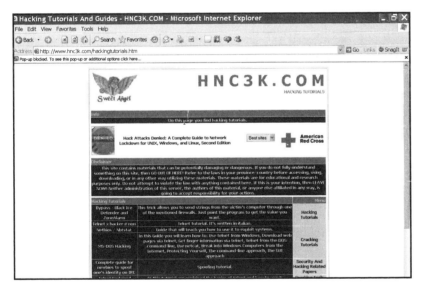

Figure 9.1

This is the HNC3K.com Web site. The site claims to be for informational purposes only; however, there is no way to restrict how the information on the site is used.

Notice in the picture that the site makes a disclaimer that the information contained on the site is for educational purposes only, but a disclaimer doesn't stop someone with ill intentions from using the information for criminal activities. And there's plenty of information on the site. Tutorials on the site include how to bypass firewalls, spoof identities on *Internet Relay Chat (IRC)*, and hack systems through common Windows vulnerabilities.

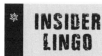 **INSIDER LINGO** Internet Relay Chat: IRC is a communication program that works like instant messenger and can be used to communicate with a group of people or individuals.

It's easy for anyone with the desire to hack into your system to find the information to do so. There are instructions on the Internet for everything from conducting phishing attacks to spoofing and defacing Web sites. And there's little or no control over these types of instructions. In part, it's difficult to prevent this type of information from being displayed on the Internet because preventing it is a violation of our inherent right to free speech. However, even if there were laws that allowed regulators and law enforcement agencies to prevent this type of information from appearing on the Web, it would still be available. There's an entire underground Web where such information and the results of hacking activities are traded.

To compound the problem, it's easy for hackers to do what they do. The information and tutorials that are found online wouldn't be possible if computer systems weren't naturally vulnerable. But they are. Computer systems and networks that are based on Windows operating systems are especially vulnerable because hackers tend to target Microsoft products.

It's a statement. Microsoft is considered a monopoly in the hacking community, and by their way of thinking, not enough credit is given to *open source* operating systems like Linux. Those in the hacking community also take exception to the fact that Windows is a closed-source operating system, meaning that the Microsoft corporation won't share source code with the computing community.

INSIDER LINGO Open Source Software: This is a type of software that has its source code available for other people to examine, manipulate, and add to as their needs dictate. Often, open source software is free, and there are communities that share all of a program or just aspects of the program.

It's funny to think, as you begin to understand more about hacking, that in truth, the computer revolution that took the world by storm was aided by a hacker. Steve Jobs, of Apple-Macintosh fame, was a hacker, working out of his garage at one time. The work done in that garage eventually led to the computer society that we have today.

Opinions run the gamut from the belief that phreaking and hacking aren't dangerous as long as these activities are carried out by responsible individuals to the belief that all hacking is dangerous.

Regardless of which stance you take in that debate, what it all comes down to is that phreaking and hacking are dangerous activities when they're conducted by criminals.

Phreaking is typically an activity that's targeted at organizations as hackers try to circumvent fee-based services such as long distance telephone calls. However, phreaking is becoming more consumer-targeted. If a hacker can use phreaking techniques to gain access to your personal financial information or personal information, that will give the hacker access to your financial capabilities.

Phreaking techniques make it possible for a criminal to monitor your Internet activity or, if you have VoIP, your telephone calls. And hacking is the equivalent of the keys to the kingdom. It encompasses any technique used to gain access to your computer from viruses to phishing and pharming.

That makes the threat from phreaking and hacking all-encompassing. If you have personal information on your computer, and 80 percent of computer users do, or if you use your computer to transmit personal information, and again about 80 percent of computer users do, then you're at risk from phreaking and hacking.

In their most benign forms, phreaking and hacking pose little or no risk to you personally. However, it's rare to find these activities conducted in their most benign forms anymore. Today, the majority of computer crimes are committed not to gain access and not to show off skill, but to capture personal information that leads to monetary gain of all kinds for a wide variety of groups and individuals who would rather steal from you than do an honest day's work.

Anatomy of Phreaking

Today a phreak is more likely to try gaining access to a computer network to utilize free Internet service or to have a look at what's on your hard drive or to monitor what you're doing while you're on your computer.

To do this, phreaks use a number of different pieces of equipment and software programs. And that's where you're most at risk. The technology of today makes it easy for a phreak or other hacker to put a small program or application on your computer which makes it easier for him to gain access to your machine if you're not fully protected. Once there, the phreak uses the application to open up a doorway to your computer.

Another rising area of interest for phreaks is network hacking, especially where wireless networks are concerned. In one iteration of phreaking that involves wireless networks, hackers drive around residential areas with specialized equipment in the seat beside them that sniffs out vulnerable wireless networks. This is called *war driving*, and when the phreak finds an unprotected network (and any wireless network that has been connected straight out of the box is vulnerable), he can park outside on the street and use a signal booster to gain access to your wireless network.

INSIDER LINGO

War Driving: This is the process of driving around looking for vulnerable wireless networks which the hacker can tap into to do his work. Hackers may also use war driving techniques to steal information from vulnerable computers or to load malicious software onto networks and computers.

Once on the network, the phreak has access to everything that's on your network, including any computers that are connected through the network and your Internet connection. While connected to your network, a phreak can copy your hard drive or load software onto your computer that will allow him to access the computer or Internet connection remotely.

That remote connection is often used for later access to conduct DOS attacks, or to send spam or viruses through your e-mail program. In many cases, you don't even know that your network, computer, or Internet connection has been compromised. If you do find out, it's usually through someone else who has received a virus-laden e-mail from you.

Tell-Tale Signs

The most dangerous thing about phreaks is that they very often do their work without your knowledge. You may never know that a phreak has gained access to your network or computer, because the signs that indicate a phreak has tapped your system are the same signs that you'll find with many other types of computer issues.

For example, if someone is accessing your computer remotely, the programs might run slower than usual, but that can often be attributed to other computer problems, like low memory or temporary files that are bulging at the seams.

Other symptoms that you might notice if a phreak has gained access to your computer include:

* Weird behavior in your applications.
* Changes in settings that you didn't make.
* Bounced back e-mails that you didn't send.
* Access denied to your computer.
* Slower than usual network or Internet connections.

All of the symptoms listed above can also be symptoms of virus or *malware* infections, and other types of security breaches on your computer. It's hard to know when you've been targeted and accessed by a phreak, which is why it's so vitally important to keep your computer properly protected with firewalls and other security applications at all times.

 **INSIDER LINGO** Malware: This term literally translates to "malicious software," and defines a piece of software or an application that is specifically designed to complete some malicious task, from stealing usernames and passwords to logging all of your Internet activity.

Anatomy of Hacking

Hacking is another of those activities that's hard to define. Many of the same problems that you encounter with phreaking are the problems that you encounter when a hacker has used some other method of gaining access to your computer. The hacker uses whatever resources that he has available to gain access to your system. It's what that hacker does once he's gained access to your computer or network that makes all the difference.

Hackers gain access to your computer or your applications with the express intent of gathering information they can use for monetary gain. That information might be usernames and passwords. It might be account numbers or even your social security number. But the hacker doesn't have to have that information. If a hacker can gain access to some simple information like your name and address and the names of the credit card companies that you do business with, then it's easy for the hacker to collect any additional information he might need to gain access to your financial accounts.

Some hackers aren't even interested in your financial information. Especially in cases where hacking takes place in the corporate environment, what the hacker is after is corporate secrets that can be sold to the competition—sometimes for millions of dollars. And if hackers are breaking into government systems, the information they gain there could be used for terrorist acts.

Hacking isn't a crime that's easily defined. You can't simply say first this happens and then this happens and that's the result of those actions. There are too many variables. A hacker can get in through e-mail or through vulnerabilities in operating systems or applications. And once the hacker has access to the system, he might gather information, or he might simply use your computer resources for some other criminal activity he is conducting. There are no absolutes, so you have to always be aware of your computer system and network and watch for any tell-tale signs that you might be the victim of hacking.

Tell-Tale Signs

Hackers don't have to be good at what they do to hack into your system. All they need are the right opportunities and the right instructions. That's what's made hacking an activity that is growing at such a rapid rate. Anyone can be a hacker, if they have the desire. And any system can be hacked, no matter how well protected it is.

It's knowing that you've been hacked that's such a difficult feat. There are some signs, like those you'll see when you get a computer virus, that are very obvious. There are other signs that you might miss completely, such as those described in the section on phreaking. But one symptom isn't enough to know that you've been hacked, and if a hacker doesn't want you to know that your system has been invaded, you might never find out.

In short, the tale-tale signs depend on why the hacker has invaded your system or your network. However, some of things that you might notice if a hacker has gained access to your system include

※ Your computer may begin operating slower than it usually does. It's not a gradual slowdown in operating time, either; it's sudden. One day your computer is working fine. The next you may boot it up only to find that it takes forever to boot or that applications take forever to load.

※ You begin to experience frequent errors with applications. Some hackers gain access to computers and networks to use the resources to conduct other criminal activities. This might cause your applications to begin to error out because there are not enough resources for the applications to function properly. This could also be a byproduct of a malicious piece of code planted on your hard drive that is destroying bits and pieces of the application.

※ Your computer begins to behave strangely. Lucy went in to work one Monday morning and booted her computer up. As the computer was booting, she got an error that told her the system was restarting. Fifteen minutes later, the computer had rebooted numerous times, but it still had not completed the boot process. When the technical support team finally gained access to the computer, they found that a virus had been planted on the hard drive, and after further investigation they found the virus was planted by someone accessing the network from outside the company.

※ Your computer crashes frequently. A computer crash can be defined as applications freezing up to the point that the computer must be restarted to release the frozen programs. If your computer doesn't usually freeze up but starts to suddenly, a hacker has probably been at work, and there's probably damage to your computer's hard drive.

Examples of Hacking

It hasn't been that long since the IRS Web site was hacked. Hackers gained access to the Web site and put graffiti on the site. And that's most often what you hear when you hear about hacking. But there are so many other ways that it can be done.

For example, in mid-2003 a hacker broke into a credit card company's network. The hacker gained access to thousands of credit card numbers, which he copied. What he intended to do with those credit card numbers is anyone's guess, but selling them to the highest bidder is probably a fair assumption.

Examples of hacking that happened to individuals are a little harder to come by, mostly because people don't realize they have been hacked unless they have discovered a virus or some other type of malware that's obvious. But hacking does happen to individuals.

For example, a computer user in Mississippi learned she'd been the victim of hacking when she tried to access her Internet connection and kept getting denied. She ended up on the telephone with technical support that helped her determine that someone had hacked into her system, gained access to her Internet account, and locked her out of the system.

It happens a lot in instant messaging programs, too. One young man reported to me that he often got locked out of his instant messaging program because he has friends who think it's funny to hack into the programs and change passwords.

These are mostly annoyances, but the implication of these actions is very serious. If it's that easy to hack into your system, to gain access to your Internet connection or your instant messaging program, then it's not much more difficult to gain access to your hard drive and everything that's stored on it. If you're one of the millions of people who keep your financial records on your computer, that could mean serious heartache for you.

Protecting Yourself

It's been said that there's not a computer or network built that can't be hacked into if the hacker has the right equipment and plenty of time. In fact, some hackers have proven this point by hacking into computers with some of the most sophisticated protection on the planet. But that doesn't mean you shouldn't protect yourself. And where hackers and phreaks are concerned, the best protection you can hope to have is a good *firewall*.

INSIDER LINGO   Firewall: This is a piece of software or a hardware device that monitors the traffic into and out of your network or computer and allows or denies that traffic based on rules set by the manufacturer or user.

Firewalls are covered in more detail in Chapter 13, but understand that a good firewall doesn't have to be expensive or hugely complicated. It's enough that the firewall protects your system and keeps intruders out.

Intrusion detection systems are another way you can protect yourself from hackers. An intrusion detection system specifically monitors traffic for intrusions from unauthorized users. Intrusion detection systems are very similar to firewalls, and in some cases, firewalls fall under the category of intrusion detection systems. However, an intrusion detection system doesn't usually have the capability to prevent unauthorized access, only to detect it.

> **❅ INSIDER LINGO**   Intrusion Detection Systems: These systems are specifically designed to monitor traffic on your network or on the Internet for unauthorized intrusion into your system. If an unauthorized user attempts to access your system, these applications provide a warning mechanism.

Encryption is another technology that will serve to keep you safe from hackers. Like all of the other protection methodologies that you'll learn about in this book, it's not foolproof. However, encryption technologies in effect scramble information that you send over the Internet. Anyone who gains access to that information must have the right *encryption key* to unlock it. It makes it harder for a hacker to get at your information, even if he manages to intercept it.

> **❅ INSIDER LINGO**   Encryption: A method of obscuring information, usually by using a code or an algorithm that scrambles the information. Once encoded or scrambled, the information cannot be accessed without the proper encryption key.

> **❅ INSIDER LINGO**   Encryption Key: An encryption key is like the key to a lock. It provides the necessary information to unlock information that has been encoded or scrambled by an encryption program. Without the key the information simply appears as gibberish.

Keep in mind that encryption technologies won't be of much help if a hacker gains access to your computer system. However, if he only has access to your network and is capturing information such as e-mails as you send them out across your network, then you have another layer of protection that just might make a hacker's job more difficult than he bargained for.

Beyond firewalls, intrusion detection, and encryption technologies, your next most effective method of protecting yourself is to ensure that your protection technologies are configured properly. Many people assume that a firewall right out of the box is enough protection. Unfortunately, it's not.

The standard configuration of most software is not enough to protect you. And in fact, the standard configuration is known to most hackers, so they are prepared to circumvent that configuration. That also means that any loopholes that are available in the standard configuration are open to hackers who know what to look for.

Therefore, it's important that you change the configuration of any protection methodologies that you put in place. Be sure to read through the documentation that comes with the hardware or software that you're using. The developers explain what each of the settings means and how it should be configured in the documentation.

Protecting yourself from hackers and phreaks, and any other type of security risk, for that matter, requires that you take a few steps to protect yourself. Fortunately, there are security devices and applications that make protecting yourself a little easier.

10 } Auction Fraud

Everybody loves a good auction. If you don't believe it, check out eBay, U-Bid, or some of the other auction Web sites that have sprung up on the Internet. Auctions offer a way for consumers to find the goods and services that they are looking for, usually at a better price than they could find on the same item in the real world.

For example, Cindy's husband lusted over a chess set that he'd seen in the mall. The chess set had a price tag of $2,500—way more than Cindy was willing to pay for it. Instead, she found the same chess set listed at an auction Web site for $200. She purchased the chess set through the site and her husband had a wonderful Christmas that year.

Not everyone who does business at an auction Web site is as lucky as Cindy (or her husband). And for that matter, Cindy hasn't always been that lucky. One item that she bid on and won at auction, an antique piece of jewelry, was never delivered to her. And she also never received a refund for the item. It was a small amount, only about $15, but it was a loss to Cindy nonetheless.

That's auction fraud for you, or at least, it's one form of auction fraud. You find an item that interests you, bid on it, and win, and it never shows up. Estimates are that auction fraud costs consumers more than $500 million each year, and that about 250,000 people fall victim to auction fraud every day.

It's one of the most prevalent cybercrimes out there, and what makes it worse is that finding the people who commit auction fraud and prosecuting them is sometimes very hard to do. It's far easier if you just protect yourself from auction fraud from the very beginning.

What Is Auction Fraud?

Purchasing goods and services at auction—especially large or expensive items that require the services of a third party, like an escrow service—sounds like a difficult way to do business, and it is a little risky. However, while auction fraud is one of the most prevalent crimes on the

Internet, in the bigger picture, there are only a small percentage of auctions that result in fraud of any type.

One military serviceman serving in Germany found and fell in love with a Harley-Davidson motorcycle that was being auctioned online. He bid on and won the motorcycle, and after making special arrangements to have the motorcycle delivered to his father's house, he wired the money for the motorcycle—more than $5,000—to an *escrow account* that the seller specified.

The only problem was that the buyer's father never received the motorcycle, and when the buyer tried to get his money back from the escrow account, which was supposed to keep his money safe until the motorcycle was received, he found the escrow service was a fraud as well. The military serviceman was out more than $5,000, and the authorities were never able to find the thief.

INSIDER LINGO

Escrow Account: A special account, usually managed by a financial company, where money (or in some cases, property like software source code, a deed, or valuable artworks) is deposited until special conditions are met. Once the conditions are met, the money or property is delivered to the correct recipient.

There's more than one way to lose your money in an online auction. This list illustrates the different ways that criminals can take you for a ride through Internet auction sites.

* You purchase an item in an auction and never receive it. It happens more than most people like to admit. You win an item at auction, pay for it, and the item never arrives. This is one of the top ways that auction buyers fall victim to auction fraud.

* You purchase an item in an auction, but the item that arrives is not the same item that you thought you were bidding on. A good example of this is an auction that took place on eBay for Xbox game systems. Several bidders won these game systems during the first holiday season after they were released. However, when the item arrived, it was nothing more than the outer shell of the game system. All of the inner parts had been removed. Unfortunately, it took eBay a while to get this seller because he was following all of the rules in selling the shells. There were disclaimers in the listing; most people just missed them or misunderstood them.

* You purchase an item in an auction and later find out that the seller was artificially increasing the price of the item. *Bid shilling* happens frequently in online auctions. The seller uses multiple usernames or has friends who drive up the price of an item and then withdraw their

final bid or offer a "second chance" opportunity to the next highest bidder in order to increase the price.

❋ **INSIDER LINGO**   Bid Shilling: This is a technique used by dishonest sellers to drive up the price of an auction. The seller either uses multiple usernames to bid on an item, driving the price higher, or the seller asks friends who have no intention of buying the item to bid on it. If a friend happens to win the auction, the seller offers it to the next highest bidder under the guise that the winning bidder changed his mind or didn't pay.

❋ You begin bidding on an item only to have a different seller try to sell you their merchandise, usually through a transaction that takes place away from the auction site. Then, when the purchase is complete and your money has been sent, the merchandise never arrives. Unfortunately, because you completed the purchase outside of the protection of the auction Web site, there's usually nothing that can be done about it. This technique is called *bid siphoning*.

❋ **INSIDER LINGO**   Bid Siphoning: This is a technique that sellers use to draw buyers away from the protection of an auction site. The seller, a criminal, will send an e-mail to a person bidding on a particular item offering them the same item at a substantially lower price. The buyer usually jumps on the transaction and sends money to the criminal, but the buyer never receives the merchandise for which he paid, and there's no recourse because the transaction took place outside the protections of the auction Web site. Criminals who use this technique have often been banned from auction Web sites.

❋ You purchase an item and are asked to put the money in a specific escrow account for safekeeping until the item arrives, or if you sold the item, the buyer puts the money in an escrow account until the buyer receives the item. The item is never received and the escrow service ends up being fraudulent, or you ship the item but when you try to collect your money from the escrow service you find it's a fraud.

❋ Some auction fraud happens even when you aren't bidding on an item or selling an item. Some criminals steal auction user's IDs to fraudulently bid on items to drive the price up, or to conduct fraudulent auctions. Some may even sell black market or gray market goods that were obtained illegally. If you don't use your auction profile frequently, it could take a month or longer to realize that your auction identity has been hijacked.

Online auction fraud is a serious crime. Victims can be taken for a few dollars or thousands of dollars, and in some cases, the criminals are next to impossible to trace. And because there are a number of ways that a criminal can take advantage of you during an auction transaction, you have to keep your guard up all the time.

Who Is Affected?

Many people think that cybercrimes typically only affect the younger generations, but that's not entirely true. The largest group of Internet users are those people between the ages of 20 and 40, and because they are the largest group, they are most often the victims of cybercrimes. However, that doesn't make people older or younger exempt from these crimes. It doesn't matter how old you are; you can fall victim to cybercrime.

Auction fraud victims can be any age and any economic group. Victims don't even have to use auction Web sites to buy or sell goods. Anyone who does is at risk, but even those who don't can have their identities used for fraudulent auctions and transactions. Fraudsters don't pick people by age or economic group. They shoot for anyone who is vulnerable to their scam.

Most often, that's new auction users. However, even a seasoned auction user can fall victim to these scams, as Cindy (her story was told on the first page of this chapter) found out when she fell victim to a less-than-honest seller after she had been doing business through online auctions for nearly four years. It can happen to even the savviest of auction users.

Fortunately, you can take action to protect yourself. And even if you can't stop auction fraud completely, you can make it much harder for a criminal to take advantage of you.

Anatomy of Auction Fraud

Auction fraud happens in a number of ways. However, it's a little easier to spot this crime than it is some other cybercrimes. What might be harder is getting back whatever money you lost in the transaction.

Melissa is a tech-savvy magazine editor. She's used the Internet for more than a decade, and she's been an eBay user for years. During that time, Melissa has purchased and sold dozens of items. So, it came as a real surprise to her when she received an e-mail from another member of the auction community that she uses warning her that a laptop she was bidding on was being sold by a seller that had cheated dozens of people out of their money and never sent the items those people won in the auctions.

It really surprised Melissa because she wasn't bidding on anything in an online auction at the time. Someone had hijacked her auction identity, and it took months to get it straightened out. She finally had to start over completely, creating a new identity, and she lost all of the *feedback* that she'd worked for four years to gain.

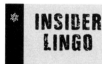

INSIDER LINGO

Feedback: This is a method through which buyers and sellers are rated on their performance. Some auction sites use stars while others simply let you write a short description of your experience. In the auction community, feedback defines how well your sales or purchases go.

Melissa's story is just one representation of the many ways that auction fraud can take place and how it can be discovered. Typically, if you're buying something at auction and fall victim to the form of auction fraud in which you never receive the item, once the auction is over, you pay for the item that you've won and then wait. Only, the item that you're waiting on never arrives.

After a respectable amount of time, you can begin the process of tracking down the item, usually by communicating with the seller. In the event that's not effective, then you can turn to the owners or administrators of the auction Web site for help. Finally, if that doesn't work, you can report the crime to the FTC or other fraud tracking agencies. Unfortunately, if it turns out that you can't work things out with the seller, it's a pretty good bet that your money is gone for good unless you have some protection from your credit card issuer or payment service.

Auction fraud that involves a hijacked user identity is a little harder to spot. However, if someone does hijack your identity you'll probably find out in one of two ways. You'll either try to sign in to your account and find that the criminal has blocked you out of it, or you'll receive a bill or have a payment drafted from your checking account for the fees associated with the sales that the criminal has been making with your stolen identity. It's also possible that someone will contact you to question why they haven't received an item that they bought from the criminal when he was using your identity.

Tell-Tale Signs

Unfortunately, spotting auction fraud before you get taken isn't easy to do. If you're bidding on an auction that a user with high feedback is running, it's difficult to know whether the user has been hijacked by some criminal. By the same token, it's hard to know if the escrow service that the seller requests you use is real.

You may not be able to spot auction fraud before you're taken advantage of by it, but here are some things you can look for.

❋ Watch your auction closely. If there is a person or people who make bids and then retract those bids, it's possible that there's something shady going on behind the scenes.

❋ Beware of any seller that e-mails you directly offering the same product that you're bidding on at a better price. It's possible the seller is on the up-and-up, but it's also possible that it's a criminal trying to take advantage of you. Why risk it?

❋ Check the status of your account frequently. If a criminal steals your auction identity, the fastest way to find out is to sign into your account once a week, even if you don't want to purchase or sell anything. If your account has been hijacked, you probably won't be able to access it.

❋ Beware of auctions that seem too good to be true. It's possible to get great deals on auction sites, but the more unbelievable the deal, the more likely it is that there really is no deal and you're being targeted for a crime. Always use caution!

Examples of Auction Fraud

Throughout this chapter you've seen stories of the different types of auction fraud. But there are hundreds more where those stories came from. All you need to do is ask a mailing list if anyone has been taken by an auction fraud, and probably at least one person will have a horror story to share.

A student of Radford University bid on a laptop on an auction Web site, and when he won the auction for $1,500 he sent the money to the escrow account that the seller specified. He waited three weeks for the laptop to arrive, during which time he contacted the seller several times. Each time he contacted the seller, the seller assured him that the laptop had been shipped and should arrive any day. The seller even provided a tracking number one time that turned out to be a bogus tracking number for an item that was shipped to an entirely different state by an entirely different company.

Finally, the student gave up and tried to contact the escrow account to request a refund of his money since the laptop never arrived. What the student found, however, was that there was no escrow company. When he researched the background of the escrow company, he found that it never really existed, and he had been victimized by an elaborate scam. On further investigation, the student learned that there were many people who had been victimized by the same scam.

What made the preceding crime even more difficult to spot was that the seller had a very good feedback rating. But that's often what criminals do. They conduct bogus auctions and have friends bid on those auctions and then leave positive feedback. Once a good "reputation" has been established, the fraudster will begin his games, and before negative feedback starts appearing on his record, he's already done all the damage he intends to do and has set up a new user ID and started the process over again.

In some cases, it could take months or even years before the person committing the auction fraud gets caught, and even if he does get caught, it may be difficult for you or the auction administrators to get any satisfaction from the law. Laws surrounding cybercrimes of all types are slowly but surely getting better, but there are still many loopholes that make it hard to prosecute some cybercrimes.

Protecting Yourself

If you take nothing else away from this book, take away the understanding that you should be skeptical of everything when you're doing business online. So the first step you can take in protecting yourself from auction fraud is to be skeptical of everything: feedback, item descriptions, sellers, buyers, auction services—the whole shebang.

Other steps you can take to protect yourself:

* Pay by credit card. Federal laws give you some protections from fraudulent transactions. If you use your credit card to pay for an item that you win at auction and the item never arrives, you can report the fraudulent transaction to your credit card company and you have some repercussions, and a chance to get some, if not all, of your money back. If you pay by check or money order and don't receive the item, chances are your money is just lost.

* Check the feedback rating of anyone you do business with. This includes taking time to read through some of the feedback that other people have left. Usually, feedback ratings have space for some description of the transaction as well as a visual rating system (like a defined number of stars to represent how well you thought the transaction went). As you're looking at feedback, look too at how long the person has been active in the auction community. The newer the seller or buyer, generally, the higher your chances of becoming a victim of auction fraud.

* Check auction listings for insurance and additional protections. Depending on what auction site you use and what payment method you use, sometimes your purchases are protected by insurance that those companies have in place. In other cases, you can pay a small fee to add insurance to your account to protect yourself in the event that a fraudster tries to take advantage of you. Be sure to read the fine print on the insurance, however. Most insurance policies have certain requirements that must be met before you can be reimbursed for losses.

* Never agree to participate in a transaction away from the protections of the auction Web site on which you choose to do business. Once you take a transaction to a private party, you lose all of the protections that the auction site has put into place. In essence, you're taking your safety and the security of your transaction into your own hands. Not every private transaction is fraudulent, but why risk it when you can conduct business in a manner that ensures you're protected?

* Beware of auctions that seem too good to be true. If an item seems to be priced far below its actual value, or if the seller makes claims that seem unrealistic, avoid the auction. Your instincts will usually tell you when something doesn't sound right. Listen to that instinct. In most cases, if it seems too good to be true, it is.

* Avoid making purchases on "second-chance" offerings. In many cases, second-chance offerings come to you because the seller or a friend of the seller has artificially inflated the price of the auction. When the auction ends, the seller will go back to the next highest bidder and offer the item to him at the highest bid that bidder made. If you're offered a second chance at winning an auction that you were outbid on, it's possible that the price has been artificially inflated, just so the seller could learn your highest bid. Decide what the item is worth to you. Then, if you lose the auction, move on and don't make the purchase on a second chance offer unless you're okay with the idea that you may have been manipulated to pay a higher price.

Even if you follow all of these guidelines and are very careful about the people you do business with on an auction Web site, it's possible that you'll still fall victim to auction fraud. In part, that's because criminals keep figuring out better ways to separate you from your money, but the other part of it is simply the volume of transactions that take place on auction Web sites.

It's like driving a car. If you drive a car every day of your adult life, the odds are pretty good that you're going to get into at least one accident in your lifetime. The same can be said for auctions. If you participate in enough online auctions, you're bound to fall victim to a fraudulent auction at one time or another. The best you can hope for is that you can recover from the crime quickly.

Reporting Auction Fraud

Some people, when taken advantage of by auction fraud, feel helpless, and often those people don't do anything about it. Especially in cases where the amount of money lost is small, people don't pursue action beyond possibly leaving bad feedback or maybe contacting the auction site to report the bad seller.

There are others, however, who feel that reporting auction fraudsters isn't nearly enough. These people take other efforts, like setting up Web sites and mailing lists dedicated to warning potential victims of auction fraud.

Regardless of whether you think the crime isn't worthy of reporting or that reporting isn't enough, you should still report the fraud to the proper authorities. It's possible that you're only one of many people who have been victimized by the criminal or criminals that are behind the auction fraud.

How to Report Auction Fraud

Reporting auction fraud isn't that difficult. In some cases, all you need to do is fill out a form online. In other cases, you might be asked to fill out a paper form and fax it to the organization to which you're reporting. It all depends on which organization it is.

However, the information needed is pretty standard across all of the complaint organizations. Your name and address will be required. An e-mail address is usually also required, but telephone numbers might be optional. Other personal information will also probably be optional.

> You should not be asked to provide your social security number when reporting auction fraud. If you are asked to provide your social security number, ask why it is needed, and if necessary, file the complaint in another manner. Some Web sites won't let you move forward if all of the fields on a form are not filled out. If you have trouble with online forms that request your social security number, use paper complaint forms instead and leave your social security number off.

In addition to your personal information, you'll need to provide details about the fraud, including what items were included in the auction and how much you paid for the items. If you have had any communication with the seller, include that information, too.

Finally, keep track of the auction number. Every auction is assigned a transaction number. If you have access to that number, write it down and keep it in a safe place, as you will likely need to refer to it often during the reporting and investigation process.

To Whom Should You Report Auction Fraud?

A good starting point is the Web site that the auction took place on. Most auction sites have a reporting form or forum for suspected fraud. Fill out the forms that are available there, and follow any instructions that the auction site has provided for problem resolution.

Then, if you don't find any help through the auction site, take the time to report the crime to your local authorities, but don't expect your police department to be of much help. They might file a report (which you'll need if there is any insurance governing the transaction), but unless the fraud ring is local and there have been a lot of complaints, they probably won't take the manpower away from more pressing crimes to investigate your losses.

Once you've reported the crime to the local authorities, then it's time to start reporting the crime to some of the national organizations that have been set up to protect you. Some of the places that you might want to submit a complaint include.

- ✻ The National Fraud Center: http://www.fraud.org
- ✻ The Internet Fraud Complaint Center: http://www.ifccfbi.gov
- ✻ The Federal Trade Commission: http://www.ftc.gov

Finally, consider sending a note to any of the consumer groups that focus on the type of scam to which you have fallen victim. There are not consumer groups for all of the fraudsters out there, but there are consumer groups for the ones that do the most damage. A Google search should show you if there's anyone out there that's been victimized by the same scam you have.

Auction fraud is one of the most prevalent crimes on the Internet. Protect yourself. And if you do fall victim to auction fraud, take the necessary steps to report it to the proper authorities so they can stop the criminals before they take advantage of someone else.

11 } Viruses, Trojans, and Worms

If you haven't had one already, you're a rare Internet user. They affect millions of people every day, and these nasty little bugs cost industries more than $55 billion each year. They are viruses, Trojans, and worms. And they are perhaps the greatest security threat to the Internet.

In the past, viruses were not much more than an annoyance. If you got a computer virus, you suffered from serious computer issues, but that's usually where the damage ended. Today computer viruses and their counterparts, Trojans and worms, are much more serious. These programs, and even just bits of programs, are the main method by which hackers and other criminals get to your computer and your personal information. Once they have that information, those criminals have control of your finances, and in some cases, your life.

What's a Virus?

Most people are familiar with the term *virus*. You know that a virus is a piece of malicious programming that is passed from computer to computer, usually through e-mail. What you may not know is that viruses are dangerous to more than just your e-mail program. They modify existing software so that when the software runs, copies of the virus are spawned. What's more, a virus can search across a network to find other programs to infect, it can destroy data, and it can destroy other software programs on the computer.

INSIDER LINGO Virus: A virus is a piece of executable code that inserts itself into programs and can cause a host of problems on your computer or network. What separates a virus from other types of malicious software is the amount of damage that a virus can do, and like medical viruses, these can be very nasty bugs to deal with.

Each iteration of a virus on the Internet gets more sophisticated. Viruses that used to be programmed to replicate and send themselves to other people in your e-mail program's address book are now programmed to replicate themselves and attach to other programs and capture information about you or your Internet and computing habits and return that information to the criminal. Viruses today don't need your address book to replicate and send themselves to thousands of people in a matter of minutes. Viruses today don't need you to do anything other than look at an e-mail. And the worst part is, it's getting harder and harder to stop viruses.

The first viruses were coded into programs that were passed around on disk. When you tried to load the program to your computer, you also loaded the virus with it. Today, a virus can arrive in your e-mail box unnoticed and begin to replicate itself and insinuate itself into your programs, files, and e-mail messages without you ever knowing it's happening.

What's more, viruses that used to take weeks or months to spread now spread globally in a matter of minutes. This is what makes it so difficult to stop them before you're infected. Antivirus programs and other methods of protection can be programmed to watch for signs that something might be a virus, but until the virus is first released and then captured and examined, there's really no sure way to protect yourself. At best, you can hope to follow some safety guidelines that make it a little more difficult for the virus to get through.

More than 63 percent of the Internet users in the US have fallen victim to a virus at one time or another, and that has a lot to do with the way that viruses behave. A *virus writer* writes the virus and then releases it into the wild. Eventually, it makes its way to you in an e-mail, and when you open the e-mail, the virus goes to work replicating itself and sending copies out to everyone in your address book. More sophisticated viruses don't even need an address book. They work on an algorithm that allows them to use spam techniques to devise e-mail addresses that are likely to be active. You may not even realize that you have a virus on your computer until you start getting bounce back notices from your e-mail provider that tell you messages you've tried to send out are not reaching their intended destination.

INSIDER LINGO Virus Writer: A virus writer is a hacker who does nothing more than write viruses. Some virus writers do it for fame, while others do it for financial gain.

What makes viruses different from Trojans and worms is the extent of the damage that they can do. Viruses are usually much easier to spot than a Trojan or a worm, and the delivery mode for viruses is usually e-mail, although they can be included in programs that you load from a disk. The biggest difference between a virus and a Trojan or a worm, however, is that viruses are capable of self-replicating, a feat that neither of the other types of malicious code can accomplish on their own.

What's a Trojan?

When you hear the term *Trojan*, you might think of the scene from the movie *Troy* where Brad Pitt's comrades trick the inhabitants of Troy with a large wooden horse. The night after the horse is pulled into the city, thousands of soldiers come streaming out of the horse to lay siege to Troy.

 **INSIDER LINGO** Trojan: A Trojan is a malicious piece of software that masquerades as legitimate software or that is completely invisible to your system until it begins to do damage. Much like its wooden namesake, a Trojan is designed to catch you off guard until it's too late to do anything but repair the damage.

That's a pretty accurate picture of a Trojan that affects computers, too. It's a small piece of software that you either don't notice or that seems to be benign. However, once it's loaded onto your computer, the software begins to behave in the most malicious sort of way. It will rearrange and delete programs, icons, and documents. It will monitor and collect information from your computer, and it might even take snapshots of all the programs and activity on your computer and send them back to the hacker or criminal who created the Trojan. This person then uses the information gathered to gain access to your computer, your financial accounts, or even your life.

It's only over the last few years that Trojans have become a serious problem on the Internet, and as with all Internet threats, the sophistication of these programs is growing. For example, there are Trojans, such as Subseven, that create a backdoor into your system that can enable a hacker to gain access to your system and control your mouse, open and close your CD-ROM, and delete or upload and download software without any input from you at all. Others can contain viruses or worms, which then spread more damage.

Trojans are even more difficult to track than worms because they work quietly, behind the scenes. You either don't see them at all, which is often what happens when you open a blank e-mail—a Trojan is secretly installed in the background—or you download the program, under the guise that it's some legitimate piece of software like a game, music, or a screensaver, and the Trojan goes behind the scenes to do its damage.

What's a Worm?

As if viruses and Trojans weren't enough, there are also malicious programs called *worms*. Worms are similar to viruses and Trojans; however, worms are self-contained programs that remain hidden and propagate via e-mail and duplication.

Usually, worms are delivered to your computer in the same manner that viruses and Trojans are. The real difficulty with worms is that they behave just as their name would imply. These malicious programs dig into your system, moving from place to place, leaving large holes through which hackers can access your system. As they move through your system or network, they also propagate themselves, spreading to other systems in multiples.

Worms are often used in Denial of Service attacks and other malicious actions against Internet Service Providers or corporations. You as the victim of the worm are not really the target. You are actually a by-product of the target. You're a victim all the same, but in the hacker's eyes, you're a means to an end.

That brings to mind the question, why do hackers write and send out viruses, Trojans, and worms? The answer is simple. They do it for two reasons. The first is a throwback to the old hacking ethos: use your skills to prove your skill level, nothing more. Unfortunately, while some "Gentleman Hackers" do still exist, they're quickly being replaced by criminals looking to make a buck.

And that's the second reason most hackers send out viruses, Trojans, and worms. They want access to your personal information. Whether it's financial information, your name and address, your social security number, your marital status, or even the size of your family, all information is valuable on the Internet, and in the right hands, any amount of information can be dangerous. Even the smallest piece of information can lead a savvy criminal to all of the keys to your identity.

A Note about Malware

One term that you've probably heard on the Internet from time to time is malware. Malware is a shortened version of the term "malicious software," and it encompasses any and all software that's written with the intention of using it for malicious purposes. Malware can be viruses, Trojans, worms, spyware, keyloggers, and any other type of software that hackers use to gain access to your personal information or to do damage to your computer or network.

The catch with malware is that it's also something more than any single type of malicious software. For example, malware includes those hybrid and combination types of malicious software that plague the Internet all the time. One such combination is a virus that delivers as a payload a *keylogger*. The keylogger is installed at the same time that you get the virus; then the virus begins replicating and sends itself out to other people.

This makes protecting yourself all the more difficult. Add to that the fact that criminal hackers and virus writers are joining forces. They are more dangerous now than ever before, and over time the threat can only become more pronounced. Many people assume the threat has peaked now, but with the rapidity of technological change, the peak of Internet dangers is still in the future.

The Real Threat from Malicious Code

There's a lot of talk about viruses and other malware. You hear about them at every turn. It seems that a new virus warning circulates every day. Magazines and newspapers devote huge amounts of column space to warning you about viruses and telling you how to repair the damage from them. Despite all that, unless you've fallen victim to a serious cybercrime like identity theft or credit card fraud, you may not realize just how dangerous these bugs are.

Viruses, Trojans, worms, and other malware *are* dangerous, however. And if you get one, it could take days or weeks and hundreds of dollars to get rid of it. When you do get rid of it, there's the possibility that it will turn back up, often repeatedly, until you finally give up and erase everything on your computer, including the operating system. If the malware is especially malicious, you could even find yourself replacing part, or even all, of your computer.

One issue that makes all types of malicious software even more dangerous is the misunderstanding that surrounds them. Viruses, Trojans, malware, keyloggers, and all of the other code-based threats on the Internet are all lumped together under the label "virus." When a user installs antivirus protection, he assumes *that* protection keeps him safe from all types of viruses, even those that aren't really viruses but are called viruses.

The truth is, just any old antivirus program isn't good enough for all of the threats that you face. You need a combination of technologies to protect yourself from these threats. But you'll learn more about that in Chapter 14.

Anatomy of a Malicious E-mail

The delivery of most viruses, worms, Trojans, or other types of malware is through e-mail. The file comes attached to or imbedded in an e-mail, and you either have to download the attached file or open the infected e-mail. The rest is automatic; everything from that point forward happens without your assistance at all.

The problem with this scenario is that there are some pieces of malware that you'll never know exist. An e-mail that appears to be blank can contain malicious code. A greeting card that seems to come to you from a friend or family member can include malicious software. The link that your co-worker sent to you in an e-mail so you can look at her wedding dress could lead you straight into a hacker's domain where you are infected through your Web browser with a piece of malicious software.

In short, there is not just one way that you can be infected, so what follows is one scenario of many.

It starts when you receive an e-mail. In the case of the Love Letter virus, the e-mail made reference to an attached file. In most cases, the e-mail comes from someone you know, and it might include a short note that says something along the lines of "Thought you might like to see this" or "Here's the file that you requested."

So, because you know who sent the message, you open the file or download it, and in that one action, the virus or malware is installed to your computer. It then goes about doing its own thing. Perhaps the virus begins propagating itself, and the next time you connect to the Internet it sends a batch of files to everyone in your address book. Or maybe it just sits quietly on your hard drive, collecting all of the keystrokes that you make while using your computer. Then, when you connect to the Internet, all of the information that has been collected is delivered to a Web site, an anonymous e-mail address, or some other storage place until the criminal can pick that information up or until the criminal sells it and someone else picks it up.

It all seems pretty innocuous. And the truth is, it really is. Until the damage starts. Then it's anything but innocuous. You may not even realize in the beginning that you've been infected with a virus, but it's usually not too long before some tell-tale signs begin to show up.

Tell-Tale Signs

The problem with viruses and other malware is that you may not even realize you've been infected until well after the fact. After a while, though, you'll begin to notice that something isn't quite right with your computer, though you may not be able to put your finger on exactly what's wrong.

Some of the indicators that you might notice include

* Your computer begins to run slower than usual. Programs might take longer to load. It might take longer for your computer to boot up. No matter how you notice it, a decrease in operating speed is one sign that you might have a piece of malicious code at work on your machine.

* Your computer begins to lock up frequently. It happens when you're working on a document in your word processing program. It happens when you're trying to load a Web page as you're surfing online. Maybe it even happens when you're just opening your mail program.

Regardless of when it happens, if you start to notice that your programs are freezing up more than usual, you might be infected by a virus or other malicious code.

✺ Your applications begin to operate strangely. A good example of this is a report one woman gave about her computer. She downloaded what she thought was an update for her Internet Explorer, but after the installed the update, she started experiencing serious issues with the program. One of the strange things the program was doing was closing and then reopening itself while she was surfing the Internet. It took the woman a while to track down the problem, but eventually she figured out that she'd received a virus with the update, and that was the cause of all the strangeness with the program. That strangeness isn't limited to one type of application, or even to just one application. Depending on the virus that you get, it's possible that you could experience this kind of weirdness with any or all of the applications that are installed on your computer.

✺ Your computer shuts down on its own and then doesn't operate properly or won't restart at all. Computer shutdowns for no reason are a pretty good sign that something's wrong. There are other issues that can cause your computer to shut down, but it's likely to be caused by a virus or other piece of malicious software.

✺ Your computer begins to restart itself every few minutes. Computers don't restart themselves without help, despite all the buzz about computer gremlins that work completely of their own volition. While your computer might shut itself off from time to time if there's a problem, it's not likely to restart itself. So, if your computer begins to restart itself often, don't call Ghost Busters. Instead, call the computer repairman, because you probably have a virus or other piece of malware at work.

Any time your computer begins to suddenly act differently than it usually does, there's probably something wrong with the machine. That's when it's time to break out the heavy arsenal.

Examples of Malicious E-mail

If you have any doubt about the severity of the threat from viruses, Trojans, worms, and other malicious software, just log on to Google and search for the term "virus." Thousands of pages are returned, on which you can find tomes of information about the viruses that threaten Internet users.

It's estimated that anywhere from 150 to 300 new viruses are released into the wild each day. And there are somewhere in the neighborhood of 4,000 vulnerabilities on the average computer system at any given time. That makes it easy for these pieces of malicious code to spread quickly and without much notice.

The BugBear virus is a good example of this principle. Actually, BugBear is not a virus, but a worm that replicates and sends itself out to all of the people in your address book. It also sends out old e-mails that you may not have deleted from your system, and in general this little bug creates all kinds of havoc. It was released into the wild in 2002, and in a matter of hours the majority of PCs worldwide were infected. If you missed out on this nasty gift, you're one of few lucky people.

Another worm that's a little more current is the ZoTob threat that began circulating in August 2005. Although ZoTob didn't spread as quickly or as widely as BugBear, the virus was a pain nonetheless. Once activated on your computer system, ZoTob opened a backdoor through which hackers could access your system, making it just as dangerous. And getting rid of these kinds of threats isn't easy either. Even the ZoTob worm, which was rated as a low threat by most antivirus providers, was rated as moderately hard to remove.

In layman's terms, moderately hard to remove means you either need a degree in computer science or a really good tech support person. If you don't have the right protections in place to keep you safe from worms, viruses, Trojans, and other pieces of malware, you should consider keeping your local computer repair service on speed dial. It's a pretty good bet that you're going to need them.

Protecting Yourself

It almost sounds as if there's no hope of protecting yourself from all this malicious software floating around in cyberspace, but that's not the case. It takes some caution in the way you handle e-mails and downloads, and it's a good idea to have some protection technologies, but you can protect yourself.

Here's what you can do to protect yourself from viruses, Trojans, and worms (and other malware, too).

❋ Your first step to being protected is to ensure that all of your applications, including your browser and your operating system, are currently updated, and that all of the patches that have been issued for those programs have been installed. The greatest risk to your computer is through vulnerabilities in the software that operates the computer. Unfortunately, patches and updates are a pain to download and install, and very often they're the last thing you think about when doing routine maintenance on your computer. However, a flaw found in an operating system or application is an immediate risk. Take the time to download and install all updates and patches. And if you're one of those people who's just too busy to think about it, consider enabling the automatic update function on your computer. Most computers and operating systems have this function, and it takes the chance out of staying updated.

❋ Never, ever open an attachment that arrives from someone you don't know. And it's even better if you only open attachments that you're expecting from the people that you do know. Too often, a virus is passed from friend to friend, because the assumption is that a file that comes from a friend is safe. If the friend doesn't know she is infected with a virus, however, the file might not be safe, and you take a risk when opening anything that comes from her. If you have a personal policy not to open anything that you aren't expecting, then you greatly reduce your chances of being infected with a piece of malicious software.

❀ If your e-mail program automatically downloads messages, change the setting so that it won't. It's inconvenient, but if you regulate the mail that is downloaded from your mail server, then you reduce your risk of infection. The same is true if your e-mail program has a preview pane that shows you a portion of the message without opening it. Often, this snippet of a preview is enough to activate the download and installation of the malicious code contained in the message. If you have a preview option in your e-mail program, especially if you're not using Web-based e-mail, change that setting so that you don't see a preview of the message.

❀ Use a firewall. There are many great firewalls available on the Internet for free, and some firewall is better than none at all. Of course, if you purchase the full version of one of the software firewalls that you can download online, you'll be getting better protection. There's more information about firewalls and what's available on the Web in Chapter 13.

❀ Install and subscribe to a good antivirus software program. It's not enough to install an antivirus and forget about it. You also need to have a subscription to the antivirus provider's virus definition service. New viruses appear on the Internet every day, making it necessary for the software to be updated every day. Without those updates, you may not be protected from some of the most recently released viruses. Get a good antivirus program (and you'll learn more about what constitutes good in Chapter 14), and then make sure that you keep that program up to date, all the time.

Viruses happen. So do Trojans, worms, and other malware. What makes the difference between getting infected and staying safe is what you do to protect yourself. Use caution when you're handling e-mail and downloads of any kind, and make sure you're using the right protection technologies to keep your system safe.

12 } Spyware

No one likes to be watched, and that's true on the Internet, too. You don't want anyone to have a record of where you go and what you do online unless you give them specific permission to keep record of certain preferences, and even then, you want restrictions put on the type of information that a company can keep about you.

Hold on to your hats, however, because there's an entire classification of software, called spyware, whose whole purpose is to collect information about you and what you do while you're online.

It's called spyware and it's code that is hidden on your computer or installed as part of another program without your knowledge. It's used to gather customer data, display advertising, track computer usage, and in the worst-case scenario, to take control of your computer. Some spyware is relatively harmless. It is used to keep track of your preferences or collect non-personal data that advertisers use to tailor your experience with them to meet your needs and satisfy your tastes. Other spyware can be very dangerous. Hackers use this harmful spyware to gain access to your social security and credit card numbers, your address, and other personal information.

Any program on your computer that collects data about you and your Internet habits is generally referred to as spyware. The most prominent concern about this type of software is that even the most benign type of spyware invades your privacy. It can also affect the performance of your computer and interfere with the programs that you use. Spyware can also change your browser's default homepage, modify your security settings, display windows that can't be closed, launch viruses, and log all of your keystrokes. It's also a growing choice of tools among hackers who steal identities.

In an effort to curb the growing prevalence of spyware, there have been several attempts to create legislation that makes the use of spyware illegal. Utah even passed a law to combat spyware, but opponents stopped the law, claiming that it was too broad and infringed on the rights of legitimate businesses. Since then, no further legislation has been passed.

Corporations within the technology industry have even jumped on the anti-spyware bandwagon. Microsoft, Earthlink, McAfee, and Hewlett-Packard, among others, have joined forces and formed the Anti-Spyware Coalition. The purpose of the organization is to define and classify spyware and standardize the uses for spyware. Even the FDIC is involved in educating consumers about spyware. It's a serious threat to anyone who uses the Internet.

What Is Spyware?

How many times have you logged on to a Web site only to have dozens of pop-up windows thrown at you advertising a variety of different products that may or may not be of interest to you? The program that makes this type of advertising possible is spyware, and beyond being an annoyance, it's a dangerous piece of software that threatens your privacy and your security.

Spyware is a general term used for software that is used in some types of advertising, like pop-up windows. This software is also used to collect personal information or change the configuration of your computer, and usually those changes are made without your consent. One type of spyware that you're probably very familiar with is *adware*.

INSIDER LINGO   Adware: Software that collects your personal or sensitive information and uses it to display advertisements that are supposed to be tailored to you. More often than not, those advertisements are not tailored to you, but instead are a real nuisance.

More malicious types of spyware will make changes to your computer that can be annoying or can even damage your system. This malicious spyware can cause your computer to slow down or crash. It may even have the ability to change your Web browser's home page or add additional components to your browser that you don't want (or need). And changing your settings back to the way they were before the spyware insinuated itself on your computer may require restoring your operating system to an earlier time.

There are a number of ways spyware or other unwanted software can get on your system. A common trick is to covertly install the software during the installation of other software you want, such as a music or video file-sharing program. When you install software on your computer, make sure you read all the documentation that goes along with that software, including the license agreement and privacy statement. Sometimes the inclusion of unwanted software in a given software installation is documented, but it may appear at the end of a license agreement or privacy statement.

There are three main ways that spyware can end up on your computer:

    ❋   Some spyware might be bundled with free software programs that you download from the Internet. These programs could require that you accept pop-up advertising as part of the service that's provided. For example, many file-sharing applications include agreements with their license agreements that state you will allow pop-up advertisements to be displayed on your computer. This type of spyware isn't illegal, but it does seem a little underhanded. You should always completely read the license agreements of any programs that you install on your computer.

❈ Some spyware is installed on your computer before you can use a specific Web site. Usually, you'll be prompted to install an application before you're allowed to enter this site. This could be spyware, and it's usually the sites that offer free products that use this method to trick you into downloading spyware. The spyware is then used to gather information about your or your habits and to push advertisements to you.

❈ Some spyware is installed when spyware makers exploit security holes using viruses, fake e-mail messages, Trojan horses, and ActiveX controls. This type of spyware is most likely to be malicious in intent and to lead to crimes such as identity theft. A good antivirus program combined with a good anti-spyware program can help to keep this type of spyware at bay, though it's not completely foolproof.

More and more spyware is appearing on the Internet and infecting people's computers. The presence of spyware or adware is often not disclosed when you download or install software, and if it is disclosed, it's buried so far down in the license agreement that you're very likely to overlook it if you don't know what you're looking for. That makes it very easy for unscrupulous companies and individuals to take advantage of you.

Why Should You Care?

As bad as spyware is when companies use it, it's even worse when criminals use it to get at your personal and private information. Some spyware is very similar in nature to a virus and you face some of the same risks from spyware that you do from viruses. Some spyware can even leave behind or install malicious code that damages your computer system in addition to wreaking havoc with all of the other actions that it takes.

Your operating system can be affected, and you can suffer computer crashes if the software is uninstalled or if pieces of the software are left behind when you uninstall it. And the damage that's done by spyware can be very costly. It's estimated that more than 75 percent of all computers that connect to the Internet are infected with spyware of some type. And the damage that spyware can do to your system could cost you hundreds of dollars to repair.

How Do You Get It?

One of the most frustrating issues with spyware and adware is the way in which you end up being infected with it. Many times you don't even know you have spyware or adware on your computer. It's installed on your system without your knowledge.

> Amanda heard about a file-sharing program that would allow her to download music and burn it to disc. She was excited about the idea because she loved music, but purchasing entire albums for a single song gets very expensive. So, on the advice of a friend, Amanda downloaded the file-sharing software and installed it on her computer.
>
> The frustration started almost immediately. First she started getting strange errors when she tried to boot certain programs, and then pop-up windows started plaguing her machine. No matter how often she closed the pop-ups, more would just replace them. The final straw was when she opened her Web browser and found that her home page had been changed. She tried multiple times to change it back, but the page kept reverting back to the unwanted Web site. Finally in frustration Amanda uninstalled the file-sharing software.
>
> If only it had all ended there. Even after uninstalling the file-sharing software, Amanda continued to have problems with her computer. Finally, out of desperation she called in a computer technician who wiped the system down completely and reinstalled her operating system. She lost everything on the hard drive in the process.

Amanda's story is just one way that you can get spyware on your system. Many times you agree to download it and just don't realize it. Other times, it's installed on your computer without your knowledge or consent. You can even get spyware by clicking through a link in an e-mail. When you click through the link, the spyware is downloaded in the background without your knowledge.

No matter how you end up with the spyware on your system, however, it's very hard to get rid of. And sometimes even understanding the way that spyware works doesn't help the removal process at all. Spyware is just one persistent piece of software.

Anatomy of Spyware

Any computer that has ever been connected to the Internet could potentially be infected with spyware. In fact, anti-spyware proponents claim that nearly every computer that's connected to the Internet is infected or has been infected by spyware. Unfortunately, like many other types of malicious code, there's no single way to end up with spyware installed on your computer. Once it's there, however, getting rid of it could be a nightmare.

No matter how you get the spyware on your computer—by clicking on a link, agreeing to download it with another application, or through some other method—there are a number of ways it can impact your system. Some of the results you can expect from downloading spyware include.

❊ You might experience poor performance after spyware is installed on your system because your system's resources are bogged down by running the spyware. If your computer is slow, crashes frequently, freezes up often, or is otherwise unstable, it might be sign that there's spyware gumming up the works.

❊ Spyware might cause unwanted or strange browser behavior. Spyware hijacks your browser and could change your default home page or redirect you to search results on pages you don't recognize. You may even notice that your toolbars have been replaced with toolbars or icons that you've never seen before.

❊ Spyware might cause pop-ups to plague your system, even when you aren't on the Internet. Or, if you're getting pop-ups even with software that's supposed to block pop-ups installed and running, then it's likely that spyware has infected your system.

❊ Spyware might even cause you to experience problems when you're using secure Web sites like the page you use when logging in to your e-mail program. Any unexpected trouble in these areas could be spyware, or it could be another type of security issue.

The real conundrum with spyware is that it's possible you won't notice any difference at all in the performance of your computer. Spyware can infect even healthy computers, and you might never know it's there. Your best chance of keeping yourself safe from spyware is to know what to look for and then to use a good anti-spyware program, even if you don't believe that you've been infected.

Tell-Tale Signs

One advertising agent spent many hours working from his home computer. The system worked well and never showed any signs that anything out of the ordinary was happening, but a friend suggested that the advertising agent switch to a new security software suite that included an anti-spyware program.

Because he was worried about viruses and other malicious types of code, the advertising agent decided to give the security suite a try. He installed it and ran both a virus scan and an spyware scan. He was amazed when the spyware scan showed there were more than 1,000 pieces of spyware on the computer, many of which were from pornography Web sites. Since the agent had never been on a pornography Web site, he was confused by the spyware that was found.

It's not unusual for spyware to be related to pornography and other types of seedy materials. It doesn't necessarily mean that the user has been on one of these sites, only that the spyware draws that type of material to the computer. Spyware seems to have no logic or reason, but there is logic and reason to it. Sometimes it's just very obscure, and in the case of pornography, it's one of the most frequently accessed types of information on the Web; therefore, it makes sense to some people that spyware should be linked to pornography.

Regardless of where it comes from or what type of content that it might offer or contain, spyware can be spotted in a few ways. Many of them have already been listed in this chapter, but here are a few more that might help you determine if there's spyware on your system.

- Pop-ups are everywhere, and they're not even related to the Web pages that you're surfing. Those pop-ups might even be related to pornographic Web sites. One of the main ways to spot spyware is through an abundance of pop-up windows. If they start appearing more often, especially when you're using a pop-up blocking software, then you probably have been infected by spyware.

- If new components begin to appear in your Web browser that you don't recognize or remember installing, you might have a spyware infection. Some spyware can add components to existing programs, like your Web browser, so keep your eyes open to details.

- Spyware can cause your system to start experiencing errors that you've never seen before. If your computer begins to suffer from more frequent errors, especially if they are new errors that you haven't seen in the past, you may have spyware on your system. Spyware consumes much of your system resources, so errors and sluggishness are to be expected with a spyware infection.

Spyware is one of those threats that's only serious in the wrong hands, but unfortunately, it can end up in the wrong hands fairly easily, which makes it risky business. Not all spyware is threatening. Some of it is just a nuisance.

The real issue is that all spyware preys on your computer resources. Some of it just takes more than computing power. Stay alert for changes in your system and use the right technologies to keep your information, and your computer, safe from this nuisance.

Examples of Spyware

Spyware can come in many shapes and forms. Then add legitimate programs, like adware that you might prefer wasn't installed on your computer, to the mix, and you have a serious problem that you could overlook if you start having problems with your computer. It's a confusing mess that could leave you with plenty of technological heartache.

When Shawn first started noticing the changes in his computer, he just thought the machine was starting to show its age. He'd had the computer for a little over a year, and it wasn't the latest and greatest thing on the market. But after talking to a friend he found out that his system was still pretty current and shouldn't be experiencing these problems.

So, Shawn did the only thing he could do, he called in an expert to find out what was wrong. What the computer tech told him was that his system was infected with spyware. Dozens of spyware programs were gumming up the works. But Shawn didn't understand where the spyware was coming from.

After talking to the computer tech, he realized that his son's surfing habits were probably to blame. His son is a teenager, and he likes to frequent anime sites and chat rooms. Shawn learned that these are places where it's possible to get spyware. Additionally, his son liked to download free games and play them until the trial period expired. The computer tech told Shawn that many spyware programs come bundled in that type of free software.

Shawn's story could be repeated in millions of households in the US. Spyware is out there, and it's easy to pick up. Many younger computer users frequent Web sites that aren't secure and are at risk for hackers and other malcontents to plant their software on. And because younger users don't fully understand the risks of the Internet, they are more likely to download the types of programs that have software included or to click-through links that might activate software.

The best way to protect yourself from this kind of threat is to understand the danger of the threat and then watch your surfing habits. Try to stay away from sites that might be prone to spyware. Additionally, educate all of the users of your computer about the risks from spyware, and be sure those users know how spyware gets on your machine. Finally, install the proper protection technologies. There are resources that make protecting yourself much easier.

Protecting Yourself

Privacy is a major issue with Internet users. Spyware puts that privacy at risk, but even more important, spyware adds greater risks to the mix by making it possible for hackers and criminals to collect information about you that leads them to steal your identity. And that's on top of the fact that spyware is generally a pain in the computer! It can invade your privacy, it can bombard you with pop-ups, and it can be responsible for computer crashes and other problems.

Here are some strategies to help you keep spyware off your computer.

❋ Be sure all of your software is up to date. Spyware may exploit vulnerabilities in your operating system and other programs, so one of the best ways to protect yourself from spyware (and other threats) is to stay updated and patched. Use your operating system's automatic updates if necessary to stay current.

❋ Use the right protection technologies. Antivirus programs and firewalls are essential to protecting yourself from spyware. Although it's not technically a virus, some antivirus programs have anti-spyware capabilities, and firewalls will protect you from unwanted intruders that spyware might let into your system. Anti-spyware applications are also a requirement for protecting yourself. Find a good anti-spyware program and use it to scan your computer for spyware regularly. Once a month is good, once a week is better.

❋ Make sure your Web browser's security settings are adjusted to the right level to protect you. If you're using Microsoft's Internet Explorer, you can set your security settings to allow only the information that you want to accept. You can view your current Internet Explorer settings by going to the Tools menu and clicking on Internet Options. Figure 12.1 shows the dialog box that appears. Select the Security tab and your security settings will appear. From that window you can change them as you like.

Figure 12.1

The Internet Options dialog box.

❋ Use safe practices when surfing the Web and downloading programs. Most of those safe practices are ones that you've probably heard a dozen times: Don't download files from people you don't know or Web sites you don't trust; be wary of free programs; don't click Okay or Agree to close out of pop-up windows; and be sure to read all the documentation that comes with software *before* you download and install the software. It's also wise if you remind other computer users in your home of these basics frequently.

Protecting yourself isn't difficult. However, even the most diligent Internet user can end up with spyware on her computer. The real issue with spyware is that it is often very hard to remove. Once it gets into your system, it digs in, and getting it out could take some serious effort. That's if you do get it all. And in the process, you're likely to delete something that you need, and then you'll find yourself with a real mess on your computer.

Your best option is to find a spyware removal tool like SpyBlaster or SpyBot to find and remove spyware for you. Your ISP might be able to recommend a spyware removal tool that it thinks is very effective, or you can surf through technology sites like CNET to find out what spyware removal tools technology editors recommend.

There are now even some ISPs that provide security tools like spyware removal tools for you, and the cost is included in your monthly service fee. Comcast cable Internet service is one of those companies. Comcast provides its members with a comprehensive security suite from McAfee that includes tools to help with spyware removal and antivirus protection.

 Be careful about downloading spyware removal programs that are free. There are some very good free spyware removal tools that come from reputable software distributors. A tool offered by an unknown distributor could be a virus or even spyware rather than a protection technology, so use caution and do business only with well-known and respected companies.

Once you have the removal tool downloaded and installed, then you need to run it regularly to protect yourself. Most security experts recommend scanning your computer for spyware at least once a month. However, it's more effective if you scan for spyware weekly, especially if you use the Internet frequently or if there are multiple users on your computer.

When your removal tool is finished running, you'll probably be shown a list of spyware that it found on your computer. You have to select which programs you want deleted and which you want to stay. Delete them all. The spyware removal tool won't bring you anything that's essential to your computer, and no spyware is really good spyware, so let the program dispose of everything that it finds.

 If you've downloaded free programs from the Internet that are infected with spyware, after you use your spyware removal tool, using the free programs will re-install any spyware that came with them to your computer. If you're really worried about spyware, consider not using freeware programs at all.

Although some spyware is benign, it's likely to become more of a threat as criminals and hackers continue to search for ways to get at your personal information. Protecting yourself from spyware, like protecting yourself from any cybersecurity threat, is a requirement if you want to stay safe online.

III } Understanding Protection Technologies

There are two ways to protect yourself from cybercrimes. The easiest way is to alter the way you behave when you're surfing the Web and using e-mail. But behavior modification is only useful to a point. At that point it doesn't matter how closely you monitor your behavior and habits—risk becomes threat.

That's where protection technologies come in. Firewalls, antivirus programs, and spyware protection are all technologies that are designed to keep your computer and your network safe.

In addition, there are some strategies that you can put in place. How you create your passwords, for example, can make all the difference in how well protected you are. Having a personal security plan is another of those areas where you can make a major difference in your online safety.

Those are all topics that are addressed in this section of the book. The technologies are explained and suggestions are made for using them. Strategies are suggested for other steps you can take to keep yourself safe, and an explanation of how to develop and implement a personal security plan is included.

By the time you finish this section of the book, you should have all the tools you need to keep yourself safe from cybercrimes.

13 } Firewalls

Many houses have firewalls—special protective spaces that help prevent fires from spreading. Cars have firewalls—protective barriers between the passenger cabin and the engine compartment. Why shouldn't computers have firewalls? If yours doesn't, it should.

Firewalls provide protection against outside attackers by shielding your computer or network from unnecessary and malicious Internet traffic. They can be configured to block some data or traffic while allowing other data and traffic through.

When the Internet first became popular, most people connected via a dial-up modem that required an open telephone line to connect to the Internet. By its very nature, dial-up Internet access was safer than today's always-on, broadband Internet connections, because Internet users were connected to the Internet for a limited amount of time. When not using the Internet, the dial-up connection would eventually terminate automatically.

The broadband Internet connection is always open. Hackers who were dealing with dial-up Internet connections were constantly under threat of being disconnected, but now hackers who gain access through a broadband connection have an unlimited amount of time in which they can carry out whatever mission they are currently pursuing.

That's where a computer firewall comes in. The firewall acts as the sentry that stands just outside the door to make sure that no one who doesn't have clearance makes it through the door. Firewalls are one of the most critical pieces of your protection arsenal. But simply having a firewall isn't enough. You must also have the firewall active and properly configured to ensure that it's providing the right protection to meet your needs.

What Is a Firewall?

A firewall is a piece of hardware or software that is designed to keep malicious intruders out of your computer and your network, if you have one. The catch is that the firewall has to be configured properly in order to provide the protection that you need.

Firewalls block malicious attacks and protect your computer from outside threats, including Trojans and hostile applications that seek to take over your computer. There are even software firewall packages that are designed specifically for personal use and are inexpensive. Most of these programs require little setup on your part, but it's a myth that they are entirely plug-n-play. If you don't configure the settings on your firewall properly, then you're leaving gaps in protection that come with standard manufacturer's settings.

When you're connected to the Internet, information is sent in small units, called packets, every time you click to navigate a page or send an e-mail message. Each of these packets contains your IP address, the recipient's IP address, and a piece of data, request, command, or other information about your interactions on the Internet.

These packets, like any type of mail, are pieces of information that you want to have access to. However, you may not want anyone else to have access to that information, because it could be private or personal. A firewall examines these data packets as they travel to and from your computer to see if they meet certain criteria.

The packets then are either passed or blocked according to the criteria defined in your configuration and the capabilities of the firewall. Anything sent or received by your computer must go through the firewall, which filters those packets based on IP addresses and packet content, as well as the specific functions of an application.

There are several types of firewalls. Some of the distinctions that separate one type of firewall from another include

* Some firewalls filter traffic by packets. Every packet must be examined and approved as it moves from your computer to the Internet or from the Internet to your computer.
* Some firewalls filter at the circuit level, which means that only communication that comes from approved computers and Internet services is allowed to enter or exit your computer.
* Stateful inspection firewalls examine configuration of packets as they move into or out of the computer and approve or reject those packets based on that configuration.

Fortunately, choosing a personal firewall doesn't require an in-depth understanding of these types of firewalls, as they are mostly used by corporations. Personal firewalls have all of the packet level, circuit level, and stateful characteristics necessary to keep your computer safe. They don't require the stronger protection technologies that corporate firewalls do, and personal firewalls are designed with your personal protection (and habits) in mind.

How Does It Protect You?

A firewall is simply a program or hardware device that filters the information coming through the Internet connection into your computer system or home network. If, based on the configuration of your firewall, a packet of information is flagged by the filters, it is not allowed past the firewall.

This is how you're protected from hackers and criminals who are trying to gain access to your computer.

Without a firewall in place, your computer is accessible to anyone on the Internet. A person who knows what he is doing can probe the Internet looking for unprotected connections that can be exploited to gain access to your machine. Once he finds a small chink in your armor, it only takes a few minutes and some keyboard time to have access to any information that's on your computer or that you access with your computer.

With a firewall in place, your computer is much more protected, and it's much harder for hackers and criminals to find a way to get in. Once they do, the games begin and it's not long before you realize that you've been victimized. When it gets to that point, there's little that you can do except try to stop the abuse and repair the damage as quickly as possible.

Firewalls may use one or a combination of several different methods to control traffic flowing in and out of the network.

❋ Some firewalls control traffic using packet filtering. Packets are analyzed against a set of filters, or rules, and those that make it through the filters are sent on to their destination. Those that do not are discarded.

❋ Some firewalls control traffic using a proxy service. Information from the Internet is retrieved by the firewall and then sent to the requesting system, or information is retrieved from the system and sent to the Internet. These requests and inspections are based on guidelines laid out within the firewall.

❋ Some firewalls control traffic using a process called stateful inspection. This is a method of inspection that doesn't examine the contents of each packet but instead compares certain key parts of the packet to a database of trusted information. Information traveling from inside the firewall to the outside is monitored for specific defining characteristics, then incoming information is compared to these characteristics. If the comparison yields a reasonable match, the information is allowed through. Otherwise it is discarded.

Even having a firewall in place isn't guaranteed protection. Hackers and criminals will try a variety of ways to gain access to your computer and to gather personal or sensitive information about you. Some of those methods of attack include

❋ **Remote Login:** Hackers gain access to your computer remotely through a hole in your defenses. Once logged on to your system, they can view or access your files and even run programs on your computer.

❋ **Application Backdoors:** Some applications are actually designed with a feature that allows for remote access. Those that don't can be infected with a virus or other bug that provides a backdoor, or hidden access. Hackers and criminals use that backdoor to gain access and control applications or programs.

❄ **SMTP Session Hijacking:** SMTP is the most common protocol used for sending e-mail over the Internet. By gaining access to a list of e-mail addresses, a hacker or criminal can send spam to thousands of users. This is usually done by redirecting the e-mail through the SMTP server of an unsuspecting host, making the actual sender of the spam difficult to trace.

❄ **Denial of Service:** You have probably heard this phrase used in news reports about attacks on major Web sites. This type of attack is nearly impossible to counter. The hacker or criminal sends a request to the server to connect to it. But when the server responds with an acknowledgement and tries to establish a session, it can't find the system that made the request. By inundating a server with these unanswerable session requests, a hacker causes the server to slow to a crawl or eventually crash.

❄ **E-mail Bombs:** An e-mail bomb is usually a personal attack. Someone sends you the same e-mail hundreds or thousands of times until your e-mail system cannot accept any more messages.

❄ **Viruses:** A virus is a small program that can copy itself to other computers. This way it can spread quickly from one system to the next. Viruses range from harmless messages to programs that can erase all of your data or completely shut down your computer.

❄ **Spam:** Spam is unsolicited e-mail that is typically harmless but always annoying. It's the electronic equivalent of junk mail, and under the right conditions, it can be dangerous. Some spam includes Web site links that actually install a piece of code called a *cookie* that provides a backdoor to your computer.

❄ **INSIDER LINGO**   Cookie: A small piece of software that, when installed on a computer, monitors and tracks the movement of the user as he surfs the Internet. This information is stored or transmitted to the organization that uses the cookie for the purpose of creating a more targeted user experience.

That's a short list of the attacks that you face, just from surfing the Internet. Some of those items are very hard, if not impossible, to filter using a firewall. To ensure that you're protected from all eventualities, you should install antivirus software on your computer as well. You'll learn more about antivirus software in the next chapter.

The level of security you establish with your firewall will help determine how many of these threats can be stopped. The highest level of security would be to simply block everything, but that defeats the purpose of having an Internet connection. Instead, a good rule of thumb is to block everything, then begin to select what types of traffic you will allow. You can also restrict traffic that travels through the firewall so that only certain types of information, such as e-mail, can get through.

Are There Pitfalls to Using a Firewall?

Your firewall is your first line of defense against criminals and hackers who want access to your computer, and therefore to your personal information, but you should be aware that using a firewall isn't always a walk in the park.

One of the biggest pitfalls of a firewall is that it can block even the things that you do want to allow to have access to your computer. For example, if you have a remote access program that allows you to access your desktop from another computer, your firewall might block it if the firewall isn't configured to let it through. The easiest way around these types of frustrations is to set permission for all of the programs that you want to be allowed access.

Another pitfall that you might face is trouble setting up a home network. Firewalls are designed to keep people out, and networks are about connecting people. Many users find themselves frustrated when they try to establish a home network because the firewall won't grant access to the other computers on the network. Fortunately, this is a configuration issue, and it's usually easy enough to figure out just by reading the software's documentation.

In all, firewalls are very effective safety applications. The frustrations that you might encounter when using a firewall are far outweighed by the protection benefits of the firewall, so don't get discouraged. Without your firewall it's almost certain that you'll fall victim to a cybercrime in short order.

Choosing a Firewall

Choosing a firewall can seem complicated. In truth, however, it's not all that difficult. The first thing you need to understand is the difference between a hardware firewall and a software firewall.

A hardware firewall is a separate appliance running a firewall. A software firewall is software that operates directly from your PC.

There are advantages and disadvantages with both camps. A hardware firewall usually sits between your PC and the Internet, and can protect all the computers on your network. If you are running more than one computer on your network, then a hardware firewall allows you to just have one firewall protecting every machine, rather then needing a firewall installed on each individual computer.

A software firewall runs directly on your PC and can serve only that one computer. By default a software firewall will prevent any application from accessing the Internet that you haven't given explicit permission to. So, for example, the first time you try to check your e-mail, the software firewall will ask you if your e-mail application is allowed to access the Internet or not. This allows a higher degree of protection from spyware and viruses by controlling what goes out as well as what comes in.

Not all firewalls are created equal, and a firewall doesn't have to be expensive to be effective. Following are explanations of the different types of firewalls available to you.

Freeware

Freeware is just what it sounds like—free software—and there are many free versions of firewalls available that will help to protect you from hackers and criminals when you're using the Internet. For example, if you're using a recent version of the Windows operating system, you probably already know Microsoft has included a personal firewall as part of its systems package. This firewall will do a fair job of protecting your computer, and if you don't have any other firewall installed, this freeware is better than none at all.

The Windows firewall prevents worms and other malware, as well as some routine hacking attempts, from entering your machine through open ports and the like. It does not check outgoing traffic, so if a worm or virus gets into your machine, or if some other type of malware attempts to communicate with the outside world, the Windows firewall will do nothing to stand in its way.

There are freeware versions of firewalls that you can download from the Internet that will stand in the way. For example, one is ZoneAlarm from Zone Labs (www.zonelabs.com). The free version of this highly regarded firewall is available for personal use with a simple download. Zone Labs includes an automatic update feature that will prompt you when a new version of their software is available and take you to a download site.

ZoneAlarm, even in its free version, is a full implementation of a personal firewall. While there are limits to what it can do, it will prevent intrusion by worms or hackers, and it will prevent them from getting out if they do get on your machine.

Software

Some operating systems include a built-in firewall; if yours does, consider enabling it to add another layer of protection even if you have an external firewall. If you don't have a built-in firewall, you can obtain a software firewall from your local computer store, software vendor, or ISP. Because of the risks associated with downloading software from the Internet onto an unprotected computer, it is best to install the firewall from a CD, DVD, or floppy disk.

Any of the firewalls that major security vendors offer will work well to protect your computer, but which one you choose depends on what else you have on your computer and what you're doing with it. For example, if you're already using an antivirus product, you might consider getting a firewall from the same vendor. In some cases, the vendor will offer a suite of security applications that provide all of the protection that you need. This combination of protection technologies makes it easier for you to manage all of your security functions from a central location.

Hardware Firewalls

Hardware firewalls are external devices that are positioned between your computer or network and your cable or DSL modem. Many vendors and some ISPs offer routers that also include firewall features. Hardware-based firewalls are particularly useful for protecting multiple computers, but they also offer a high degree of protection for a single computer.

Hardware-based firewalls have the advantage of being separate devices running their own operating systems, so they provide an additional line of defense against attacks. Their major drawback is cost, but if you look, you can probably find a hardware firewall that's reasonably priced.

So what do hardware firewalls do exactly? More than anything, they stop malicious software from gaining access to your system. To do this, hardware firewalls employ numerous functions.

❋ **Network Address Translation (NAT):** Every system on the Internet has an IP address which is used to connect with other computers across the network. NAT prevents unauthorized connections by giving computers behind the firewall a set of private addresses while presenting to the world a single, public address. The disguised IP address makes it difficult for others to get through the firewall to an individual computer.

❋ **Port Management:** By default, most hardware firewalls close unsolicited access to all ports on your computer. So if a hacker or criminal tries to form a connection with TCP port 80 (used for Web connections) or TCP port 25 (used for outbound e-mail), the firewall would ignore the request. As far as the inquiring software can tell, there is simply nothing there. On the other hand, firewalls can let you open specific ports to link up with other systems across the Internet.

❋ **Stateful Packet Inspection:** A firewall can do more than simply prohibit packets from a specific source and take action based on the content or behavior of packets. For instance, a stateful firewall can tell if an incoming packet was unsolicited or if it arrived in response to a request from the local network. This prevents intruders from sneaking into your computer without your knowledge.

❋ **Virtual Private Networking:** A virtual private network is a method for establishing encrypted, point-to-point connections across the Internet. A good firewall will block the encrypted connection between a remote device and the virtual private network software. Firewalls with support for virtual private networks can pass through these encrypted links.

❋ **Content and URL filtering:** Firewalls can also offer higher-level features for blocking access to URLs that contain a specified string of letters or to any sites that fall outside of a list of accepted Web domain names.

A hardware firewall offers some advantages over a software firewall, but unless you have very sensitive information that could be dangerous if it falls into the wrong hands, there's probably no reason for you to go to the extra expense of installing a hardware firewall. Most software firewalls will provide all of the protection that you need.

Installing and Configuring Your Firewall

Installing your firewall will probably be a very easy task. In most cases, all you need to do is insert the disk into the disk drive and then follow the prompts that the installation program provides.

However, if you're using the Windows XP operating system, before installing your personal firewall, be sure that the firewall built into Windows XP is disabled. Never use two software firewalls at the same time. Completely uninstall one before installing another.

Use the vendor's uninstall utility or the Windows XP add/remove software tool in the control panel. After you install a firewall, be sure to check it with a service like the Security Space Desktop Audit to make sure that it is configured correctly. Testing your firewall is the only sure way to tell that your computer is really being protected.

Installation Guidelines

Nearly everyone understands the need for antivirus software, but it may not be clear why a firewall is also needed. The two reinforce each other and back each other up. Firewalls use safe computing rules to protect your computer from intrusion, while antivirus software scans your file system for known malware that has slipped through the firewall, then removes it when found.

Fortunately, installing a firewall on your computer is fairly easy to accomplish. Here are the steps you should follow to get your firewall installed.

1. Insert the software disc into your CD drive.

2. If the disc doesn't run automatically, select Start > Run.

3. In the Run menu, select the drive where the CD is, and click OK.

4. The program should begin to install on your hard drive. Simply follow the prompts in the installation wizard.

5. When the installation is complete, you may need to restart your computer to get the firewall to take effect.

It's really that simple. However, once the firewall is installed you might find it takes a few days to get it configured to allow you to work as you normally would. When your firewall won't let you do something, resist the temptation to shut it down completely. Take the time to define the different programs and applications that should be allowed access to your computer or the Internet. And don't turn the firewall off. Once the firewall is down, it will take hackers or criminals only seconds to locate your unprotected computer and begin trying to gain access to it.

Configuration Guidelines

Most commercially available firewall products, both hardware- and software-based, come configured in a manner that is acceptably secure for most users. Since each firewall is different, you'll need to read and understand the documentation that comes with the firewall you've chosen in order to determine whether or not the default settings on your firewall are sufficient for your needs.

Additional assistance may be available from your firewall vendor or your ISP. Alerts about current viruses or worms sometimes also include information about restrictions you can implement through your firewall.

Properly configured firewalls may be effective at blocking some attacks, but don't be lulled into a false sense of security. Although they do offer a certain amount of protection, firewalls do not guarantee that your computer will not be attacked. In particular, a firewall offers little or no protection against viruses that work by having you run the infected program on your computer, as many e-mail-borne viruses do. However, using a firewall in conjunction with other security technologies will help protect you against many attacks.

Firewalls are not a silver bullet that will shield you from all threats, but they do help keep your system safer. The firewall will not detect or block specific threats the way an antivirus program does, nor will it stop you from clicking on a link in a phishing scam e-mail message or from executing a file infected with a worm. It simply restricts the flow of traffic into and out of your computer to provide a line of defense against programs or individuals who might try to connect to your computer without your approval.

Many firewalls, by default, will block most incoming traffic and restrict attempts by programs to communicate with the Internet. You can usually add or remove programs that should be allowed to communicate through the firewall, or you can open up specific TCP/IP ports so that any communications on those ports will be passed through the firewall.

As a general rule, whenever you install a new security technology, like a firewall, you should review all of the default settings to ensure that they provide enough protection for your computer. Many applications are set to the lowest level of protection, leaving your computer vulnerable on some levels. By using the application's administrative functions, you should be able to adjust the security settings of your firewall to provide you with the protection that you need.

The default settings of your firewall will provide some protection for you. In some cases, they may even provide more protection than you want. Take the time to learn about the settings and adjustments available through your firewall, and then adjust them to suit your own personal needs.

Troubleshooting

Any software application can give you fits at times, and firewalls are no exception. Sometimes, the configuration of your firewall conflicts with the configurations of other applications that you use. If this is the case, try adjusting the settings of your firewall until you find a happy medium that allows you to remain protected and still have access to all of your applications.

If you have doubts as to whether you've properly configured your firewall, there are some vulnerability tests available on the Internet that you can use to test your firewall and find out how protected you really are. A few of those testing sites are listed below.

* Shields UP!— https://www.grc.com/x/ne.dll?bh0bkyd2
* PC Flank—http://www.pcflank.com/about.htm
* Sygate Tests—http://scan.sygate.com

Once you run these tests on your computer you should have a good understanding of why you need a firewall and how well your firewall protects you from the threats that you face on the Internet.

There is no single protection technology that will keep you safe from every security threat that you face online. However, a firewall is a good first step in getting your computer, and therefore your personal and confidential information, protected. Just take the time ensure that you install and configure the firewall in a manner that will balance the need to keep your computer safe with your need to have access to the Internet and all of your applications.

14 } Antivirus Software

According to industry experts, between 150 and 300 new viruses are released every day. Viruses are one of the most prolific threats on the Internet, so what are you to do?

When you consider that the term virus actually encompasses more, and more dangerous, threats than just viruses, the only logical thing to do is to use whatever means necessary to protect your computer. Fortunately, it's not that difficult to get protected and stay protected from viruses, worms, Trojans, or other types of malware.

Part of that protection comes in the form of antivirus software, and you don't have to pay a lot to get great protection. There are many programs available that offer a variety of protection levels. What's most important is that you have an antivirus program, and that you keep it up-to-date.

The types of viruses that you face will change daily. There may be viruses that hang around forever, simply because they are well-constructed and hard to get rid of. However, as long as you have up-to-date virus protection, you are protected from those viruses and from the new ones that threaten you every day.

What Is Antivirus Software?

Antivirus software is an application that helps to protect your computer against most viruses, worms, Trojans, and other types of malware by recognizing and rendering that malware harmless. These malware programs perform malicious acts, such as deleting files, accessing personal data, or using your computer to attack other computers.

There are many levels of antivirus software available. Some ISPs provide antivirus software with their monthly Internet service. The fee for this type of antivirus is included in the monthly service fee that you pay for your Internet service, and the quality of the antivirus software is usually very good. And for good reason. If your ISP provides you with quality antivirus software, that reduces the liability to the ISP for damage done by viruses and other types of malware. That cost can be very high, too. On average, viruses cost businesses more than $55 billion each year.

To be effective, your antivirus software should have current virus definitions or descriptions. Those definitions are how the application recognizes the virus and quarantines it so that it's not capable of doing any further damage to your system. The antivirus software also removes the malicious software from your computer so that it can't do any further damage, and it removes it in such a way that no other programs or applications are harmed.

To accomplish this, antivirus software has to have a way of cataloging virus information to be used to locate and remove viruses. To do this, antivirus software tracks viruses using either a dictionary approach or by looking for certain suspicious behavior.

In the dictionary approach, when the antivirus software examines a file, it refers to a dictionary of known viruses that the authors of the antivirus software have identified. If a piece of code in the file matches any virus identified in the dictionary, then the antivirus software attempts to repair the file by removing the virus, quarantines the file so that it's inaccessible and cannot replicate, or it deletes the infected file.

To be successful, the dictionary approach requires periodic downloads of updated virus dictionary entries. As new viruses are discovered and identified, they are included in existing listings of virus information, also called virus dictionaries.

Dictionary-based antivirus software typically examines files when the computer's operating system creates, opens, closes, or e-mails them. This way the software can detect a known virus immediately upon receipt.

The dictionary approach can effectively contain virus outbreaks in the right circumstances; virus authors have tried to stay a step ahead of such software by writing viruses that are partially encrypted or otherwise modified as a method of disguise. When disguised like this, the virus doesn't match any of the listings in the dictionary, so it goes unnoticed until the newest iteration of the virus is recognized and cataloged.

Another approach is the suspicious behavior approach. This approach doesn't attempt to identify known viruses, but instead monitors the behavior of all programs. If one program tries to write data to an executable program, for example, the antivirus software can flag this suspicious behavior, alert the user, and ask what to do.

Unlike the dictionary approach, the suspicious behavior approach provides protection against brand-new viruses that do not yet exist in any virus dictionaries. Unfortunately, this approach to protecting you against viruses also creates a number of false alarms which leads users to become desensitized to all the warnings over time.

Because this type of antivirus works on the behavioral patterns of viruses, if the user accepts the recommended course of action on every warning, then the antivirus software effectively restricts all operations to the point of being useless. This problem has worsened since 1997, since many more non-malicious program designs came to modify other .exe files without regard to the issue of false positives. Today antivirus applications are using this type of recognition less and less because it's becoming less and less effective.

The purpose of antivirus software is to find and quarantine or remove viruses from your computer. Unfortunately, there may be times when viruses get past the antivirus program, so it's always a good idea to use caution when downloading files or viewing your e-mail.

How Does It Protect You?

Although details may vary among packages, antivirus software scans files or your computer's memory for certain patterns that may indicate an infection. The patterns it looks for are based on the signatures, or definitions, of known viruses. Virus authors are continually releasing new and updated viruses, so it is important that you have the latest definitions installed on your computer.

Once you have installed an antivirus package, you should scan your entire computer periodically. Your antivirus software protects you in a couple of ways.

❈ Most antivirus programs have automatic scans that review specific files or directories and prompt you for action if anything out of the ordinary is found. Automatic scans can be arranged to take place at any time that is convenient for you.

❈ Antivirus programs will also have manual scanning capabilities so that you can scan files you receive from outside sources before opening them. This includes saving and scanning e-mail attachments or Web downloads rather than selecting the option to open them directly from the source, and scanning floppy disks, CDs, or DVDs for viruses before opening any of the files.

Each package has its own method of response when it locates a virus, and the response may differ according to whether the software locates the virus during an automatic or a manual scan. Sometimes the software will produce a dialog box alerting you that it has found a virus and asking whether you want it to remove the virus. In other cases, the software may attempt to remove the virus without asking you first.

This process may differ depending on what product you choose, so find out what your antivirus software requires. Many antivirus packages include an option to automatically receive updated virus definitions. Because new information is added frequently, you should take advantage of this option. See Appendix C for a link to some of these resources.

Installing antivirus software is one of the easiest and most effective ways to protect your computer, but it has its limitations. Because it relies on signatures, antivirus software can only detect viruses that have signatures installed on your computer, so it is important to keep these signatures up-to-date and use additional types of protections to catch the files that might get past your antivirus software.

The Pitfalls of Antivirus Software

It seems that any software that you install on your system these days has some kind of drawback. For example, many programs are riddled with flaws that make your computer vulnerable to all kinds of security threats. Antivirus software isn't exempt from the pitfalls of software.

One of the difficulties that you may experience with antivirus software is that it can weigh heavily on your performance quality. Some antivirus software uses so much of your computer's resources that it can have many of the same effects on your computer that viruses and malware have.

Unfortunately, because the software creates problems with the operating system, some users may disable the program and leave themselves vulnerable to all the bugs that are out there. It's not enough simply to have the antivirus software on your computer; you must also keep it active and up-to-date for it to protect you.

Another issue is that there are various methods for encrypting and packing malicious software that make even well-known viruses undetectable to antivirus software. Detecting these viruses requires a special feature that can decrypt the files before examining them. Unfortunately, many popular antivirus programs do not have this feature and are often unable to detect encrypted viruses. So, while you think that you're protected, in actuality, you're not *entirely* protected, and you can still be infected by viruses.

Finally, some software installations require that antivirus software be disabled before the installation begins. This creates two issues. First, the very fact that the antivirus program has to be disabled creates security risks. If the antivirus program isn't scanning for viruses and other types of malicious software, then what's stopping criminals and hackers from putting malicious software on your computer as you install your new program? It could even be bundled with the new program.

The second issue is that ignoring the warning to disable your antivirus software could prevent the software that you're installing from installing properly. So it's a conundrum. You're in danger if you do disable your antivirus protection, and you're in danger if you don't. The best you can do is follow the instructions for installation and then reactivate your antivirus software immediately.

No software comes without some disadvantage. And antivirus software may have some of the same disadvantages that other types of software have. However, the tradeoff between the advantages and disadvantages is worth some frustration. The damage that can be done by malicious software such as viruses, Trojans, and worms is considerable, and antivirus software will help protect you from some of that damage.

It won't protect you from all of it. There is no single software protection program that will. The best that you can hope for is to create a combination of programs that help keep you safe while you're using the Internet and e-mail programs.

Choosing Antivirus Software

There are many vendors who produce antivirus software, and deciding which one to choose can be confusing. All antivirus software performs essentially the same function, so your decision may be driven by recommendations, particular features, availability, or price.

There is no real right or wrong answer when it comes to choosing antivirus software. Make your choice based on recommendations, and take the time to try a few different antivirus programs before you decide to buy a full version. You may find that although everyone you asked recommends a particular package, when you install it on your computer it begins to create issues with your operating system, while a different package that someone mentioned in passing fits well with your normal usage and doesn't consume all of your resources.

Consider features and price when you're evaluating software, too. Prices are pretty similar across the industry. Most antivirus programs will cost you around $50 for the full suite. But there are some antivirus programs that are very good and won't cost you a thing. The features that you need, of course, will depend on how you use the Internet and what types of protection you're looking for. Most antivirus programs protect from more than just viruses. Check with the vendors that you're considering to find out exactly what protection you can expect from their products.

Installing any antivirus software, regardless of which package you choose, increases your level of protection. However, you should be suspicious of e-mail messages that claim to be from your ISP and have an antivirus program attached. It's true that many ISPs are providing antivirus software and firewalls for their existing customers; however, there are scams playing on that fact, and these e-mails that appear to be from your ISP are actually from hackers and criminals, and the attachment that claims to be antivirus software is actually a virus or other piece of malicious code.

ISPs won't send out antivirus software to all of their users. Instead, these companies may send you an e-mail telling you that these programs are available on their Web site. As with all types of cybersecurity threats, use caution when opening any attachments that you aren't expecting.

Choosing an antivirus program isn't that difficult. And once you decide what program will work best for you, the hard part is done. All that's left is installing it and getting it working for you.

Freeware

Freeware is software that's available for free on the Internet. There are some freeware antivirus programs that work very well. For example, Grisoft makes an antivirus program called AVG that is highly recommended and very efficient at protecting you from malicious software, including viruses.

The AVG software is easy to install and easy to use, and the cost is just right. If you want to know more about the AVG antivirus software, you can find out more at http://www.grisoft.com.

Of course, AVG isn't the only freeware program on the Internet. There are several that are very good and very easy to use. To find additional freeware antivirus programs, use Google to search for "free antivirus."

Just use caution when downloading free antivirus software. Some hackers and criminals think it's funny to provide you with malicious code or even a bogus program that offers no protection at all when you think you're downloading antivirus protection. Use only software provided by reputable companies. To find out if the software that you're looking at comes from a reputable vendor, search for the vendor and the name of the software online. Any derogatory experience that users have experienced with that company or product will probably show up in that search.

Software

Antivirus software isn't difficult to find. There are many different types of antivirus software available on the Web or at your local office supply store, and your favorite software vendor probably also carries antivirus software. Finding it is the easy part.

In an effort to protect themselves, many ISPs have moved to providing antivirus software to their users free of charge. This software is the same that you would receive if you were to buy it directly from an antivirus software provider, and it will protect your computer just as well.

Some people still prefer to have their own antivirus separate from their ISPs. If that's the case, you can find a good program without a lot of difficulty. However, note that you can't run two separate antivirus programs on your computer without creating conflicts. Decide on one antivirus program and remove the other from your system.

Once you've chosen the software, all that's left is installing and configuring it, and that's not all that difficult to do either.

Installing and Configuring Your Antivirus Software

Software today is so much easier to install than it was in the past. There was a time when installing any kind of software was a major headache that led to frustration and sometimes even caused users to give up completely because they couldn't figure it out. Fortunately, software installations have matured over time.

Today, installing any program is as easy as inserting the program CD into your CD drive and following the prompts that appear. If you're installing software from a downloaded file, then all you need to do is double-click the file, and the installation will start. Then, simply follow the prompts provided by the installation wizard, and in no time at all your antivirus software will be installed and protecting your system.

Installation Guidelines

Installing your antivirus program should be fairly easy to do. However, with antivirus software, installation doesn't end when the program is installed on your computer. The software is only as effective as its latest definitions, which is the list of viruses the software can detect. So, it is imperative that you keep the software updated and keep the current definitions downloaded and installed.

Because of the high number of viruses for Windows, most Windows antivirus software has a capability built in to the program to automatically update its definitions on a set schedule. You can set the frequency of those updates from daily to weekly or monthly, whichever time frame works best for you. If you have an always-on broadband connection, you should definitely set your updates to take place daily. If you use dial-up Internet, you probably still want to have the updates done daily, but you can get away with doing them once a week if you find that it gums up the works to do the updates so frequently.

Before you install any antivirus program, be sure to uninstall any existing antivirus software on your computer, including previous versions of any antivirus software that you're currently using.

To install the new antivirus program, insert the disc in your disc drive. If the disc doesn't auto-read, then you'll need to go to the Start menu, select Run, and then select the drive the disc is in. This should start the installation process; then all you need to do is follow the prompts from the installation wizard. When you launch the software for the first time, you'll probably be prompted to configure how you want to install updates and virus definitions. You can learn more about this by reading the documentation that comes with the software.

Configuration Guidelines

All antivirus programs will have an administrative screen or control panel of some kind. From this control panel you can set how you would like the software to perform, from blocking everything to allowing anything. How strong or weak you want your antivirus software to be is up to you.

Regardless of the settings that you choose for your antivirus software, unless it's updated regularly, it won't be of much use to you. Out-of-date antivirus software is ineffective antivirus software. The software relies on regular updates to help protect against the latest threats. If you aren't subscribed to these updates, your computer may be vulnerable to attacks by malicious software. Here are some tips for making sure your antivirus software stays current.

❊ Purchase an annual subscription from your antivirus software company to make sure your antivirus software stays current and effective. If you have purchased a subscription, most antivirus software will update itself when you are connected to the Internet unless you've changed the default configuration for updates. You can change how often you want updates to be downloaded and installed, and you can usually change the way you are notified about the need for or delivery of those updates. For example, if it's time to receive updates to your antivirus software and you haven't signed online for a while, the program can remind you to go online so the update can be completed. Or, if you prefer to have actions like this happen automatically without your knowledge, you can turn the notifications off completely.

❋ To ensure your software is up-to-date, open your antivirus program from the Start menu or the taskbar notification area and look for the update status. If you still aren't sure if your antivirus software is up-to-date, contact your antivirus software provider. Fortunately, most antivirus programs will tell you if they are out of date.

The following settings should be enabled by default when you install the software and shouldn't be disabled for extended periods of time. If you do have to disable these settings to install new software or for any other reason, be sure to re-enable them as soon as possible.

❋ If your program allows for real-time scanning, and it should, then that feature should be enabled on your administrative panel. If you disable real-time scanning, you leave your system open to vulnerabilities. Real-time scanning provides examination of everything that you're doing, in real time. This includes sending and receiving e-mails and downloading files.

❋ Your program should have a schedule for regular scanning of your hard drive. Be sure this schedule is set to happen frequently. Once a week is fine, but daily is better.

❋ Your antivirus program should also be set to scan your e-mail in real time. Since e-mail is one of the greatest areas of threat, if you scan them as they are coming in and going out, you're staying one step ahead of the game.

Configuration can seem like an overwhelming task when you're installing your antivirus protection. When in doubt, use the most protective settings on the program. You can always go back and change them if you find that those settings are too restrictive. To change them, simply pull up your program's control panel by clicking the program icon in the icon tray at the bottom of your screen, or by double-clicking the icon for the program on your desktop.

Antivirus by itself is just software. In order to be effective, you must have the program actively scanning your files, and it must be current and updated with the latest virus information. It's not as much work as it seems like it would be. Fortunately, antivirus software designers understand that you and I already have more things to keep up with than we ever have any hope of maintaining, so they've made configuration and maintenance for these programs easy to accomplish.

Troubleshooting

Despite all of your best efforts, there may be times when you experience difficulties with your antivirus software. For example, even though you have set up automatic updates for your antivirus software, you may notice after a while that those updates don't seem to be occurring. It's possible that changes to your ISP's configurations could prevent these updates from happening, so it's wise to check periodically, just to make sure that your updating service is working properly.

If you're using a firewall, it's possible that the firewall might also be blocking the updates because it appears that they are not from a trusted site. Adding the update service and the security company's Web site to your trusted sites and trusted actions should alleviate this problem.

Another problem that you might experience is that the antivirus software conflicts with other programs or applications running on your computer. This is a very frustrating problem, and it occurs often when there is a wireless network involved. Try updating all of the firmware for your wireless router and then configuring your software to allow access from the wireless router. It's a frustrating process, but you'll find that once you get the settings right, you won't experience any further problems.

Antivirus software is one of those have-to-have programs that you just can't afford to be without. It's like a Web browser or an e-mail program. Without it, your computer won't function properly for very long.

Try a few different types of antivirus software before you settle on one. You may find that a freeware program provides everything you need, but you might find that it takes something a little more sophisticated to protect you. It all depends on your needs and how you use your computer.

Once you have the software, install it and keep it current. And keep it active all the time. It's not enough to simply have the software on your hard drive. The software must be active for it to protect you.

15 } Spyware Protection

Spyware is one of the biggest threats you'll face on the Internet. In fact, if you don't currently have spyware on your computer, you're either very lucky or you've been very diligent in both your Internet usage habits and in your computer maintenance.

Spyware and its big brother *adware* have been around for a while, but over the last few years, spyware has been making a steady shift from a marketing tool to a criminal software program, deployed to gain access to your personal information. It's become such a problem that over half of the computer crashes reported to Microsoft in 2004 were attributed to spyware infestations.

INSIDER LINGO   Adware: Software that companies store on your computer to track your Internet habits. That information is reported to the sponsor company, which then uses the adware to push relevant advertisements out to you or to personalize your online experience with the organization.

By some estimates, more than 76 percent of consumers' PCs are infected with spyware. Further, most of those people have no idea they're even infected, much less what the spyware is doing to their machine. And once obvious signs of spyware are evident—a new home page or new toolbars keep showing up in your browser, new icons appear on your desktop, or your computer slows dramatically and begins crashing more frequently—the spyware infection is so bad and has been going on for so long that it will be difficult to get rid of.

Your best defense in the war against spyware is to protect your computer from it as completely as possible. Begin using good Internet and surfing habits, and put spyware protection technologies in place on your computer. Then use them frequently.

Those technologies can be confusing. It's hard to know which application is best and the best ways to use it. This chapter clears up that confusion by answering all the questions you might have about spyware protection technologies.

What Is Spyware Protection?

Using the Internet puts you at risk, and using the Internet without proper security measures leaves you open to all kinds of malicious software. Spyware is one of the most difficult of those types of malicious software, and it can result in an invasion of your privacy or expose your computer to other dangers. Spyware is tracking software put onto your computer without your consent. The purpose of spyware is to gather and steal your personal information. This is usually accomplished without your knowledge or permission. You may never even know that you've got spyware installed on your computer until some obvious change is made to the computer.

Spyware protection helps to detect and remove spyware applications from your computer before they become a serious problem. Spyware protection is also called anti-spyware—a program that operates much like an antivirus program. So, why isn't antivirus protection enough to keep spyware off your computer? The answer is that antivirus and anti-spyware protection technologies look for different things. Antivirus, for example, looks specifically for an application or code that behaves in a manner, or has *signatures*, that indicates the code is a virus. On the other hand, anti-spyware protection technologies look specifically for code and applications that behave like spyware.

 **INSIDER LINGO** Signature: The binary pattern of a virus or other malware. This pattern is very much like a fingerprint—each piece of malware has a different signature.

Many antivirus developers have begun to add expanded capabilities to their programs that allow those applications to detect malware other than viruses. However, it's only recently that they have begun to add anti-spyware support. That means you need to have a separate program to detect and remove spyware.

How Does It Work?

Anti-spyware helps protect your privacy on the Internet by eliminating spyware or adware on your computer. It works similarly to antivirus applications by scanning your computer's memory and the drives on your computer. If spyware is found, it is logged and then can be deleted. You control that process, and you can determine which pieces of spyware should be removed and which should not.

This is an important feature in spyware protection tools because these tools don't usually differentiate between spyware and adware. You don't want spyware on your computer, but some types of adware make surfing the Internet more enjoyable and more relevant to your needs. Having the ability to decide which you want to leave on your machine and which you want to have removed is a big plus.

Firewalls also don't protect your computer from spyware. It can bypass your firewall and stay hidden for long periods of time without your knowledge. However, your firewall protects you from many other threats, so don't forgo the firewall in favor of anti-spyware technologies. There are several spyware protection technologies that are free, so you can afford to have both types of protection.

Finally, spyware protection is similar to antivirus programs in the need to update frequently. Spyware, like viruses, changes frequently. Each change brings a new and different piece of code or signature, and the only way to stop it is to include those signatures in the spyware protection program. To do that, anti-spyware programs usually update daily.

 Just as antivirus programs don't protect your computer from spyware, anti-spyware programs don't protect your computer from viruses. Make sure you have the proper protection technologies installed to protect yourself from all sides. These include firewalls, antivirus, and anti-spyware technologies.

Pitfalls of Spyware Protection

There's probably no technology or application on the market that doesn't have some downfall, and spyware protection technologies are no different. For example, one of the biggest downfalls of anti-spyware applications is that some clever criminals have discovered that they can use these types of protection to actually plant spyware on your computer.

Here's how it happens: You realize you need some form of anti-spyware application, so you search the Web for a free program. When you find one that looks pretty good, you download and install it on your computer. Only, it's not really anti-spyware; it's spyware, disguised to look like it's protecting your computer. Under the guise of a protection technology then, the spyware is free to carry out the actions of spyware: collecting and reporting information about you, your Internet habits, and maybe even your financial information or buying habits, including numbers for the credit cards that you use online.

So, it's important to be wary of the protection technologies that you choose to download from the Internet, especially if they are free. Always get your software from well-known sources, and check out any program thoroughly before you download it. One way to check out a program is to do a Google search on the name of the application. If it's a scam, it's pretty likely that you'll find information that's been posted by other people who fell for the scam.

The other real downfall with spyware protection technologies is that every program looks for something different. What one anti-spyware program detects and removes, another will miss completely. Program designers use detection methods that are as varied as the spyware that infects your computer.

To overcome this problem, it's best if you have two anti-spyware applications installed and running on your computer all the time. Unlike many antivirus programs, most anti-spyware programs can co-exist, so it's safe to install and run more than one. The two applications will probably catch many of the same instances of spyware, but it's also likely that each one will catch spyware that the other application missed. By having two installed, you dramatically reduce your chances of having a piece of spyware slip under the radar.

Finally, some anti-spyware applications can be real resource hogs. Fortunately, most anti-spyware vendors give you a free trial period (if the application you choose isn't freeware), so take the time to check the application out before you purchase the full version. Check for compatibility as well as for ease of use and how well it operates on your computer. If you find that it causes your computer to slow down dramatically, or if you begin to experience crashes and freezes more frequently than you have in the past, uninstall the program and try something different.

Choosing Spyware Protection

Some companies will go to great lengths to keep you from removing their adware or spyware from your computer. In light of that fact, the old adage "An ounce of prevention is worth a pound of cure" applies to both spyware and adware. Fortunately, a few simple precautions will go a long way toward keeping spyware and adware off your computer, and the best part is that these strategies don't cost you a thing.

❋ **Make sure your computer won't install programs automatically.** You also need to ensure that your e-mail program doesn't automatically launch programs when you open a message. To do that, follow these steps:

1. Make sure that your system is currently up to date with all patches and upgrades.

2. In Microsoft Windows, open Microsoft Internet Explorer, and then from the main toolbar select Tools > Internet Options > Security. This will open the Security tab in the Internet Options dialog box shown in Figure 15.1. Once there, adjust your security settings so that your Internet security zone is High.

❋ The High security setting will cause some Internet pages not to be displayed. If these are sites that you want to see, and you know they are safe, you can add them to your safe sites list by going to Tools > Internet Options > Security > Trusted Sites and typing in the URL for the Web page that you want to view.

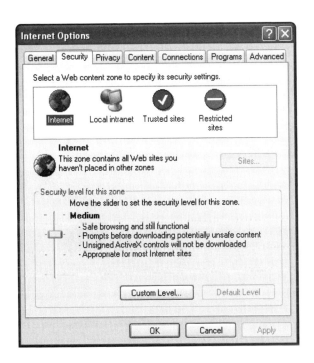

Figure 15.1
The Security tab in the
Internet Options dialog
box.

3. To secure your e-mail program in Microsoft Outlook 2003, select Tools > Options > Preferences > E-mail Options and then select Read all standard mail in plain text. Then click OK.

❋ **Keep your operating system fully patched against any known security vulnerabilities at all times.** The Microsoft Windows Update site at http://www.update.microsoft.com is the place to find these updates. At the site, you have two options: Express, which lets you install the most critical updates, or Custom, which lets you choose which updates to install. Your best course of action is to select Express and follow the prompts from there. You should check for updates at least monthly to ensure your operating system is fully protected against known exploits.

For example, spyware and adware commonly change your Internet Explorer startup page to a different site. This is accomplished when the application exploits a vulnerability in the Internet Explorer program. That vulnerability was first patched by Microsoft in January 2001. However, many users have not updated their computers, so this vulnerability remains a common way in which criminals gain access to computer systems. And there are hundreds of other similar vulnerabilities in the Windows operating system that leave your computer vulnerable.

※ **Disable Windows Messenger Service.** Windows Messenger Service is as vulnerable to exploits as any other Windows application. There is also a critical exploit in Windows Messenger Service that could allow malicious attackers to remotely run code on your computer if it is left vulnerable. If you disable the service, you prevent spyware from being installed on your system. To disable Windows Messenger Service

1. Select Start > Settings > Control Panel.

2. Then go to Administrative Tools > Services > Messenger.

3. The Messenger Properties dialog box appears, as shown in Figure 15.2. In the Startup Type menu select Disabled and click OK. Windows Messenger Service will be disabled.

Figure 15.2

The Messenger Properties dialog box.

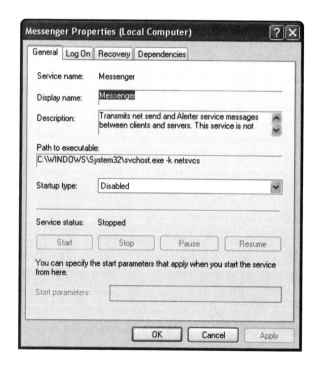

※ **Always use safe Internet habits.** Avoid unsavory Web sites (especially pornography sites and gambling sites). Don't download attachments unless you are expecting them and you know who they are from. And perform regular maintenance on your computer. You can even set the maintenance to take place automatically, as long as it gets done.

Once you've taken steps to ensure your system is configured properly, then use caution any time you're prompted to allow an application to install itself to your computer. You should see a prompt that asks if you want to allow installation when a piece of software is attempting installation on your computer. Don't select OK, Yes, or Run This Program when this prompt appears unless you fully understand what's being installed and why. Furthermore, if you deliberately download an application, read and understand the End-User Licensing Agreement before you install it. Spyware and adware details are often buried in the fine print of the agreement, and if you simply click Yes or Accept before reading the agreement, you might be agreeing to install an unwanted application on your system.

Even with the best surfing habits, however, you're still probably going to end up with spyware on your computer at one time or another. So, for protection you should have at least one, and preferably two different, anti-spyware applications installed and running on your computer. Those applications can be free, or they can be fee-based. It doesn't matter as long as you have some kind of protection.

Freeware

Chances are you have spyware on your computer. If you're using Microsoft Internet Explorer, if you surf the Internet, or if you've ever clicked on a pop-up offer of any kind, you can just assume you're infected. Even those pop-ups that ask if you want to check for spyware aren't safe—they're actually spyware in most cases.

So it's best if you can keep spyware off your computer to start with. Even if you manage to keep most of it off your computer, however, you're bound to have some spyware. Fortunately, getting rid of it isn't difficult, and in many cases, you can get a spyware removal tool for free on the Internet.

One free tool that's well-known and widely used is LavaSoft's AdAware SE Personal. This tool does a great job of searching out and removing spyware and adware from your computer, and it's relatively easy to use. AdAware also has a couple of versions that are fee-based. Those versions either are for businesses or they offer additional features that the free version does not. Which version you choose should be determined by your specific needs. You can learn more about AdAware on the Web at http://www.lavasoft.com, and you can search downloads.com for the free AdAware SE Personal version.

Spybot Search and Destroy is another free anti-spyware program that you can find on the Web. Spybot is part of a volunteer effort to fight spyware and similar problems, and you may receive a request to make a donation to cover their costs. It's not required, but if you like the software, a small donation ensures that it will continue to be improved and updated.

Spybot has many of the same features as AdAware, though all spyware programs will differ slightly from one vendor to another. Regardless of the differences, however, Spybot does a good job of finding and removing spyware from your computer. You can learn more about Spybot at http://www.spybot.info.

Many spyware programs don't differentiate between *tracking cookies* and spyware, so check the reports that your spyware program generates carefully.

INSIDER LINGO

Tracking Cookies: Small packets of information placed on your computer when you visit a Web site. The cookie is used to track your movements and behavior on the site and in some cases in other places on the Internet. This information is used by organizations to push more relevant content to you under the guise of improving the user experience. Tracking cookies are generally harmless.

Tracking cookies are placed on your computer by Web sites tracking how you use their site. They're not spyware in the strictest sense of the term; however, they may create some privacy concerns, so anti-spyware programs may pick up these legitimate bits of software. The result is that your computer appears to have more spyware than it actually does. You can go through and pick and choose what you want to keep and what you want deleted. Unfortunately, it's often hard to distinguish the good from the bad. If that's the case with your cookies, let the spyware program remove them all. It will be a little inconvenient. Web sites where you have a username and password and have set up preferences will have to be reset each time you do this. However, giving up that personalization may be a small price to pay for keeping the more dangerous types of spyware off your computer.

SpywareBlaster, which can be found at http://www.spywareblaster.com/ is another free anti-spyware application, but this application acts very differently from most other types of anti-spyware. It doesn't detect and remove spyware; it prevents it from being installed on your computer in the first place by determining how spyware is using ActiveX controls. Using this interesting technique, the program actually prevents the install of ActiveX controls that work with spyware without interfering with legitimate ActiveX controls, so your normal surfing activities aren't stopped or prevented in any way.

Keeping spyware off your computer shouldn't be difficult, and it shouldn't be expensive. And it's far better for you to use one or two of these free spyware programs to keep your computer clean than to use nothing at all. In fact, freeware should meet your needs without much difficulty. Just remember to use caution when choosing a freeware anti-spyware program, because there are some spyware programs that masquerade as protection technologies.

Software

There is some great freeware available to help protect your computer system; however, you may decide that you prefer to have spyware protection that you've purchased through your security solutions provider. McAfee offers an anti-spyware application, and Symantec plans to offer one in the near future, but just the fact that these two major security providers are this far behind in providing anti-spyware applications illustrates how quickly spyware became a major problem.

Even if they are behind, however, there are some benefits to purchasing an anti-spyware solution rather than using a free one. For example, being familiar with a vendor is an important consideration because of the tendency for criminals to try to use anti-spyware applications to trick you into downloading their spyware.

Many fee-based applications also offer added features, like differentiating between adware and spyware. Fee-based anti-spyware applications are also more reliable than free programs. With fee-based anti-spyware software, there's a much better chance that the vendor will be around for a while and will continue to support and improve the application.

One software program that's currently free but will likely be fee-based in the near future is the Microsoft AntiSpyware Beta 1.0. The program was purchased from Giant Software Company in December 2004, and at the time of this writing it is still in the Beta testing phase. What that means to you is that there may still be bugs in the application. However, it also means that Microsoft is working to clean up any remaining bugs, and it shouldn't be long before it makes it to the final release version.

The best feature of Microsoft's AntiSpyware Beta is that it's easy to download and install. In addition to that, it offers a real-time monitor, automatic updates, and a data sharing mechanism that helps to protect against new spyware attacks before many other applications are even aware that a problem exists. If you'd like to try the application, you can download it from http://www.microsoft.com/athome/security/spyware/software/default.mspx.

Spyware can be controlled in a number of ways. Freeware and software programs are available to help you keep from becoming a victim of a spyware infection. Whether it's a free program or a fee-based program, what really matters is that you have some kind of anti-spyware application running on your computer all the time, and it would be even better if you have two programs.

Installing and Configuring Spyware Protection

Installing and configuring most anti-spyware programs is pretty much the same as installing and configuring antivirus software. In Windows all you really have to do is follow the prompts from the program.

Still, there are a few changes that you may decide you need to make to the standard installation, so in this section you'll learn how to install and configure your spyware protection. Please note that every program is slightly different, and what works for one may not work for another. To make it easier for you, I'll walk you through installing and configuring the Microsoft AntiSpyware Beta 1.0 program.

Installation Guidelines

One of the best things to happen to software is the installation wizard. All you have to do is double-click (or download and run) an executable file, and an installation wizard walks you through the process. And especially where Windows is concerned, the process is as simple as point and click. Well, okay, it's almost that simple.

Microsoft's AntiSpyware Beta 1.0 installs with an installation wizard in just a few steps. Since it's relatively indicative of how most software applications will install, it will be the general example for this book. Here's how you install the program.

1. Download the file from http://www.microsoft.com/athome/security/spyware/software/ default.mspx. When prompted, select Run.

2. A Welcome dialog box appears with an explanation of what you're installing. When you've finished reading the text in the dialog box, select Next.

3. The license agreement appears. Be sure to read the entire license agreement and then click the radio button beside I Accept and click Next.

4. The next dialog box, shown in Figure 15.3, prompts you to select the folder in which you want the program placed. In most cases, it will automatically select the correct folder. However, if you want to change the location for the program, you can do that by selecting Browse and then navigating to the folder where you want the program installed. When you make the decision about where to install the program, click Next.

Figure 15.3

The Folder dialog box.

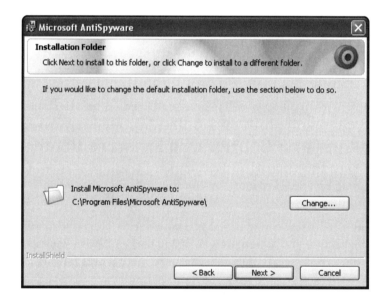

5. The Installation dialog box appears, as shown in Figure 15.4. Select Install.

6. Installation proceeds automatically, as Figure 15.5 shows.

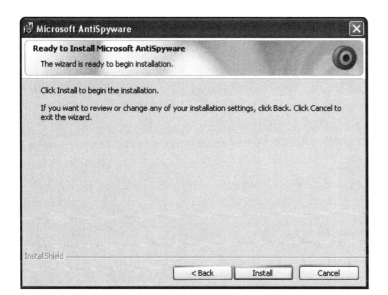

Figure 15.4
The Installation dialog box.

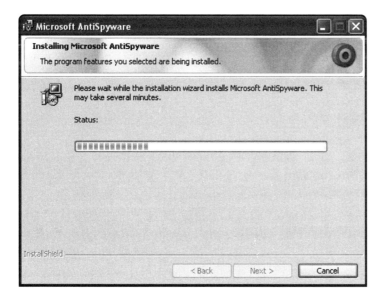

Figure 15.5
Once you click Install, the installation proceeds automatically.

7. When the installation is finished, a final dialog box appears that tells you the installation is finished, as shown in Figure 15.6. There's also a checkbox on this dialog page that you should check to launch the program when the dialog box closes. Click to check that box, then select Finish to finish the installation process.

Figure 15.6
The final dialog box in which you choose to open the program when installation is finished.

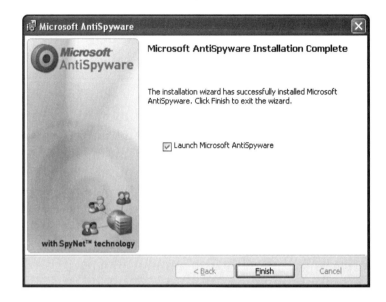

That's it. It's that easy to install Microsoft's AntiSpyware, and most other programs will be that simple, too. Of course, not every application is going to be that easy. There may be more steps or more choices to make, depending on the program that you choose to use, but it still shouldn't be difficult because the point of the installation wizard is to make it easier to install and run programs on your computer.

Configuration Guidelines

Once you get the program installed, the next step is to configure it to work optimally. This is where most programs vary widely. Some have more capabilities than others, and some are more difficult to configure than others. With Microsoft's AntiSpyware Beta 1.0, there's not a whole lot that you have to configure.

The first time you pull up the program, whether it's immediately after you install it or at a later time, you'll be taken to a Setup Assistant that looks like the screen shown in Figure 15.7. After you read through the text on the screen, click Next.

The setup for this program is basically a three-step process. Once you start the setup process, the first screen you come to allows you to determine if you want to program to Auto Update, as shown in Figure 15.8.

Now spyware is constantly being developed, so it's a good idea to have your AntiSpyware program set to automatically update the definitions it uses to detect spyware. New definitions are released often, and the AutoUpdater ensures that you always have the most current definitions installed. Unless you have a very good reason not to, you should enable the AutoUpdater and then click Next.

Figure 15.7
The Setup Assistant is the first screen you'll encounter as you configure Microsoft's AntiSpyware program.

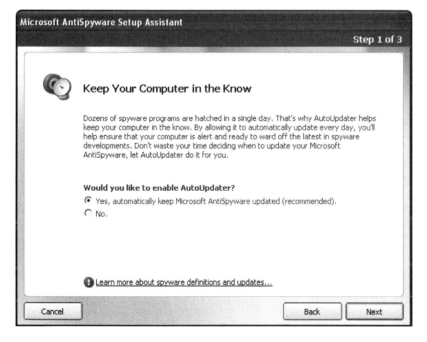

Figure 15.8
The first screen in Microsoft AntiSpyware's setup process prompts you to set automatic updates.

> ❊ You can update your anti-spyware definitions manually in most programs, including Microsoft AntiSpyware. However, if you rely on your own memory to remember to update, you may be vulnerable when new spyware begins to circulate. Use the automatic update feature to ensure that your anti-spyware definitions are always current.

The second step that you'll go through is the Real-Time Security Agent stage. To ensure that the program always has the most recent anti-spyware information, the AntiSpyware program uses security agents and checkpoints, shown in Figure 15.9, to monitor your system, applications, and Internet activity for suspicious activity that could be indicative of spyware. These agents will allow unthreatening changes to your system, applications, and Internet attributes, they will block known spyware threats, and they will prompt you to make a decision to allow or block items that are possibly threatening. Select Yes to enable the real-time security agents, and then click Next.

Figure 15.9
AntiSpyware's security agents monitor your system, applications, and Internet activities for suspicious activities that indicate possible spyware.

If you receive an alert from AntiSpyware, the alert box will appear in the bottom right-hand corner of your computer screen. It provides information to help you make a decision about blocking or allowing the activity that seems suspicious.

The final step in the configuration process is shown in Figure 15.10. In this step, you're asked to participate in the AntiSpyware Community. The community is basically a network of computers that use industry standard security methods to connect together to form an anti-spyware network. When one computer on the network finds what appears to be spyware, all of the machines on the network are updated to protect against the spyware.

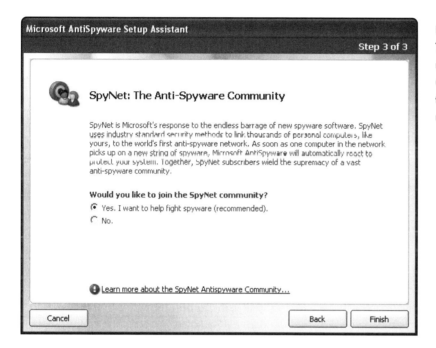

Figure 15.10
The AntiSpyware community network is a group of users connected together to form an anti-spyware network.

The AntiSpyware community allows real-time agents to catalog and update the anti-spyware system that protects you and the other Microsoft AntiSpyware users. To participate in the network, select Yes, and then click Finish.

❋ Participating in the AntiSpyware community shouldn't put your privacy at risk; however, you should know that your computer use will be monitored as part of the program. When suspicious activity occurs, that usage is reported to software agents to help build and increase the protection provided by the application.

After you've completed those three configuration steps, you'll be prompted to run a quick scan on your computer, as shown in Figure 15.11. You can choose to run that scan at a later time; however, it takes less than five minutes to run that first scan in most cases, and it will immediately get you started protecting your computer. If you'd like to scan your computer, select Scan Now and then click Next. When the scan is complete, you'll see a quick summary of how many files were scanned and how many pieces of spyware were found on your machine.

Figure 15.11
When the configuration process is complete, you'll be prompted to scan your computer for the first time.

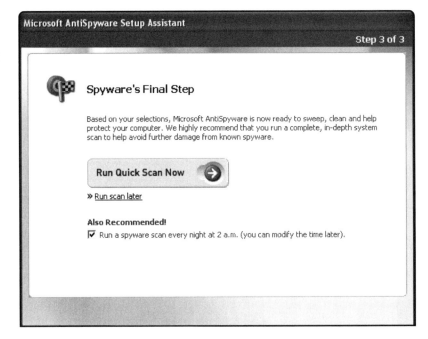

In addition to the main configuration that you'll go through when you set up the program, you can also change some configuration attributes using the interface commands on the application. Here are some of the options you can change.

* **Scan Options.** Go to the front page of the AntiSpyware application and select Scan Options on the right side of the page. As shown in Figure 15.12, you can select an Intelligent Scan or a Full Scan. The Intelligent Scan takes less than five minutes to complete, but the Full Scan is a more complete scan. The only caveat with the Full Scan option is that it can take more than 20 minutes to complete. You can use the Intelligent Scan most of the time, and run the Full Scan one time each month just to be certain that nothing is being overlooked in the shorter scan.

* **Advanced Tools.** Advanced tools gives you access to options like System Explorer, Advanced File Analyzer, Browser Hijack Settings Restore, and Tracks Eraser. The Tracks Eraser is an interesting technology (shown in Figure 15.13). It allows you to erase your tracks for

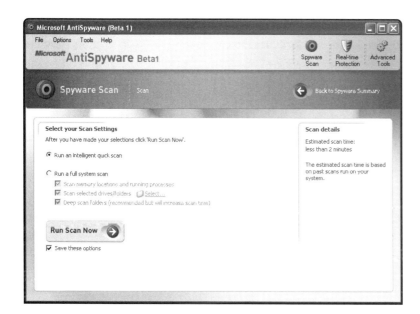

Figure 15.12
The scan options in Anti-Spyware's front page allow you to determine what type of scan you want to have performed on your computer.

certain activities like Internet history, cookies, and saved passwords, among other things. Explore these features to see what they allow you to do.

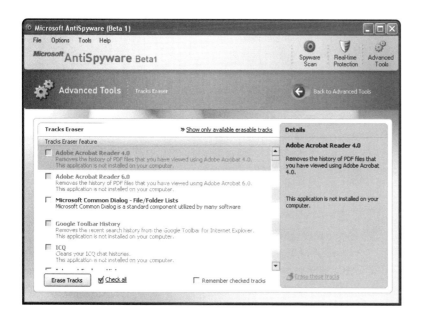

Figure 15.13
The Advanced Tools options allow you to make several changes to the AntiSpyware application.

❋ **Change Scan Time.** The time the scan runs is automatically set to around 2 a.m., since that's usually a time when most computers are not in use. To change this time, go to Tools > Settings, as shown in Figure 15.14. From this screen, you can also access the AutoUpdater, Real-time Protection, Alerts, SpyNet Community, Spyware Scan, and General settings to make changes so that the program operates in a way that's useful to you.

Figure 15.14
The settings control panel allows you to make changes to scanning times and many other options in the AntiSpyware program.

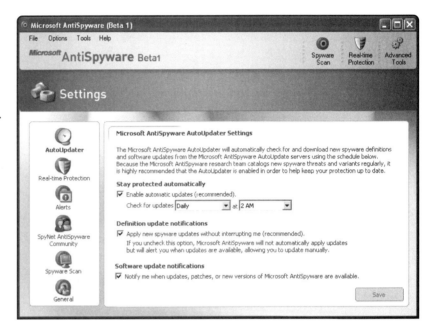

Microsoft's AntiSpyware program is just one of many programs that are available, both free and paid. In general, any anti-spyware program will have a variety of settings that you can control in whatever manner suits you. A general rule of thumb for these settings is to set them at the highest protection level available to begin with. You can always go back and make changes to those settings if you find that they don't work well with how you use your computer.

Troubleshooting

Any application that you download and install to your computer is bound to have a glitch now and then. Unfortunately, because every application is different, it's hard to pinpoint exactly which problems you're likely to have. However, there are a few problems that occur frequently. Following are a few of the issues that you might encounter as you download, install, and use an anti-spyware application. These are not specific to any application, but in general are a good place to start if the application isn't working exactly like you expect it to work.

❄ **The program doesn't seem to be scanning my machine on a regular basis.** If you don't see some notification that the program has scanned your machine, you may begin to wonder if it's actually working. If you're not seeing a scan notification, one of two things could be wrong. It's possible that your notifications are turned off, in which case you simply need to go into your control panel and turn those notifications on. Or it's possible that you've turned off the automatic scan function, which can also be turned back on from your control panel.

❄ **The program keeps displaying pop-up boxes prompting for me to allow or deny access to a specific program.** If it seems that you're constantly being prompted by a particular program, then it's possible that there's spyware installed on your system that isn't being completely removed by your anti-spyware tool. Try installing and running another anti-spyware program to remove the spyware that's causing the problem.

❄ **Despite having an anti-spyware program, your computer is still acting strangely or continues to bog down.** Some free downloads that claim to be anti-spyware programs are actually spyware, so instead of protecting your machine, they only make the programs worse. Try downloading and running a different anti-spyware program to see if it helps.

❄ **Installing a new anti-spyware program results in the computer freezing up or crashing.** Some anti-spyware isn't compatible with the other systems on your computer. If you're consistently having trouble downloading and running a spyware protection program, try a different program to see if the problem is in the compatibility.

❄ **The program scans your system regularly, but there's still evidence that there is spyware on your computer.** If you see evidence of spyware—unusual icons on your desktop, new toolbars or a new home page that you didn't assign in Internet Explorer, or general sluggishness in your computer that increases over time—it's possible that your anti-spyware program isn't updating regularly. Perform a manual update to the program and run it again, then check your automatic update setting to ensure that the application is updating when it should.

Spyware is one of the biggest and most dangerous threats to your security on the Internet. Don't let spyware control your computer and Internet experience. There are a variety of free and fee-based anti-spyware tools available. Install at least one program on your machine and make sure it's set to automatically update and scan your computer. Two programs are better, as each catches different spyware.

You don't have to be at risk, but to keep yourself from being at risk, you have to take some steps to protect yourself. In some cases, the protection is a little inconvenient. However, it's a lot more inconvenient to have a criminal or hacker gain control of your computer, identity, or financial information, so take the time to protect yourself from spyware. If you don't, you will become a victim of cybercrime in some form.

16 } Updates and Patches

Would you live in a house that was built in the early 1900s without improving the locks or replacing the windows and doors? You might, but it's more likely that you would make changes to the security of the place to protect yourself and your personal belongings. The world we live in today is no where near as safe as it was then.

You can consider your security in the cyberworld in the same light. Many people don't think anything of leaving the windows and doors of their operating systems and applications wide open. Unfortunately, the dangers of leaving your virtual house unprotected are equally as dangerous as leaving your physical house unsecured.

That's where regular updates and patches come in. Updates and patches are the equivalent of locks on your doors and windows, and keeping your operating system updated is the most important thing you can do to protect yourself from viruses, spyware, and the other security threats that you face on the Internet. It only takes a few minutes to update and patch your computer.

Microsoft Windows is known for having large numbers of security holes through which hackers and criminals can gain access to your computer and your personal information, plant viruses on your machine, or even steal resources to use for other criminal activities. However, regularly updating your computer system software helps to keep you safe.

You do have to update more than just your operating system, however. You also need to update your other applications, and even your protection technologies like firewalls and antivirus programs. This chapter gives you all the details on patches and updates to help you keep your computer safe from flaws and errors at the code level.

What Are Updates and Patches?

You hear about them all the time, especially as you're looking at ways to protect your computer. Someone is always telling you to be sure that your computer is current on all of the updates and patches that it needs. But what are updates and patches, really?

In the most general of terms, updates and patches are small pieces of software that repair flaws in operating systems and applications. To be more specific, a patch is a piece of code that repairs software that doesn't behave exactly as it's intended to behave. Updates are pieces of software that add missing functionality to an operating system or application.

If you understand software development cycles, you'll understand the function of updates and patches. In today's information driven world, software developers are pushed hard to release more useful versions of all kinds of software as quickly as possible. To accomplish this, developers design and create applications, and then run them through a testing cycle.

However, it's not at all uncommon for the testing cycle to miss some of the minor glitches that exist in the code as a result of the short time frame of many of today's development cycles. Patches and updates are the solutions provided to address those glitches.

The problem exists in the glitches that aren't repaired with a patch or update. Criminals and hackers use these vulnerabilities in software to gain access to the applications and to your computer.

For example, port scanning is a technique that hackers and criminals use to take advantage of unprotected ports on a computer. These ports are usually unprotected because of a glitch in the operating system that's running on a computer. However, there's a patch that closes those ports, making it nearly impossible for a criminal to gain access to your computer through the port.

It all seems a little arbitrary. After all, if these kinds of problems exist in software development, why not take more time during the development and testing phases to make sure no issues that would need to be patched or updated exist? It's one of those catch-22 situations that seem to plague the Information Age. Users need these applications and programs right now. They don't want to have to wait six more months to get the tools that help them accomplish the task at hand.

So, users push for new releases and new applications. However, rushing to get the next big thing on the market means that there are bound to be small details that are missed, and often those details won't be discovered until a user actually puts the software to use in the course of her normal daily workflow. Fortunately, most software developers are quick to respond to issues that users report, and it's not at all unusual for a program to frequently need to be patched or updated to keep up with the flaws that are discovered.

Why Are Updates and Patches Important?

Software systems grow more and more complex every day, and it's common for security-related problems to be discovered only after a piece of software has been released and is in use by a large number of users. Although most vendors try to address known flaws in a timely manner, there is still the opportunity for intruders to take advantage of existing flaws and mount an attack on your computers and networks.

To keep your risk at a minimum, you need to stay abreast of any updates or patches that may apply to your system and take immediate steps to reduce your exposure to the vulnerability. Those steps include disabling the affected software and applying the pertinent patches and updates that vendors provide.

Regularly installing applicable updates can reduce your vulnerability to attack. You need to stay informed of vendors' security-related updates to their products, which may be called updates, upgrades, patches, service packs, hot fixes, or workarounds. Whenever an update is released, you need to determine if it is applicable to your computer, and if it is, install it.

When Should You Update and Patch Your Software or System?

It's no secret that many applications today are constantly in need of repair. In fact, on any given week, you can browse through the technical publications online and hear stories of yet another patch that's been released for some very well-known and widely used programs.

It's because there is so much proliferation in those software programs that you should get your patching and updating routine in hand. If you don't perform those updates and patches regularly, you're effectively opening the door to any criminal who wants to come snooping through your computer.

So, here are a couple of rules to guide you in updating and patching your software and computer system.

❋ **Rule 1:** Develop a regular schedule to check for patches and updates, and have that schedule apply to all the software and applications on your computer, from the operating system to the program level.

❋ **Rule 2:** Where possible, allow your updates and patches to take place automatically. However, be aware that automatic updates can only happen if your computer is turned on and connected to the Internet. So, while automatic updates are a great idea, they can give you a false sense of security if you haven't made sure the update or patch is actually being taken care of.

Scheduling Regular, Automatic Patches and Updates

The majority of computers in homes and offices throughout the world are based on the Microsoft Windows operating system. As part of that system, Microsoft's Windows Update site, which can be found at http://update.microsoft.com/windowsupdate/v6/default.aspx?ln=en-us, is the easiest way to get rid of the software flaws and bugs that circumvent the security of your Windows-based computer. If you don't use this update site to keep your computer currently patched and upgraded at all times, a criminal could gain access to your computer, files, or accounts by exploiting the known vulnerabilities in your software or operating system.

The first time you patch or update your machine will be the hardest because there will be a lot of updates and patches that you need to download and install. You may even have to go through the process several times, but after the first time, it gets easier.

When you're ready to begin the patching and updating process, shut down all other programs, and try not to run anything else during the update process. The updates are going to bog down your machine because they use a lot of resources. If you're running multiple programs while you're trying to go through this process, you're more prone to freezes and crashes, or you could corrupt the file that you're trying to download and install, so it's best if you don't try to work on anything else while you're updating or patching your system. Here's how to get started with the updating and patching process.

1. Open Internet Explorer and go to Microsoft's Windows Update Web site at http://www.update.microsoft.com. You can also get there from the toolbar in Internet Explorer by going to the Tools menu and selecting Windows Update.

2. When you get to the site, which is shown in Figure 16.1, you have the option of getting Express Updates or Custom Updates. Express updates are the most critical updates that your computer needs at this time. Custom Updates allows you to choose which of the needed updates you want to download and install. It's recommended that you use the Express Updates option to install all recommended updates.

Figure 16.1

The Microsoft Windows Update Web site walks you through the Windows updating process.

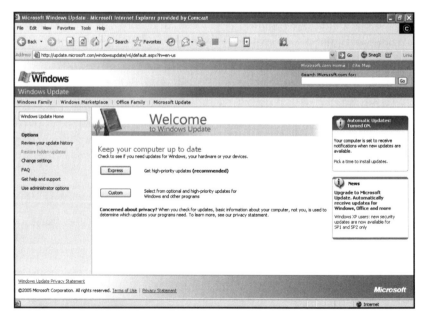

❋ It may be necessary to download a small piece of software from the Windows Update Web site so that the site can analyze your computer to see which updates are necessary. If you're prompted to download this software, authorize it so that the site can tell you which updates you need.

3. When you click the Express Install button, Windows Update will analyze your computer to see what updates are available, as shown in Figure 16.2. In Figure 16.3, you can see an example of the recommended updates displayed when the process is complete.

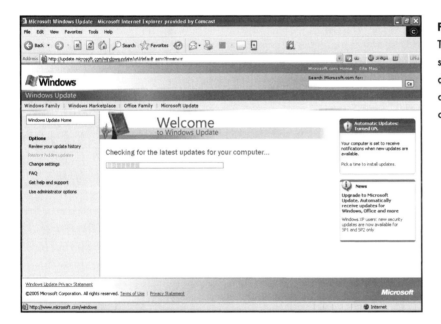

Figure 16.2
The Windows Update site scans your computer to determine which updates are necessary for your computer.

4. When the system is finished and you have a list of all the updates you need, click Install Updates. Figure 16.4 shows the necessary updates being installed on your computer. Be patient with the update process, as it could take a while to complete. The time it takes depends on the number of updates that need to be downloaded and installed.

Figure 16.3

When Windows Update has finished scanning your computer, it shows you a list of the updates that are needed for your computer.

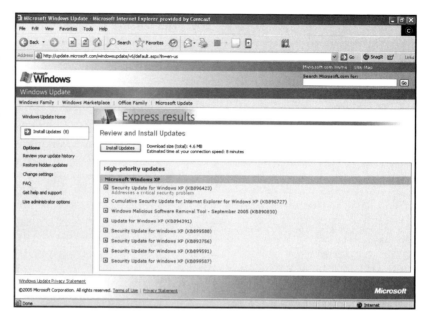

Figure 16.4

When you click Install Updates, Windows Update installs the necessary updates to your computer.

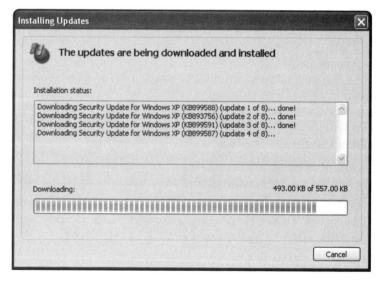

If you have never done an update, you may find that there are dozens of them that need to be done. These all represent defects that threaten your privacy and security. If multiple updates are available, Windows Update will download and install all of them at once whenever possible. However, some updates can only be installed separately. If that happens, a pop-up window will tell you. Either way, you should go through the update process from beginning to end several times until you get notification that there are no current updates needed on your computer.

5. When the updating process is complete, there may be some updates that require you to restart your computer before the update can take effect. If, as in Figure 16.5, you are prompted to restart your computer when the update installation is complete, click Restart Now. After your computer restarts, go back to the Windows Update Site to make sure there are no more critical updates.

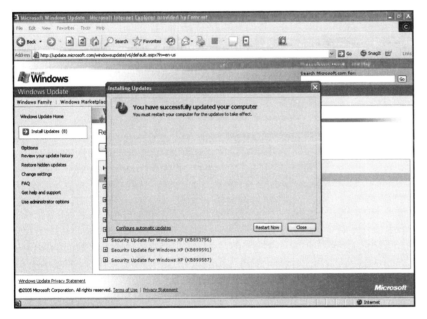

Figure 16.5
After the installation of your updates is complete, you may be prompted to restart your computer so those updates can take effect.

✳ After your computer restarts, go back to the Windows Update Web site and repeat the process until you are told there are no more critical updates needed. Otherwise, you will still be vulnerable. Some updates can only be applied after earlier ones are applied, so it's not at all uncommon to have to repeat this process two or more times, especially if you have never updated your computer before.

Windows Update will help to protect your computer from software and people trying to exploit vulnerabilities. However, it doesn't protect your computer from software and people exploiting the normal operating capabilities of your computer, like weak passwords, bad configurations, viruses, Trojans, and other malicious software. Updating is not a cure-all, but it's certainly a strong dose of medication that will take you very far along the path to maintaining a healthy computer.

You can also configure your computer to automatically check for the availability of critical updates. When you automate this process, your computer scans for updates and notifies you with a pop-up window when one is available. To enable automatic updates, go to Start > Control Panel > Automatic Updates. As shown in Figure 16.6, the Automatic Updates dialog box appears, and you're given the choice to update your computer automatically, download updates but only install them when you say to, receive notification when updates are available, or turn automatic updates off completely. You should choose one of the first three options, depending on which suits you best, and then click Apply > OK. If you choose to have the updates done automatically, you'll also need to decide what time of day you want to have those updates happen.

Figure 16.6
The Automatic Updates dialog box lets you choose when and how you want your automatic updates to take place.

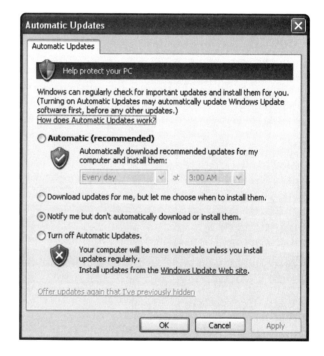

Remember that when you set up a time for the automatic updates to occur, your computer must be on and have an Internet connection available for the updating process to complete successfully. If you plan to enable automatic updates, be sure to set them for a time when you know that both of those requirements will be met. If you use dial-up Internet access, a better choice for you might be to enable notifications for when new updates are available.

Of course, Windows isn't the only operating system in use, and all operating systems need to be updated periodically. If you're using another operating system, the operating system manufacturer probably provides some software applications or updating tool that you can use to keep your operating system healthy.

If you do not keep your computer securely patched and up-to-date, you run the risk of having your computer attacked and compromised. Your computer could be rendered inoperable, be used for a criminal or hacker's storage site, or be programmed to attack other computers or cause network interruptions such as a denial of service attack.

It's advisable to keep all your other software programs up-to-date as well—not only to get the latest features, but also for improved security. Updating software programs is similar to updating your operating system. Most software programs have an update option, as shown in Figure 16.7. Usually, you can find that update option by going to the Help menu for the program. When you click the update option on the menu, you're often taken to a Web site where current updates are available.

Figure 16.7
Most software applications, like the Dragon Naturally Speaking software shown here, have an update option that allows you to get the latest software updates for the program.

Some software programs also have a registration process that tells you when to expect and how to get to updates and patches for those programs. Be sure to read all of the information provided by your software developer and any information provided when you register your product. And be sure to register the product, because some companies notify only their registered users of necessary updates and patches.

❋ Occasionally a patch or update will make your computer behave strangely. Most of the time this isn't the case; however, it's not unheard of. Just in case you encounter this type of problem, it's a good idea to set a restore point on your computer, if you have restoration capabilities, before you download and install any updates or patches. This ensures that you'll have a place to go back to in the event that the patch or update creates unexpected issues. If you don't have a restoration option and a patch or update turns out to be a hassle, you may just have to be patient until the software developer provides a patch for the patch or update. How's that for confusing?

In general, all of your updates and patches should be available through the methods in this chapter. It can be a lot of work, and it's probably going to be inconvenient to get everything set up so that updates and patches take place with a minimum of input from you. However, the alternative is to leave your computer exposed to hackers and criminals that look for vulnerabilities to exploit to help them reach their goals. If you don't protect your computer and your software programs with regular updates, you will almost certainly become a victim of some form of cybercrime.

17 } The Word on Passwords

Hackers can gain access to most computers in less than a minute, and that's one of the reasons that you so often hear warnings about creating and safeguarding usernames and passwords. They're your key to keeping your information safe, yet many people who wouldn't go around passing out keys to their home to every stranger they come in contact with will do something very similar to that with their computers.

For example, employees of one company found out just how vulnerable their passwords where when a consulting firm used a well-known cracking program, called "John the Ripper," to do the work of breaking passwords. It took the program only about an hour to determine nearly 30 percent of the passwords for close to 10,000 accounts included in the exercise. And that's just from one exercise at an average American company. Consider how much damage could have been done if that consulting firm had been a criminal or disgruntled employee with inside access. In many cases, a trip around the office will net dozens of passwords from people who have written them on sticky notes and posted them on their computer screens.

It's true that a good password may take months or even years to break with the right technology, but year after year it's proven just how few good passwords really exist. Most people use passwords that are easy to remember, which means that they are also easy to figure out, and that one factor leaves you vulnerable to attackers. However, when you add in issues like passwords that have been written down and are sitting right out in the open, the whole situation takes on a new aura of danger and unprotectedness. It's no wonder that you constantly hear harping about how to create and use passwords. What you'll find here is an explanation of why passwords are so important.

Why Does Everyone Harp on Passwords?

The way that people choose passwords is really no mystery. Some choose words straight out of Webster's dictionary, a pet's name, or the name or birthdates of their spouses, lovers, and children. Many add a number or two on the end of their chosen word, thinking they are clever.

Unfortunately, the number is more often than not a predictable number like a date of birth or anniversary, maybe even their age. Unfortunately, none of these methods of creating a password is any match for today's computers, which are capable of trying millions of word variations per second and often can figure out a password in less than a minute.

Bad passwords don't necessarily make it easier for a hacker to break into your network, but if they gain access to your computer by other means and they have your password, the damage is already done, so it doesn't really matter. The sad truth is that many people use the same password over and over again—on all of the services on their home computer, and possibly even all of the services on their work computer. So in many instances, a criminal who gains access to your username and password can move about all of your accounts, both personal and professional, with the appearance of being a legitimate user.

That's one of the reasons that your username and password are sought out by criminals and hackers. It's also why so many viruses and worms have propagated over the last few years. It's nothing today for a criminal or hacker to send a worm or virus into your computer that will collect and send the usernames and passwords back to them. Once they have that information, they have the keys to your electronic kingdom, and they're going to lock you out and refuse to let you back in.

At one time, anyone could read the password file—the collection of encrypted keys for the system's software locks. That made it easy for hackers to copy the file and then use its contents from any computer. Fortunately, software has advanced some since that time.

Today, operating systems usually only allow system administrators access to read the encrypted passwords, forcing hackers to get administrator rights on the system before they can grab the file. Of course, the fact that most computer users use their computer from the administrator's profile means that this shift in design doesn't provide a whole lot of protection. Other features, like login rules that lock users out after three unsuccessful attempts to log in, have become common. But even those tactics provide only a limited amount of protection, because in most cases resetting the password is just a matter of providing the right information.

While such defenses have made hacking attempts based on repetitive password guesses using a list of common words less successful, such attacks are invaluable to hackers as a way of gaining access to your computer or network. Once the criminal or hacker gains access to your computer, there are many ways he can bypass other security mechanisms to gain access to any information that he might want.

The only defense is to make passwords impossible to guess and difficult to crack with an algorithm. Unfortunately, those kinds of passwords need to be selected in a totally random fashion, and that's difficult for most people to do. It comes down to being able to remember the password once you set it.

Most people usually have several passwords to keep track of, and so they often use the same password multiple times. At best, people may use one password for certain accounts, like financial accounts, and another password for personal accounts. But using passwords that are random is not a normal practice because it's far too easy to forget a random string of numbers, letters, and characters.

The sad fact is, no matter how often most people are warned about protecting their passwords, not using the same password on multiple accounts, or creating passwords that are difficult to guess, they still do all of those things. It all comes down to convenience, and safe, effective passwords aren't usually convenient, which is good news for criminals and hackers.

How to Choose a Password

Passwords are one of the biggest security problems because most users invariably choose bad passwords, making it easy for anyone attacking a computer to gain access to the machine and all of the information on it. It's a frightening fact that about a third of Internet users' passwords can be cracked in less than five minutes.

Yet, there are more than 6.6 quadrillion different eight-character passwords that can be created using the 95 printable ASCII characters available to any computer user. Eight characters is the recommended minimum length of a good, strong password, but only if those characters are random combinations of numbers, letters, and symbols.

One way to create a good, strong password is to use various *mnemonics*. A common technique, called a pseudo-random password, takes the first or last letter of each word in an easy-to-remember or familiar sentence or phrase. The phrase can be a set of words taken from a book, a song, a quotation, a statement, or anything else that you easily remember. However, it shouldn't be a phrase that anyone will associate with you. So, if you were Arnold Schwarzenegger, for example, you wouldn't want to use the phrase "I'll be back."

INSIDER LINGO Mnemonics: Techniques used to make some piece of information, like a password, easier to remember.

Some examples of pseudo-random passwords include the following:

❄ Chosen phrase: "99 bottles of beer on the wall"
Password: 99boB0tW
Derived by choosing the first letter from each word, using a mixture of uppercase and lowercase letters, and replacing one "O" with a zero.

- ❋ Chosen phrase: "Today, Tomorrow, and Forever."
  Password: 2Da2mRo&4e
  Derived by creating words with numbers and letters, replacing words with symbols, and mixing up lowercase and uppercase letters.
- ❋ Chosen phrase: "Tomorrow Never Dies—James Bond"
  Password: tWNrDS007
  Derived by choosing the first and last letter from each word, mixing up lowercase and uppercase letters, and replacing James Bond with his agent number, 007.

Strong passwords are unique combinations of lower- and uppercase letters, numbers, and symbols rather than complete words. Another type of password that you can create is called a combination password. Combination passwords are an easy-to-remember combination of two unrelated words with a mix of uppercase and lowercase letters, numbers, and symbols.

Here are some examples of combination passwords:

- ❋ Combination words: Phone Home
  Password: fONhoM
  Derived by combining the two words phone and home, changing "phone" to fON (the "o" is replaced with a zero), and dropping the "e" in home. Notice, too, that the upper- and lowercase letters were mixed.
- ❋ Combination words: Monday's Date
  Password: mONDeSd8
  Derived by respelling Monday with a zero replacing the "o" and an 8 replacing "ate" in date. The upper- and lowercase letters have also been mixed up.
- ❋ Combination words: Once Again
  Password: 1CeAgIN
  Derived by changing "once" to "1ce" and "Again" to AgIN". Again, the upper- and lowercase letters are mixed up.

Passwords are your ID cards on the Internet. Your passwords are your way to prove who you are and to gain access to different software applications, Web sites, and services on the Internet. However, if a criminal or hacker discovers your passwords, he can take on your digital identity and gain access to any of the sites, applications, or services that you could access. Unfortunately, once criminals gain access, they usually shut you out completely.

The most widely used attacks aimed at ferreting out passwords in authentication systems are *dictionary* or *brute force* attacks. In most of these attacks, the hacker or criminal must know your username, but that's not as difficult as it sounds. Many applications let you choose your own username or use your e-mail address as your username, and just as you do with passwords, you probably use the same username in multiple locations.

Many password attacks are aimed at accounts with maximum privileges so the criminal or hacker can exploit all of a system's resources. In Microsoft Windows, for example, the administrator account is especially enticing to the criminal or hacker because that account gives him more freedom to access as much information as possible.

Therefore, it's a good idea to change the username on this account to something different. You can also create a decoy account with the username "administrator," but with only the minimum enabled privileges and a strong, hard-to-discover password. This protects the real administrator account and could help you detect an intrusion attempt by using the auditing options on Windows accounts. These functions will inform you of failed authentication attempts.

❄ Another good practice is to limit all accounts that children use to surf the Web. Many computers are compromised by children who download files or visit Web sites that have malware attached to them. Some ISPs, like AOL, offer parental controls that provide age-appropriate controls. If your ISP does not, there are also programs, such as NetNanny, that provide those controls.

Usernames and passwords are not a new threat. They've been a problem for as long as there have been usernames and passwords, but if you create solid, random passwords, you reduce your risk of having your password compromised dramatically. Build strong passwords using the techniques outlined above.

Updating Passwords

One of the most overlooked password issues, even for those who have great passwords, is the need to update the password occasionally. Think about that. How long have you been using your current password? If it's been more than three months, you're putting yourself at risk.

Even the best passwords should be updated or changed periodically. A good rule of thumb is to set a reminder to change your password on all of your various applications and Web sites about every three months—sooner if you suspect for any reason that your password might have been compromised.

You could even take that one step further and change your password every month. If you choose to update your password that frequently, just remember not to write the password down any-where. It doesn't do any good to frequently update your password if it's written on a slip of paper for anyone to find. Also keep in mind that every one of your passwords should be different, which further complicates changing your passwords monthly. For both of those reasons, it's probably best if you only update your passwords quarterly, unless you suspect that someone has gained access to your system or your password.

You need to make it a point to update or change your password regularly. Good passwords will go a long way toward making sure you aren't victimized by a criminal or hacker, but why chance it? Change your password before someone can capture it and use it to gain access to your computer and your personal information.

Additional Tips for Great Passwords

It seems that the list of guidelines for creating and using passwords goes on forever. In truth, however, it's not that difficult to create and maintain great passwords; it just requires a little extra attention, and possibly a change from the way you've used passwords in the past.

One of the basic rules for choosing a password is to ensure it is at least eight characters in length, and those characters need to be relatively complex. As a rule of thumb, a good password should contain a mix of letters, numbers, and special symbols, such as those symbols that you can access by pressing the Shift key and a number on your computer's keyboard.

One of the most difficult parts of using strong passwords is that although it's not too difficult to create a good password, there are so many services that require passwords for access that remembering them all can be a problem, especially if you are using passwords created with a series of numbers and letters that are difficult to guess.

To get around this issue, many people use the same password for all of their different applications, Web sites, and services. This increases your risk, however, and if you use the same password to access your computer, Web mail, and electronic banking, an attacker only needs to have one password to access all three applications.

It's important to use different passwords, especially when it comes to services with confidential information, such as online banking services. And if you really feel the need to use simpler pass-words, or passwords that are fewer than eight characters in length, then only use those passwords with services that won't put you at risk, like newsletter or mailing list subscriptions.

Here are some tips for creating and using strong passwords.

❋ Good passwords are at least eight characters in length.

❋ Your password should contain alphabetic characters.

❋ Your password should contain at least one numeric character.

❋ Your password should contain punctuation or symbol characters. For example, any of these characters could be used in a strong password: !@#$%^&*()_+|~-=\`{}[]:";'<>?,./

❋ Your password should not be derived from your name or the names of your spouse, children, friends, or other family members.

❋ Your password should not be a word chosen from the dictionary. This includes foreign language words, slang, jargon, and proper names.

❋ Avoid using passwords that are based on your birth date, address, phone number, or other personal information. Also be sure not to use this kind of information from any other person that you're related to or associated with.

❋ Use a mnemonic combination of a phrase or sentence that means something to you.

❋ Do not use sample passwords, like the ones described in this book or in other articles or passages about creating passwords.

❋ Change your password frequently.

❋ Do not share your password with anyone, including your spouse, children, or best friend.

❋ Do not write your password down, and don't post it anywhere near your computer. That includes in your desk drawer, under your keyboard, or on the side of your computer's CPU (central processing unit).

❋ Do not store your password in a file in the computer. In an effort to be organized many people put all of their passwords in a file on their computer's hard drive. The problem with that is if a criminal or hacker finds that file, all of your passwords are compromised.

❋ Do not share the same password with other accounts either on the computer or on the Internet. This includes Web mail accounts and individual profiles that you and your spouse might have on the same computer.

❋ Be sure your password is not based on a dictionary word—in your native language or a foreign language—or a reversed word, or on common names, especially if those names belong to your friends, acquaintances, or family members.

❋ Be sure your password is not too simplistic or systematic. The more random your password is when created, the harder it will be for a hacker or criminal to crack the password.

❋ Your password should be something that you understand and can remember, but it should not be something that other people will associate with you.

Passwords are a simple method of protecting yourself. Despite the simplicity, however, when created with strength and protection in mind, your password is your last line of defense. As such, you should be sure that you create good, strong passwords that are difficult for other people to guess.

Then you have to keep those passwords safe. Don't post them on your computer screen or write them on your notepad. And don't share your passwords with other people. It's not at all uncommon for spouses to have the same password across all of their accounts. Even if you and your spouse stay together forever, there's still risk in this practice. If, for some reason, one of your passwords is compromised, then both of your passwords are compromised.

The same is true in the workplace. Don't share passwords with your co-workers, and most especially don't use the same passwords at work and at home. Create a different password for each account, and keep them all separate and unrelated.

Passwords don't have to be a hassle. There are many tricks that you can use to create a strong password without having to remember truly random characters. Instead, just make sure that you use passwords that seem random, but make sense in your own mind.

Your passwords are the keys to every account that you must log in to online and on your computer. Treat them just like you would the keys to your house. Make them unique, and keep them out of the hands of the wrong people.

18 } Your Cybersecurity Plan

Most people have some aspects of their computer secured, yet other aspects of the same computer might be lacking in protection. Usually, it's not because you don't want to be protected, but more because you either don't know you need the protection or because you don't have the time to get all of the protections in place.

One way to get past those hurdles to your personal cybersecurity is to have a personal cybersecurity plan to help guide you through the process of putting the proper protection strategies in place. Notice the word used there: strategies.

Security is about using the right strategies to keep yourself safe when you're using the computer. And it's likely that you'll use a number of different protection technologies. However, technology isn't the complete answer, so you also need additional strategies, like how you plan to use your computer, and what you personally plan to do to protect your computer, and the information on it, while you're using the computer.

In order for cybersecurity to be effective, it must be a holistic effort. A cybersecurity plan gives you the tools that you need, at your fingertips, to decide what's the best way to get protected and to keep that protection ongoing.

It may seem as if it would take a long time to create a cybersecurity plan, but in truth, it really doesn't require more than two or three hours of your time. Beyond the planning stage, you'll also need to allocate time to the technologies and strategies that you decide to put into place, but those issues have already been covered in this book.

This chapter is about building a plan, or more accurately, a set of guidelines, that leave nothing about your cybersecurity to chance. In many cases, especially where a couple or a family use the same computer, one of the biggest challenges is that you think your spouse or son or daughter is performing some of the most basic security maintenance on your computer. However, that person thinks you're doing it, and as a result, it never gets done.

The pages that follow outline some of the most important issues that you need to address, and there's a form included that helps you get through all of the activities to help make you safe. Use the form to ensure that nothing will get lost in the shuffle.

However, remember that these pages are simply guidelines. What you do with them and how you put them to use should be based on your personal style. These pages simply give you a starting point. Using them should get you on the track to security. And, if you already have security in place, then you'll have guidelines to use the next time you update all of your programs and applications or when you change to a new computer.

Ultimately, it all comes down to how secure you really are. The pages in this chapter will help you find out.

What Is a Cybersecurity Plan?

A cybersecurity plan is basically an outline of all of the actions that you need to take in order to ensure that your computer is protected. From choosing the right software applications to making sure that everyone who uses your computer knows his or her own responsibilities for keeping other users safe, the cybersecurity plan ensures that you are where you should be to be protected.

Your cybersecurity plan doesn't have to be anything elaborate. You can either create your own plan, which you can print and store in a fire safe, or you can use the plan that's in the book to check and maintain your security level.

Regardless of which way you do it, keep a copy of the plan. You should keep a copy for two reasons: The first is that you have a record of everything that you do to protect yourself. It doesn't seem like you'd need that, but if you do happen to fall victim to some hacker or criminal, having the plan to look back over will help you to re-establish any protections later on that may have been lost or compromised. In looking back over the plan, you may also find the weak areas that left you vulnerable if you were victimized.

The other reason that you may want to save a copy of your cybersecurity plan is so that you have a quick and easy reference to turn to when you're updating your security protections at some point in the future. Typically, you'll want to update/upgrade your security protections at least every six months, but if you can do it every three months, that's a much better way to stay on top of security.

> The term update/upgrade in this chapter doesn't mean to add patches and updates to whatever software that you use. While it's important to keep all of your technologies and applications up-to-date, in this case, the update/upgrade refers to reviewing your protection strategy on a regular schedule and then increasing or adding protections that match the changes in the security landscape.

In short, your cybersecurity plan is a tracking document that helps you remember all the facets of cybersecurity, and then it helps you maintain the cybersecurity that you put in place for the long term.

Do I Really Need a Plan?

Whether you actually need a cybersecurity plan is a question that has answers that are as individual as the people who need to be protected. The short answer is that everyone who uses the Internet needs some kind of cybersecurity plan in place. The long answer is that people differ, and you might be perfectly capable of staying on top of all of your security plans and implementations. If that's the case, the security plan is likely to simply be a refresher for you.

Either way, the conservative, elitist answer is yes, you do need a cybersecurity plan. Even if it's a simple page with the answers to the questions that you'll find later in this chapter, you still need some kind of cybersecurity plan. Even if you never need it, it's like insurance; you really can't afford to be without it.

The cybersecurity plan gives you a clear overall picture of all of the protection technologies that you have in place, the areas where you have additional needs, and the areas where you are more or less sitting on the fence between being protected and being vulnerable. So, even if you have a great cybersecurity plan that's perhaps not written down, it serves a purpose for you to write it all down. The simplest purpose is to keep you prepared in the event that a criminal or hacker gains access to your information.

How to Design a Great Personal Cybersecurity Plan

Designing your cybersecurity plan won't take too much—just a few hours of your time and a few sheets of paper. Beyond the physical design of the plan, however, there are some other considerations. For example, what works for other people may not work for you.

In that vein, you'll find as you're putting your cybersecurity plan together that it's a living document that changes often. Advances in criminal capabilities and enhancements in protection capabilities happen every single day. Therefore, your security needs will change every day.

That doesn't mean that your cybersecurity plan will need to be updated daily. Once you complete it and all of the technologies are in place, then the update probably only needs to happen every three to six months. However, for that small amount of time, two to four times a year, you'll find that you're better protected than you have ever been.

Determining Your Cybersecurity Needs

Probably the hardest part of the whole plan is in determining your cybersecurity needs. Do you need a firewall? Do you need anti-spyware protection? The answer is probably yes to both questions, but you won't know that for sure until you look at your specific needs and then compare those needs to protection technologies that you have in place.

In the corporate world, it's called a security assessment, and the whole purpose is to take a candid look at your existing protection and compare it to the risks that you face. Only then can you see where you might not be protected.

So, your first step is to determine what your cybersecurity needs are. Here are some questions that will help you decide what you need:

1. How many people use your computer?

2. How many users are children?

3. How many users are teenagers?

4. How many computers do you need to protect?

5. Are those computers networked together? Is it a wired or wireless network?

6. Do you have any parental controls in place?

7. What activities are usually completed on the computer (list the activities for all of the users that use each of the computers included in this list).

8. What protection technologies do you currently have in place?

9. Are all users familiar with safe Internet behaviors?

10. Do all users practice safe Internet behaviors?

11. Is there sensitive information stored on your computer?

12. Are you currently experiencing any performance issues with your computer or any of the computers on your network?

Once you have answered all of these questions, you should begin to get a better understanding of where you are at risk, and what is specifically putting you at risk—whether it's poor Internet behaviors or unprotected machines. With that in mind, you can begin to decide what additional security solutions you might need.

Selecting the Right Security Solutions

You may have heard it said before that technology is a tool, but it's not a replacement for good habits. It's true, even where security is concerned. You can put some of the best protection technologies available on your computer, but if you don't have the right behaviors in place, those technologies won't do you any good at all.

Therefore, before you can begin to choose security solutions, you should make sure that you and any other computer users in your household or on your network are surfing the Internet and using the computer in a manner that will keep you safe. Here are some of the issues that you should consider when thinking about the way you and other users behave while you're online.

* Do you or other users in your home frequently visit Web sites that are considered high risk? (Examples of high risk sites are gaming sites, pornography sites, gambling sites, and some chat rooms.)

* Do you and the other users in your home understand and practice safe e-mail strategies? (For example, does everyone understand that they should not download files attached to e-mail unless they know who the file is coming from and are expecting it?)

* Do all users understand that they should never click through a link sent in e-mail or an instant messaging service unless they know the person sending the link and are certain that it's a safe link?

* Do all users understand that they should not provide any type of sensitive or personal information via e-mail or in response to an e-mail or instant message requesting that information?

* Do all users know that they should not download free applications and programs unless they are certain that the applications and programs are safe? (For example, many file-sharing applications are free, but they come bundled with adware and spyware that can put your computer at risk.)

* Do all users understand what safe shopping habits are when online, and do they practice those habits?

How you behave when you're online has a tremendous bearing on how safe you are, despite all of the technologies that you might install on your computer. Take the time to make sure that you and all of the other computer users in your house know how to behave while online, and then periodically check on everyone to be sure those habits continue to be observed. Only then will your protection technologies do you any good.

With that out of the way, you can begin to decide what types of security applications you need to have. The top three, of course, are a firewall, an antivirus application, and an anti-spyware application. At the very least you need to have one application that performs all three jobs; however, those applications are currently very hard to find. In time they will be common, but until then you might consider getting separate applications that work well together.

In addition to those technologies, you should also ensure that your automatic updates are turned on and that your computer is currently updated. It doesn't take long to do, but this is one of those areas that is often overlooked. It's also an area where the most damage can be done, so enable the automatic updates, and then you won't have to worry about it.

As you're looking at protection technologies, keep in mind that most of the applications that you purchase for your personal computer will probably only allow you to install the software on a single computer, two at most. If you have multiple computers in your household, you may need multiple copies of all of the protection technologies that you choose to install. That can get pricey when you consider that the average price for these software applications can be around $30 each.

Finally, you should also consider the ease of use of any application that you install on the computers in your home. Some programs are very easy to use; others are very difficult. If you have the option to evaluate a protection software using a free trial period, take advantage of that option. Spend the free trial period evaluating the software. Pay attention to how easy it is to use, how it integrates into your computer system, and how well it seems to protect you.

> ✳ You should be able to tell how well some of your security applications work, because many of them have an alert system that lets you know when a virus is detected, when access to your computer has been attempted and denied, or when a pop-up window has been blocked. Watch for these alerts to see how often your security application is catching security threats and blocking them.

Once you have decided on the security technologies that you want, all that's left is for you to put your cybersecurity plan in place.

Your Complete Cybersecurity Plan

The actual cybersecurity plan can be as long or as short as you need it to be, and it will be determined by your personal needs. In general, the cybersecurity plan should be one to three pages in length. However, if you have a large number of computers in your home, or if you have more than two or three users, the length of your plan will increase. What's important is that you do what's comfortable for you while ensuring that your computers get protected and stay that way.

The easiest way to keep up with that will be to write it all down, so here's a chart that you can use to keep up with everything. Where appropriate, check the boxes that indicate where users are protected. Any area that doesn't get checked needs additional information. In addition to these areas, you'll also need to assign some ongoing monitoring and maintenance to each of the computer users covered in the plan.

Computer User Cybersecurity Plan

Activity or Technology Notes	User #1	User #2	User #3	User #4
Understands what Web sites are acceptable and what Web sites are off limits.				
Understands how to surf the Web safely.				
Understands secure e-mail strategies.				
Practices secure e-mail strategies.				
Understands safe download strategies.				
Practices safe download strategies.				
Understands security risks.				
Knows not to provide personal information to anyone online.				
Knows not to click through links in e-mails.				
Has firewall installed and active.				
Has antivirus installed and active.				
Has single anti-spyware program installed and active.				
Has two anti-spyware programs installed and active.				
Knows how to use all installed protection technologies.				

Once all of those questions are answered, add the following questions and answers to the page:

1. Who is responsible for updating your operating system and software applications?
2. Who is responsible for keeping security technologies up-to-date and active?
3. Who is responsible for ensuring that all users within the household are using safe Internet surfing practices?
4. Who is responsible for staying informed about present and future security threats?
5. How often do you plan to re-evaluate your security procedures and applications?

That's really all there is to it. By the time you get through all of the questions and the checklist, you should know what you need, where your weak spots are, and how to strengthen those weak spots. All that's left is for you to put the plan in place.

Implementing Your Plan

If you've gotten this far, implementing your plan will only take one additional element that's not already included—time. It shouldn't take more than a few hours to get your cybersecurity plan from paper into practice, even if you don't have any security technologies installed on your computer. So, all that's really left for you to do is to make that time. Don't put it off; do it right now, because if you put if off, you'll never get it done.

As you're putting your plan in place, you might want to get all of the computer users in the household together for a quick meeting. This is a great opportunity for you to say to each person, "Here are the guidelines that we're going to be following to protect ourselves from cybercriminals," and then hand them a copy of the cybersecurity plan that you've put in place.

If you pull everyone together, all at once, then you can be sure that everyone understands the cybersecurity plan and you can help clear up any confusion about who is responsible for what, whether it's simply a behavior change or actually helping to install and configure the technologies that you've chosen to keep yourself safe.

Once everyone is on the same page, then all you have to do is the physical installation and the configuration of any new technologies that you put in place. Then you're done. Hopefully everyone is on the same page, and you're protected. Now, you can move on with life and not think about cybersecurity again for a while. But only for a short while, because you'll need to update that plan again every three to six months.

Updating Your Cybersecurity Plan

It would seem that once you install a piece of software on your computer, then it's done. Unfortunately, that's not usually the case. Once you get the software installed, you might have a brief break, but there will still be times when you need to participate in your security.

From software upgrades and updating to new technologies, you'll find that the whole landscape of personal cybersecurity changes drastically a few times each year. In part, it's because technology is such a new phenomenon. However, it's more because criminals and hackers are learning that there really is money to be made if they can leverage the Internet to commit the same crimes they commit in the real world.

So, it only makes sense that you'll want to actively maintain your security applications. Keep up with what's changing and how threats are evolving, and then make sure that your protection technologies keep pace with that change.

Also, as children grow and relationships change, your computer usage will change. Take the time you need to keep up with all of those changes. In the long run, you'll be much more protected for it, even if it does cost you an additional 15 to 30 minutes of your time every week or month.

Your cybersecurity plan is your key to knowing where your security is at any given time. Take a few hours to work through the plan, and then make sure that your computers are up to the challenge, and you'll find that you're better protected now than you've ever been.

IV } Cybersecurity Checklists

Cybersecurity is one of those topics that tends to get away from you. Right now, you're reading this book because you have security on your mind and you want to do something about it. But soon something else will take precedence, and cybersecurity will slip to the bottom of your to-do list. This section of this book is designed to help you stay on top of security by presenting some of the most relevant security strategies in quick, easy-to-digest sections. It's a refresher, if you will, to help you maintain the good security habits that you've developed as you've worked your way through this book.

In this section of the book you'll find a list of dos and a list of don'ts, and a security plan checklist to use when you're putting your security plan in place or when you're updating that plan. There are also checklists that help you quickly get up to speed on e-mail protections and protection technologies.

This is a quick reference for you to come back to time and again, because although the threats change and some of the technologies will advance, the principles of protecting yourself should always remain the same. Use these tools to keep yourself safe for the future.

19 Ten Cybersecurity DOs

Protecting yourself isn't a matter of being completely locked away from any threat. Instead, it's a matter of being prepared for any threat. Here's a list of the top ten strategies you can use to keep yourself safe from any threat that a hacker or criminal sends your way.

* **Do keep your computer system upgraded.** It's very hard to secure older PCs. Operating systems like Windows 95, Windows 98, and Windows ME are no longer supported by their developers, so it only makes sense that you should upgrade to the newer version of the Windows system. Windows XP is the current operating system and is supported by the Microsoft Corporation. That means that securing that operating system is much easier for you to do. Either upgrade your operating system or purchase a newer computer that comes with Windows XP installed.

* **Do keep your computer system and software applications current on updates and patches.** Malicious hackers or criminals often attempt to exploit security holes that exist in your computer's operating system or software programs. If a security hole is discovered, the operating system or software manufacturer will quickly develop a patch to seal off that hole. Your best strategy for patching or updating your operating system or software programs is to set these utilities up to update automatically when new patches are released.

* **Do keep a current version of antivirus and anti-spyware software active on your computer at all times.** The key word here is current. Antivirus and anti-spyware programs must be updated regularly to ensure that they are equipped to protect you from the most current threats circulating on the Internet. Be sure you have an antivirus and an anti-spyware program installed on your computer. Set those programs up for automatic updates, and then don't turn them off for any reason. It takes hackers only seconds to break into an unprotected PC.

❋ **Do use complex, hard-to-guess passwords to protect your computer and your applications.** Use some form of mnemonic to develop a password that is at least eight seemingly random characters in length. Those characters should be alphanumeric, and should include symbols where possible. Remember, too, to keep your passwords safe from nosey people or criminals, and to use different passwords at work and at home, as well as varying your passwords from one application to another.

❋ **Do use a strong firewall, and keep it updated properly.** Firewalls will do you no good if they are out of date. Hackers and criminals eventually learn how to break through a firewall, so be sure that whatever firewall you choose to use is updated periodically to withstand any new or developing threats. Also remember to keep your firewall turned on at all times. If it becomes necessary to turn off your firewall for some reason, disconnect your computer from the Internet until the firewall can be reinstated.

❋ **Do be aware of the security risks that you face as you surf the Internet and use your computer.** Half of being protected is knowing where and when you're at risk. Take the time to learn about the current threats to your computer both online and offline, and then stay current with that knowledge. There are many security publications and Web sites where you can find all of the information that you need to be sure you're aware of the threats to your computer and applications. Use them to stay knowledgeable and keep yourself safe. This is especially essential as security threats continue to grow in severity and sophistication.

❋ **Do avoid click-through links included in e-mails or attachments you aren't expecting from people you don't know.** The fastest way that viruses and other malware spreads is by people clicking on a link included in an e-mail or downloading an attachment from someone they don't know. It doesn't matter how enticing the attachment might sound, don't download it if you aren't expecting it and you don't know who it's from. For links that are embedded in e-mails, rather than clicking through them, type the URL into your Web browser's address bar. This is most helpful if you go to the main page of the site you're visiting first and then navigate into the site from that front page. This helps to ensure that you know where you are and that it's the site you intend to be on.

❋ **Do avoid installing free programs or utilities on your computer unless you're certain they are safe.** Many free programs, such as file-sharing applications, toolbars, Internet accelerators, and games, contain spyware or adware in the download. You may never know that you've downloaded something that's harmful until your computer becomes so bogged down with adware or spyware that it begins to freeze up or crash on you. Avoid downloading and installing any application that doesn't come from a trusted source.

❋ **Do secure your wireless network.** Wireless networks are notorious for being major safety concerns. Most wireless network routers come with security settings that are set at their lowest protection level. Take the time to get to know your wireless network configuration, and then increase your security levels to the highest possible point that will still allow you to access the network without letting others break into your network and steal your private and personal information.

❋ **Do back up all of your important data.** Even the best-protected computers and applications occasionally fall victim to determined criminals and hackers. Protect your data by backing it up regularly on a piece of permanent storage media like a USB drive or a CD or DVD disc. Then, store that information away from your house, but not in your car. The heat in your car could damage the storage media. Your best storage site would be a safe deposit box in your local bank.

20 } Ten Cybersecurity DON'Ts

Security is a serious issue that everyone should be concerned about. However, security isn't only about doing the right things. It's also about *not* doing the wrong things. It's the combination of the two that gives you real security.

Here's a list of the top ten things that you should not do while you're using your computer and the Internet. Avoid these activities and you'll increase your security multiple times.

❋ **Don't use unsafe password practices.** Don't write down your passwords and store them under your keyboard, on your computer monitor, or in any other place that they can be found by someone else. You should also avoid sharing passwords with other people, and that means community passwords or your own password that you tell someone else. Your password is your key to your security while you're using your computer. Treat it as a secret that you wouldn't want to share with anyone else.

❋ **Don't store passwords electronically.** Some computers have a "Store my password" function. Don't use it. In fact, if you can, turn that function off so you're not tempted to use it. When you use those functions, your password is stored in a file that could be accessible to hackers or criminals if they gain access to your computer. You should also avoid storing your passwords in a file that you create on your computer for the same reason.

❋ **Don't interact with pop-up windows that appear on your computer screen.** Pop-up windows are usually activated by adware or spyware. Even if a pop-up window isn't a malicious piece of software launched by a criminal or hacker, it's still being pushed at you, usually without your permission. Interacting with pop-up windows only serves to provide more information about your computer and your Internet habits to whoever is pushing the pop-up out to you. Don't even click within a pop-up to request that you be removed from their advertising list. In most cases, that will only cause you to receive more pop-up windows.

✺ **Don't allow your e-mail program to automatically open attachments in your e-mail.** Many attachments contain viruses or other malware that puts your computer and your personal information at risk. Make sure that your e-mail program is set to prompt you before any file is downloaded to your computer. It's also wise to change your e-mail settings to text only, rather than enabling HTML messages to be displayed on your computer. This prevents hackers and criminals from slipping malware onto your computer disguised as HTML.

✺ **Don't reply to spam or click on a link to unsubscribe from the mailing list.** Spam is unwanted e-mail—the electronic equivalent of junk mail. Unfortunately, spam is a lot more dangerous than junk mail. Clicking on links inside a spam message or replying to spam messages only confirms to the sender that they have reached a valid e-mail address, and as such, the spammer will usually continue to send you messages. To make matters worse, they may sell your e-mail address to other spammers, which increases the amount of unwanted e-mail that you receive.

✺ **Don't purchase anything that's promoted in a spam message.** Even if the spam is just spam and not a disguise for a criminal who is trying to gain access to your credit card information, you don't want to purchase anything that's promoted by spam. All that your purchase will serve to do is encourage and fund the spammer to continue sending out spam messages. If an item you want to purchase is advertised in spam, go directly to the Web site to make the purchase; don't click through the link in the e-mail.

✺ **Don't reply to any e-mail message that requests personal and confidential information.** Legitimate businesses will not request that you provide such personal information via e-mail. Nor will they send you a link to click through to their Web site. Legitimate businesses have other ways to get any information that they may need from you, and that information will never be account information or usernames and passwords.

✺ **Don't be deceived by an enticing subject line.** Criminals and hackers will do anything they can to get you to open their e-mails, click through links within their e-mails, or download an attachment. Make it an unbreakable rule that you won't respond or take action on any e-mail that comes from someone you don't know. Then, extend that rule one step further to include not opening attachments from people you do know but are not expecting attachments from. Viruses and other malware spread rapidly because people open attachments they aren't expecting or from people they don't know. No matter how enticing it might appear to be, don't do it. You never know when you might get targeted for some kind of malicious attack.

✺ **Don't become the victim of a phishing attack.** Phishing attacks are becoming more and more sophisticated. In fact, even some security experts are finding it very difficult to tell phishing e-mails from legitimate e-mails. Use the utmost caution when you receive any e-mail that seems to be from your bank, credit card company, or any other institution with which you do business (including Amazon.com, PayPal, and eBay). Be sure you understand the privacy policies of the organizations that you do business with, because this is where you'll find information about how a company will or will not contact you and what information they will or will not request from you. Always be skeptical. And when in doubt, call the phone number listed on your statement or the back of your credit card (but don't call any number listed within the body of an e-mail—those numbers can be faked just as easily as the e-mail).

- **Don't share access to your computer with anyone else.** This covers a lot of ground, but basically means that you should monitor the other people who use your computer very closely. It also means that you should monitor your network closely, whether it's wireless or wired. Be sure you have the appropriate firewalls and other protection mechanisms in place, and never, ever use an unsecured wireless access point. In short, the only person who should have access to your computer is you.

21 } Security Plan Checklist

Most businesses have security plans. Those plans include policies that outline what protection the business needs and how that protection should be used. They also include procedures that outline what actions should be taken when. It helps those organizations to keep their business information and employees secure.

Security plans aren't only for businesses, however. You should have a security plan, too. You don't have to take it to the extent that a business would, but having some well-thought-out guidelines for how you plan to protect your computer and your personal information prepares you in the event that you become the target of some hacker or criminal who would take advantage of you or steal your information or identity.

A personal security plan shouldn't take you long to develop. There are a few key areas that you should give some thought to. Think about how you use your computer and what activities you use the computer for, and then use the following checklist to help you put the proper protection technologies and habits in place. This keeps you one step ahead of the criminals and hackers who won't hesitate to steal your personal information or take advantage of your computer resources.

Your security plan should also include some recovery information, like backups and copies of your personal financial information. Then, in the event that you do fall victim to some cybercriminal, you'll be prepared to recover as quickly as possible.

Answering the following questions will get you started thinking about what you need to stay protected.

1. How do you use your computer? What activities do you use your computer to accomplish (e.g., paying bills, making purchases, downloading music, etc.)?

2. What protection technologies do you currently have installed and active on your computer? Don't list protection technologies that are not currently turned on and up-to-date.

3. Is your operating system up-to-date? When was the last time you updated your operating system?

4. Is your Internet browser up-to-date? When was the last time you updated your browser?

5. Is your other software up-to-date? When was the last time your software applications were updated?

6. Are automatic updates currently enabled for your operating system? Your browser? Your other software applications?

7. Would you consider your passwords to be strong, medium, or weak? Why?

8. Do you use safe surfing habits? (Do you avoid Web sites that are prone to having malware lurking on them?)

9. Do you use a software application to limit your children's activities online? What application do you use?

10. Do you have separate passwords for all of your services that require them?

11. Do you share your computer with other people?

12. Do you keep a regularly updated backup of all the important information stored on your computer?

13. What protection level is your e-mail application set to?

14. Do you send and receive HTML or plain text e-mails?

15. Do you often receive e-mails, with or without attachments, from people or businesses you don't know?

16. Does your computer have ActiveX controls enabled?

17. Does your computer have Java controls enabled?

18. Have you ever read the privacy policy of a Web site with which you interact?

19. Do you ever make purchases online with companies that you're not familiar with?

20. Do you have a wireless network installed in your house? Have you adjusted the security settings on that wireless network?

21. How current is the operating system that you use?

22. Is your computer in a location where other people (friends, family, or visitors) can have access to it?

23. Do you ever turn off your computer?

When you have answered all of the above questions, you should have a good idea of the current state of your personal security. The answers to those questions, combined with the information that you've learned from this book should illuminate the areas where you need to improve your security and show you the areas where your security is at about the right level. Now, use the following checklist to mark off the items where you are protected. The items remaining on the list are the ones that you should address immediately.

Complete the checklist by noting if an item is already complete or attended to, or if it needs additional attention. For each item on the list, fill in the action system with the protection technology or strategy that you used. When you've completed the checklist, you should be better than reasonably sure of the security of your computer system and your surfing habits. Be sure to keep up with the checklist for future reference as you go back and re-evaluate your security every few months.

Personal Security Plan Checklist

Action item	Complete	Needs Attention	Action Taken
Operating system up-to-date			
Software applications up-to-date			
Browser software up-to-date			
Firewall installed and active			
Antivirus software installed and active			
Anti-spyware software installed and active			
Security configurations adjusted			
Administrative profile password protected			
Dummy administrative account created			
Updates and patches automated			
Read and understand privacy policies			
Stay informed about security threats			
E-mail program configurations adjusted to restrict access			
E-mail program configured to send and display e-mail as plain text			
Incoming and outgoing e-mails scanned for viruses and other malware			
ActiveX controls disabled			
Java controls disabled			
Familiar with retailers and service providers			
Wireless connection security settings adjusted			
Physical security addressed			
Backup current and stored properly			

22 } E-mail Protection Checklist

E-mail is one of the most exploited technologies in existence. Really, that's no surprise, since e-mail is a very impersonal and easy-to-use method of connecting with other people. Unfortunately, because it is very impersonal and easy to use, it also presents a major challenge to your computer's safety.

It is for these reasons that you should pay special attention to your e-mail accounts and the way you manage those accounts. The checklist below should help you determine how well protected your e-mail account is.

Once you get through the checklist, you will know the areas in which you are protected and the areas in which you are not. To use this checklist, check off the items according to whether they are true or false. For false answers, fill in the space provided with the methods or software used to improve or increase security in that area.

E-mail Protection Checklist

Action Item	True	False	Corrected	Action Taken
My e-mail is configured properly to ensure security.				
I keep the preview pane in my e-mail program closed.				
I understand how security applies to attachments.				
I never open attachments unless I know the sender.				
I never open attachments unless I am expecting them.				
I use a spam filter within my e-mail program.				
I understand that I shouldn't be asked for sensitive or personal information.				
I understand the threats that face my e-mail program and my e-mails.				

Action Item	True	False	Corrected	Action Taken
I use an antivirus application.				
I regularly update, or have automatic updates set up for my e-mail account.				
I keep my antivirus protection turned on at all times.				
I have my incoming and outgoing e-mails scanned by my antivirus program.				
I understand not to click through embedded links in e-mails.				
I understand how to create and use strong passwords.				
I keep all of my software, including my Web browser and e-mail program, properly patched and up-to-date.				
I use encryption technologies for sensitive e-mails.				
I keep my computer physically secure at all times.				

One additional note about e-mail: Web-based e-mail tends to be more vulnerable to security issues, so if you can avoid it, don't use Web-based e-mail. However, if you have no choice but to use it, take all of the precautions necessary to protect yourself.

23 } Protection Technology Checklist

All of the various technologies that are available to help you protect your computer when you're online can be confusing. Should you use a free program, or do you need to buy a program? Should you install several applications, or will just one meet your needs? It's hard to navigate all of the various issues that you'll face as you find the right technologies to keep you safe.

The following questions should help you decide what you need and whether you need more than one program. Answer all of the questions, and by the time you're finished, you should have confidence that whatever program you decide upon will meet your individual needs.

1. What do you use your computer for? For example, surfing the Web, checking e-mail, paying bills online, or other activities.

2. What type of Internet connection do you use?

3. Do you have a wireless network in your home?

4. Do you have sensitive information on your computer that would put you at risk if a criminal or hacker were to gain access to it?

5. Do you have a firewall installed and active? If yes, which one? If no, why not?

6. Do you have antivirus software installed and active? If yes, which one? If no, why not?

7. Do you have anti-spyware protection installed? If yes, which one? If no, why not?

8. Do you have any other protection technologies installed?

9. How many people use your computer?

10. Is your computer in an area where visitors who come into your home can access it?

11. What features would you like to have in a firewall?

12. What features would you like to have in antivirus software?

13. What features would you like to have in anti-spyware protection?

14. Do you currently suffer from slow response time on your computer?

15. Do you currently suffer from frequent computer crashes?

16. How much are you willing to spend on a suite of applications to protect your computer?

17. Is there a specific protection technology that you prefer over the others on the market?

18. Does that protection technology offer all of the protections you need (including firewall, antivirus, anti-spyware, pop-up blockers, and anything else you need or want)?

19. How much time do you have to devote to running each of those protection technologies to learn the status of your system?

20. Are there specific products that have been recommended to you (or that you've been warned against) by other people who are currently using those applications?

21. How often do you plan to update your protection technologies?

Appendix A

Demystifying the Jargon

Adware

Software that collects your personal or sensitive information and uses it to display advertisements that are supposed to be tailored to you.

Ankle Biter

Another name for a script kiddie. These hackers use existing hacking tools to break into networks through known vulnerabilities.

Anti-Spyware Software

A software application that locates and removes or disables spyware applications.

Antivirus Software

A software application that locates and removes or disables viruses and other types of malware applications.

Auction Fraud

The criminal activity of defrauding buyers and selling at Internet auctions by pretending to be someone you are not, or by auctioning an item with no intention of sending it. Other types of auction fraud also exist.

Authentication

The process by which a person or entity is authenticated, or proven to be the person or entity they claim to be.

Bid Shilling

A technique used by dishonest sellers to drive up the price of an auction.

Bid Siphoning

A technique that sellers use to draw buyers away from the protection of an auction site.

Blue Box

A device, built by phreaks, that plays the correct musical tones at the correct frequencies to allow the hacker to gain access to the public telephone network.

Botnet

A network of computers that have been illegally taken over with the express purpose of using those computers to complete malicious or illegal tasks.

Brute Force Attack

An attempt to break a password by using all of the possible combinations of the 95 ASCII character set.

Card Not Present

The type of retail transaction that typically occurs when a consumer is shopping online or over the phone. The credit card is authorized even though it is not present at the actual site of the sale.

Click-Through Link

A link within an e-mail or on a Web site that takes you to a different Web site.

Confidence Fraud

Fraud committed when a criminal creates confidence in his or her victims.

Contextual Clues

Signs, such as navigation panes and graphics, that make a Web site easy to use and make that site appear legitimate. These signs also guide users through a site.

Cookie

A small piece of software, used by companies and installed on your computer, that tracks certain information about you and your surfing habits and then feeds that information back to the company to be used in advertising and customization of Web sites.

Crackers

Criminal hackers who manipulate computers and programs for financial gain, usually outside of the confines of the law.

Credit Card Fraud

A crime that happens when a criminal obtains your credit card account number through illegal means and uses it to make fraudulent purchases of goods and services.

Cybercrime

Crimes committed using the Internet as a catalyst.

Cybercriminal

A person who commits cybercrimes.

Cyber Harassment

The criminal act of harassing or threatening a person with malicious intent using the Internet or Internet technologies.

Cybersecurity

Security activities and technologies designed to prevent or reduce cybercrime.

Cyberstalking

The act of stalking a person using the Internet or other electronic capabilities.

Denial of Service

A hacking attack in which a hacker inundates a server with unanswerable session requests, causing the server to slow to a crawl or eventually crash.

Dictionary Attack

Once a hacker or criminal gains access to your username, he can try a series of passwords from a set list to see if they match. This kind of attack is often carried out using a specially built application that references a dictionary as the source of the passwords to try.

Distributed Denial of Service

A denial of service attack most often conducted using a network of personal computers with broadband connections that have been taken over by hackers using viruses, Trojans, or other types of malware to infect and gain access to the computer.

Domain Name

The numerical address or URL assigned to a Web site. An example of a domain name is Thomson.com.

Dot Com Boom

That period of time from the late 1990s to the early 2000s when Internet growth and Internet company growth was disproportionately inflated by demand. During that period, the world shifted from the Industrial Age to the Information Age, placing more value on information than on products.

Dot Com Bust

The period during 2000 to 2002 when the inflation that technology brought to the stock market was corrected. Many companies failed and the value of many others was reduced greatly by decreased financial backing and demand for higher profits.

Electronic Sabotage

An attempt to shut down Internet or cell phone service by sending thousands of e-mail or text messages using an automated messaging program that has the capability of sending thousands of messages per minute.

E-mail Scams

Attempts by criminals to defraud or take advantage of Internet users by sending scams through e-mail programs.

Encryption

A method of obscuring information, usually by using a code or an algorithm that scrambles the information. Once encoded or scrambled, the information cannot be accessed without the proper encryption key.

Encryption Key

An encryption key is like the key to a lock. It provides the necessary information to unlock information that has been encoded or scrambled by an encryption program. Without the key, the information simply appears as gibberish.

Erotomania

A condition where a criminal commits a crime because he believes that he or she is in love with the victim and that the victim returns those feelings.

Escrow Account

A special account, usually managed by a financial company, where money (or in some cases, property like software source code, a deed, or valuable artworks) is deposited until special conditions are met. Once the conditions are met, the money or property is delivered to the correct recipient.

Feedback

A method through which buyers and sellers are rated on their performance. Some auction sites uses stars, while others simply let you write a short description of your experience. In the auction community, feedback is what defines how well your sales or purchases go.

Firewall

Software applications that provide protection against outside attackers by shielding your computer or network from unnecessary and malicious Internet traffic.

Flame Wars

E-mail battles, between two or more disagreeing parties, in which the e-mails are sent publicly and which often contain very derogatory statements.

Freeware

Software that's made available for free, usually because it's in a testing phase or because the company is trying to build community interest in the software. Occasionally freeware is distributed by criminals or hackers and is loaded with malware or viruses.

Gray Market Goods

Products that were obtained illegally, usually with stolen credit card numbers, which are resold for a profit.

Hacker

A person who intentionally breaks into computer systems and networks that he does not have permission to access. Some hackers break into systems because it is a challenge. Others do it for financial gain.

Hacking

The art of breaking into a computer or network that you do not have permission to access.

HTTP

Hyper Text Transfer Protocol. A Web programming language that is designed to help build Web sites.

HTTPS

Hyper Text Transfer Protocol Secure. A Web programming language that is designed to help build secure Web sites.

Identity Fraud

The act of pretending to be someone that you are not for the purpose of gaining access to some item or action that the person you are imitating is able to access.

Identity Theft

The act of stealing someone's identity for personal or financial gain.

Information Aggregators

Individuals or corporations that collect public information about you, organize it in a manner that's accessible by other people, and then resell that information to anyone who can afford the price they are asking. Information aggregation is a legal practice, and many organizations, such as creditors or employers, purchase this information during background checks and pre-employment screenings

Infrastructure

The network of interconnected computers upon which an Internet service is built. Also called a technological backbone.

Internet

A network of connected computers around the world that contain information which is shared among all of the users of the network.

Internet Service Provider

An organization that provides Internet service plans and access software to Internet users, usually for a monthly or yearly fee.

Into the Wild

This phrase refers to the release of a piece of malicious code onto the Internet. Much as an animal can be released into the wild to roam as it pleases, viruses, Trojans, and other types of malware can be released on the Internet.

Intrusion Detection Systems

These systems are specifically designed to monitor traffic on your network or on the Internet for unauthorized intrusion into your system. If an unauthorized user attempts to access your system, these applications provide a warning mechanism.

Investment Fraud

A crime that takes place when you are persuaded to make an investment in a company, stock, or other vehicle that's not real.

IP Address

The location of your computer on a network, like the Internet, usually indicated by a series of numbers. For example, 169.192.255.20

IRC

Internet Relay Chat. A communication program that works like instant messenger and can be used to communicate with a group of people or individuals.

JavaScript

A programming language often used in designing Web sites.

Keylogger

An application used to capture and record keystrokes. Originally, keyloggers were used as diagnostic tools in software development, but today, many hackers and criminals use them to collect usernames and passwords or other sensitive information as you type it into your computer.

Logic Bombs

Attacks that are similar to viruses or Trojans; however, a logic bomb is set to activate at a specific time. Once activated, the malicious payload can rewrite your hard drive and delete, alter, or corrupt data on your hard drive.

Malware

This term literally translates to "malicious software," and refers to a piece of software or an application that is specifically designed to complete some malicious task, from stealing usernames and passwords to logging all of your Internet activity.

Nigerian Letter Fraud

This scam is often referred to as the *419 Scam* because of the code in Nigerian law that it violates. The scam aims to take money from unsuspecting people by convincing them to provide account information in an effort to help the family of a persecuted political or royal family. This scam has been around for decades and originally used postal mail as a means of scamming unsuspecting people.

Open Source Software

This is a type of software that has its source code available for other people to examine, manipulate, and add to as their needs dictate. Often, open source software is free, and there are communities that share all of a program or just aspects of the program.

Operating System

The software platform installed on your computer that allows you to operate and work with other types of software.

Patch

A small piece of software that repairs flaws in operating systems and applications.

Payload

The result, or activity, that a piece of malicious software can perform.

Peer-to-Peer

A type of network that connects computer resources and distributes those resources evenly among workstations or computers.

Pharming

Also called DNS Poisoning. Altering information on a DNS server so that when users attempt to access a Web site, they're redirected to a fraudulent Web site where personal information such as usernames and passwords or financial account information is collected for use or resale at a later time.

Phishing

An attempt by a criminal or hacker to gain access to your usernames and passwords or account information so that the criminal or hacker can exploit those accounts, usually for fraudulent transactions.

Phreak

A hacker or criminal who uses phreaking techniques to gain unauthorized access to telecommunication services.

Phreaking

A technique used to gain access to the public telephone network. Phreaking is undergoing a shift from telephones to other communication services like e-mail and VoIP. The point of phreaking in the past was to gain access to free communications services. Today, phreaking is more targeted to eavesdropping on electronic communications methods for the purpose of financial gain.

Port Scanning

A technique that hackers and criminals use to take advantage of unprotected ports on a computer to gain access to the computer or to a network to which the computer is attached.

Red Box

The red box performs a similar function to the blue box. The difference is that red boxes are specifically designed to play musical tones at frequencies that trick pay phones into believing that money has been deposited into the phone. When these boxes were used frequently, there were some that were sophisticated enough to make both the frequencies required and the sound of the coins dropping into the payphone.

Script Kiddies

Hackers who don't have enough skill to write their own cracking programs. These hackers usually use hacking programs that other more experienced hackers have developed to conduct denial of service attacks and other large scale attacks.

Short Messaging Service (SMS)

A service that is available for most cellular telephones that allows short messages to be sent directly to the phone. SMS messages are usually referred to as text messages.

Signature

The binary pattern of a virus or other malware. This pattern is very much like a fingerprint—each piece of malware has a different signature.

Skimming

A process by which criminals capture credit card information that is used to create cloned credit cards. In the real world, the clerk or server to whom you hand your card swipes it through a card reader twice. The first time is to authorize your charge, the second time is to capture your information. Skimming is much more difficult to accomplish online.

Smart Card

A small electronic device, usually the size and shape of a credit card, that contains a microchip on which is encoded private and personal information.

Social Engineering

A practice hackers use to convince others that they are someone that they, in reality, are not. This trickery is often used to gain access to personal and confidential information, especially usernames and passwords or financial account information.

Spam

Unsolicited e-mails that are typically harmless but always annoying. It's the electronic equivalent of junk mail, and under the right conditions, it can be dangerous.

Spoofing

A deceptive technique in which a hacker or criminal tries to convince you that an e-mail or Web site is legitimate by making that site or e-mail look exactly like the original. Spoofing is often used to trick people into providing information that they would not otherwise provide.

Spyware

Code that is hidden on your computer or installed as part of another program without your knowledge. It's used to gather customer data, display advertising, track computer usage, and in the worst-case scenario, to take control of your computer.

Technological Backbone

The network of interconnected computers upon which an Internet service is built. Also called the infrastructure.

Text Messaging

A service that enables you to send a short text message from your cellular phone to another cellular phone. Usually only works if both parties have text messaging capabilities.

Tracking Cookies

Small packets of information placed on your computer when you visit a Web site. The cookie is used to track your movements and behavior on the site and in some cases, in other places on the Internet. This information is used by organizations to push more relevant content to you under the guise of improving the user experience. Tracking cookies are generally harmless.

Triggers

A facet of an object or situation that makes it all seem more believable or that creates a sense of urgency that the requested action should be carried out.

Trojan

A Trojan is a malicious piece of software that masquerades as legitimate software or that is completely invisible to your system until it begins to do damage. Much like its equine namesake, a Trojan is designed to catch you off guard.

Update

A software application released by software designers that offers improvements in software applications after they have been used by many people.

URL

Universal Resource Locator. An address on the Internet that tells where a particular Web site is located. For example, http://www.JerriLedford.com.

URL Rewriting

A process in which a piece of software is used to rewrite all of the links on a legitimate Web site to lead to bogus Web site. When you click through the link, you're taken off the legitimate site to the bogus site, where the hacker or criminal can control all of your movements during your Internet session.

Virus

A piece of software or code that is intended to infect your computer system so that it can replicate and redistribute copies of itself.

Virus Writer

A criminal or hacker who writes viruses almost exclusively.

VoIP

Voice over Internet Protocol. A means of routing telephone calls or voice communications over the Internet. VoIP makes it possible for people to have low-cost telephone conversations using a broadband connection.

Vulnerability

A classification based on the amount of risk that you face and how easily it can be mitigated.

War Driving

A practice where hackers or other criminals cruise around neighborhoods with high-powered computer equipment in their cars looking for unprotected wireless networks. Once the network is found, the criminal parks on the street, gains access to the network, and then uses the network resources for malicious or criminal activities. War driving is related to war dialing, an older version of the same scam in which hackers or criminals used computer programs to dial random telephone numbers until they found a number that allowed them to access the Internet.

Worm

These bugs are similar in nature to viruses and Trojans, but worms have the ability to move from one computer to another without any human intervention at all. And because worms can replicate themselves on your computer, there could be thousands of them traveling out from your system to infect other systems—all without your knowledge.

Zombie

A zombie is a computer that has been taken over by a criminal or hacker for use in malicious or illegal tasks. Zombies can be linked to create a network of zombies that encompasses hundreds or thousands of computers.

Appendix B

Cybersecurity Worksheets

Keeping up with the various elements of cybersecurity can be tough, especially in today's never-slow-down world. And all of the elements of cybersecurity take time to accomplish. In this appendix, you'll find worksheets and checklists that will help you get protected and stay that way. Use these worksheets the first time to make sure that you're protected from all sides; then use them each time you update your security and protection technologies to ensure that you don't miss anything.

Windows Security Checklist

Security Issue	Complete	Needs Attention	Action Taken	Date to Review	Notes
Password Protect Administrator's Profile					
Create Dummy Administrator's Profile					
Set Up Profiles for General Use					
User Profiles Password Protected					
Remove Guest Profile					
Windows Currently Up-to-Date					
Automatic Updates Configured					
Configured Windows Security Settings					
ActiveX Controls Disabled					
Java Controls Disabled					
Remote Desktop Disabled (if applicable)					

Virus Protection Checklist

Protection Issue	Complete	Needs Attention	Action Taken	Date to Review	Notes
Antivirus Installed					
Antivirus Active					
Antivirus Currently Updated					
Automatic Updates Configured					
All Files Scanned (Currently)					
All Files Scanned (Automatically)					
Automatic Scans Enabled					
Virus Program Configured to Remove Viruses When Found					
Audible Alert When Viruses Found					
Limit User Response to Viruses When Detected					
Enable Macro Virus Protection					
Enable Real-Time Scanning					
Enable Incoming and Outgoing Mail Scans					
Practice Safe E-mail Handling					
Block Automatic Downloading of Message Attachments in E-mail					
Educate All Users about Virus Dangers					
E-mail Program Configured Properly					
Preview Pane is Disabled (where applicable)					
Understand Threat from Viruses					
Recognize Virus-type Extensions					
Do Not Click Through Links in E-mail					

Internet and Web Browser Safety Checklist

Protection Issue	Complete	Needs Attention	Action Taken	Date to Review	Notes
Update Web Browser					
Install Firewall					
Firewall Active					
Configure Firewall for Better Protection					
Configure Web Browser for Higher Security					
Test Web Browser's Security					
Install Pop-up Blocker					
Pop-up Blocker Active					
Configure Pop-up Blocker for Better Protection					
Only Make Purchases Through Trusted Sites					
Anti-Spyware Program Installed					
Anti-Spyware Program Active					
Configure Anti-Spyware for Better Protection					
Understand and Use Safe Surfing Practices					
Educate Other Users of Safe Surfing Practices					
Regularly Review Safety and Security Settings					
Regularly Update Firewall					
Regularly Update Browser					
Regularly Update Anti-Spyware					
Automatic Updates Configured for Anti-Spyware					
Regularly Update Pop-up Blocker					

Protection Issue	Complete	Needs Attention	Action Taken	Date to Review	Notes
Automatic Update Configured for Pop-up Blocker					
Firewall Prompts Before Allowing Suspicious Activity					
Understand Security Threats When Online					

Identity Theft Checklist

Protection Issue	Complete	Needs Attention	Action Taken	Date to Review	Notes
Understand the Threats That Lead to Identity Theft					
Understand Safe E-mail and Surfing Practices					
Use Safe E-mail and Surfing Practices					
Have List of All Credit Cards and Bank Accounts					
Monitor Personal Financial Accounts					
Regularly Check Credit Report					
Avoid Downloading Unknown Attachments					
Preview Pane Disabled in Mail Program					
Have Contact List in Event of an Incident					
Keep Records of all Credit Card Transactions					
Protect Personal and Confidential Information					
Recognize Phishing Attack					
Understand How Security Lock and HTTPS Work					
Use Protection Technology to Enhance Safety					
Don't Provide Personal or Confidential Information in E-mail					
Don't Click Through E-mail Links					

Protection Issue	Complete	Needs Attention	Action Taken	Date to Review	Notes
Don't Download Unexpected E-mail Attachments					
Have Properly Configured, Active Antivirus					
Have Properly Configured, Active Firewall					
Have Properly Configured, Active Anti-Spyware					
All Users Understand Identity Theft Threat					

Investment and Credit Card Fraud Protection Checklist

Protection Method/Activity	Yes	No	Action Taken	Notes
You understand how investment fraud occurs.				
You understand how credit card fraud occurs.				
You understand securities laws.				
You understand risks when investing.				
You always research your investments before making them.				
You always make your investments through a trusted broker.				
You check the background of new investment brokers.				
You do not make investments based on emotional response.				
You make investments based on solid research.				
You make investments based on recommendations.				
You read disclosure documents about investments.				
You use traceable methods of payment when purchasing investments.				
You regularly review your credit card statements.				
You have copies of the front and back of your credit cards.				
You never respond to e-mails that claim to be from your credit card issuer.				
You always call the number listed on your card or statement for information.				
You immediately request a review of unauthorized charges.				
You only carry the necessary credit cards on your person.				
You use only specific credit cards for shopping online.				
You always print receipts from online transactions.				
You know who to call if you suspect you have been victimized.				
You keep careful records in case of fraudulent transactions.				
You're always skeptical.				

Avoiding Auction Fraud

Checkbox	Action Item	Notes
☐	You only participate in auctions on reputable auction Web sites.	
☐	You review seller feedback before bidding on an item.	
☐	You are skeptical about auction claims.	
☐	You do not participate in transactions outside the protection of the auction site.	
☐	You are familiar with the auction site's security policies.	
☐	You use a reputable escrow service for transactions over $100.	
☐	You monitor auctions closely to ensure they are operated properly.	
☐	You verify the seller through the auction site.	
☐	You use verified payment services to complete auction transactions.	
☐	You only make purchases from verified sellers.	
☐	You maintain your responsibilities during an auction transaction.	
☐	You know who to report disputes to at the auction site.	
☐	You know who to report disputes to at the payment site.	
☐	You know who to report disputes to at the escrow site.	
☐	You do not use your checking account as a method of payment.	
☐	You use a payment service instead of paying sellers directly.	

Spyware Removal Checklist

Checkbox	Action Item	Notes
☐	You understand the dangers of spyware.	
☐	You understand how spyware is installed on your computer.	
☐	You understand where spyware originates.	
☐	You have anti-spyware protection installed.	
☐	You understand the effect that spyware has on your computer's performance.	
☐	You understand how to scan your computer for spyware with the protection technology.	
☐	You understand how to use your protection technology to remove spyware.	
☐	You understand that one anti-spyware program alone won't protect your computer.	
☐	You use spyware protection from a reputable company.	
☐	You keep your spyware protection up-to-date.	
☐	You keep your spyware protection turned on and active.	
☐	You set up automatic updates for your spyware protection.	
☐	You set up automatic spyware scans for your computer.	
☐	You educate other users about the dangers of spyware.	

E-mail Security Checklist

Checkbox	Action Item	Notes
☐	You use an e-mail program instead of Web mail.	
☐	Your e-mail program is up-to-date.	
☐	You have increased the security settings on your e-mail account.	
☐	You understand safe e-mail practices.	
☐	You use safe e-mail practices all the time.	
☐	You have an antivirus program installed on your computer.	
☐	Your antivirus program is active.	
☐	You have a firewall installed on your computer.	
☐	Your firewall is active.	
☐	You have at least one anti-spyware program installed on your computer.	
☐	Your anti-spyware is active.	
☐	Your have real-time scanning activated for your e-mail.	
☐	You use all available technologies to protect yourself from e-mail borne viruses and malware.	
☐	You have the preview pane turned off on your e-mail program.	
☐	You keep your Web browser up-to-date.	
☐	You have changed to a Web browser that is not Windows-based.	
☐	You keep other users informed of safe e-mail practices.	
☐	All users understand how to operate your installed protection technologies.	

Appendix C

Cybersecurity Resources

The following pages represent a few of the different online resources in more than a dozen categories. However, all you need to do to find even more resources is a quick search on Google or your favorite search engine. Using a combination of the words "security," "personal," "virus," "phishing," "Trojan," or any of the other security-centric terms covered in this book, you'll find more resources that you'll know what to do with.

General Cybersecurity

CyberSecurity Institute
http://www.cybersecurityinstitute.biz/

Cyber Security Industry Alliance
https://www.csialliance.org/home

Microsoft's Protect Your PC
http://www.microsoft.com/athome/security/protect/windowsxpsp2/Default.mspx

Consumer Sentinel
http://www.consumer.gov/sentinel/

Crime Library
http://www.crimelibrary.com/

FirstGov for Consumers
http://www.consumer.gov/

Victim's Assistance of America
http://www.victimsassistanceofamerica.org/

FTC's Consumer Site
http://www.ftc.gov/ftc/consumer.htm

Mozilla's FireFox Browser
http://www.mozilla.com

DLL Help Database
http://channels.lockergnome.com/it/archives/20041226_dll_help_database.phtml

Browser Security Test
http://bcheck.scanit.be/bcheck/

Browser Security Tests
http://www.jasons-toolbox.com/BrowserSecurity/

PopupTest
http://www.popuptest.com/

Popup Blocker Test
http://www.popupcheck.com/

STOPzilla
https://www.stopzilla.com/

Mozilla Popup Tester
http://www.gozer.org/mozilla/popup_tester/

The Cleaner!
http://www.moosoft.com/

StaySafeOnline
http://www.staysafeonline.info

ITSecurity
http://www.itsecurity.com

Cybercrime.gov
http://www.cybercrime.gov

National White Collar Crime Center
http://www.nw3c.org/

National Crime Prevention Council
http://www.ncpc.org/

Hideaway.net
http://www.hideaway.net/home/public_html/index.php

Computer Emergency Response Team
http://www.cert.org

Computer Security Institute
http://www.gocsi.com/

Internet Security Systems
http://www.iss.net

IP Protocols Logger
http://pltplp.net/ippl/

Verified Security
http://www.verifiedsecurity.com/home/

GetNetWise
http://www.getnetwise.org/

WiredSafety
http://www.wiredsafety.org/

Microsoft's Security360
http://www.microsoft.com/events/series/mikenash.mspx

Cyberstalking and Cyber Harassment

Stalking Resource Center
http://www.ncvc.org/src/main.aspx?dbID=dash_Home

The Anti-Stalking Web Site
http://www.antistalking.com/resource.htm

WHO@
http://www.haltabuse.org/

Stalking Resource Center
http://www.ncvc.org

Phishing

MailDefense
http://www.networkingfiles.com/AntiVirus/maildefense_3.0.html

Anti-Phishing Working Group
http://www.antiphishing.org/

Spam

SpamFighter
http://www.techspot.com/downloads/203-spamfighter-standard.html

SpamCop.net
http://www.spamcop.net/

SpamPal
http://www.spampal.org/usermanual/antivirus/pccillin/pccillin.htm

SpywareBlaster
http://www.javacoolsoftware.com/spywareblaster.html

SpyChecker
http://www.webmasterfree.com/spychecker.html

HijackThis
http://www.tomcoyote.org/hjt/

Spyware Beware!
http://maddoktor2.com/index.php

SpamBayes
http://spambayes.sourceforge.net/

Spamihilator
http://www.spamihilator.com/

Scams

Snopes.com
http://www.snopes.com/

Vmyths.com
http://www.vmyths.com/

Identity Theft

Federal Trade Commission's ID Theft Center
http://www.consumer.gov/idtheft/

Fraud

US Securities and Exchange Commission
http://www.sec.gov

State Securities Regulators
http://www.sec.gov/answers/statereg.htm

North American Securities Administrators Association
http://www.nasaa.org

Federal Trade Commission
http://www.ftc.gov

BrokerCheck
http://www.nasd.com

SEC's Edgar Database
http://www.sec.gov/edgar.shtml

National Futures Association
http://www.nfa.futures.org/

National Fraud Information Center
http://www.fraud.org

International Organization of Securities Commissions
http://www.iosco.org/

Internet Fraud Complaint Center
http://www.ifccfbi.gov/index.asp

AuctionBlackList
http://www.auctionblacklist.com/

Antivirus Software and Other Malware Protection

Microsoft's Malicious Software Removal Tool
http://www.microsoft.com/security/malwareremove/default.mspx

McAfee AntiVirus
http://www.mcafee.com

Norton AntiVirus
http://www.Symantec.com

AVG Anti-virus
http://www.grisoft.com

F-Secure
http://www.f-secure.com

TrendMicro's PC-Cillin
http://www.trendmicro.com/en/home/global/personal.htm

Avast Antivirus
http://www.avast.com/index.html

EZ Trust Antivirus
http://home.ca.com/dr/v2/ec_MAIN.Entry17c?
SP=10007&PN=21&CID=198395&SID=35715&PID=1302599

Panda Antivirus
http://www.pandasoftware.com

Spyware Protection
Cyber Rights and Cyber Liberties
http://www.cyber-rights.org/

Privacy Rights Clearing House
http://www.privacyrights.org/

Spyware Warrior
http://www.spywarewarrior.com/

SpywareInfo
http://www.spywareinfo.com/

Anti-Spy Shop
http://www.anti-keylogger.com/

Computer Associated Spyware Information Center
http://www3.ca.com/securityadvisor/pest/

LavaSoft (Adaware)
http://www.lavasoft.com

Spybot Search & Destroy
http://www.safer-networking.org/en/download/

Trend Micro Anti-Spyware
http://www.trendmicro.com

SpySweeper
http://www.webroot.com

Spyware Encyclopedia
http://research.pestpatrol.com/

WinPatrol
http://www.winpatrol.com

Sysinternal's Rootkit Revealer
http://www.sysinternals.com/Utilities/RootkitRevealer.html

Microsoft's AntiSpyware Beta
http://www.microsoft.com/athome/security/spyware/software/default.mspx

Bazooka Adware & Spyware Scanner
http://www.download.com/Bazooka-Adware-and-Spyware-Scanner/
3000-8022-10247782.html

CWShredder
http://www.intermute.com/spysubtract/cwshredder_download.html

ToolbarCop
http://www.softpedia.com/progDownload/Toolbarcop-Download-8846.html

Firewall Protection

BlackIce PC Protection
http://www.digitalriver.com/dr/v2/ec_dynamic.main?SP=1&PN=10&sid=26412

ZoneLabs
http://www.zonelabs.com/store/content/home.jsp

Security Now!
https://www.grc.com/x/ne.dll?bh0bkyd2

PC Flank
http://www.pcflank.com/

Sygate Online Services
http://scan.sygatetech.com/

Jetico Personal Firewall
http://www.jetico.com/

Kerio Personal Firewall
http://www.kerio.com

Outpost Firewall Pro
http://www.agnitum.com/products/outpost/

Sygate Personal Firewall
http://smb.sygate.com/products/spf_standard.htm

PC Security Shield
http://www.pcsecurityshield.com/

Openwall Project
http://pltplp.net/ippl/

Updates and Patches

Microsoft Windows Update
http://www.update.microsoft.com

Microsoft Office Update
http://office.microsoft.com/en-us/officeupdate/default.aspx

Miscellaneous Links

Equifax Personal Solutions
http://www.equifax.com/

Experian
http://www.experian.com/

TransUnion
http://www.transunion.com/index.jsp

Answers That Work
http://www.answersthatwork.com/

AnnualCreditReport.com
https://www.annualcreditreport.com/cra/index.jsp

Better Business Bureau
http://www.bbb.org

Appendix D }

Quick Reference Guide

Even if you know personal security inside and out, there are likely to be times when you just don't remember everything that you should. This is especially true if you're in a hurry of if you've been victimized and you're scrambling to re-establish your protection strategies and technologies. The following list is meant to give you, at a glance, what you need to ensure that you're as protected as you can be. It's by no means all-inclusive; however, it should give you a good starting point and help to jog your memory about points that you might be missing.

The list is broken down by protection topic so that you can breeze through only the sections that you need, when you need them.

Cyberstalking and Cyber Harassment

* Use gender neutral and age neutral usernames and e-mail addresses.

* Avoid giving out your personal information for forum and e-mail registrations.

* Check your Internet Service Provider's (ISP's) policies about harassment, cyberstalking, and other abusive behavior to be sure that you have recourse if someone starts exhibiting abusive behaviors.

* Use caution with e-mail signatures. Use signatures for business communications, but turn them off when you're posting to online forums or answering e-mails that aren't business related.

❊ Request that your name be removed from information aggregators or location services such as 411.com, Switchboard.com, and WhoWhere.com.

❊ Use automated filtering programs, such as those included in Microsoft Outlook and Outlook Express, to block unwanted messages or messages from unknown sources.

❊ Begin collecting the communications from the person who is harassing or stalking you. If the communications are e-mails, print them off and keep them all together in a file. If they are instant messages, log and print them. For text messages, save the messages to your phone. These records are important should it ever become necessary for you to turn to law enforcement agencies.

❊ Avoid contact with the stalker or harasser. If you must, and you know who the abuser is, send a single, clear request to the stalker or harasser to cease all communications in all forms. Once that message is sent, resist the urge to respond to any messages in the future, no matter how much you might want to state your own thoughts and feelings on the matter.

❊ Report the abuse to your ISP as soon as it begins. If the ISP can't or won't do anything to help, continue reporting the abuse at regular intervals, and keep copies of all the requests that you send.

❊ Contact the police and file a report. When you contact the police, be very clear in your explanation of what's happening and be sure to let the officer taking the report know that you have supporting evidence of what's happening to you. However, don't be surprised if you don't get a lot of cooperation from your local law enforcement agencies. Most don't have the personnel or expertise to put much time or effort into cybercrimes that don't involve monetary losses.

❊ Visit SpamCop (http://www.spamcop.net) to have the e-mails that are sent from the criminal analyzed and to have the criminal's ISP contacted about the unwanted messages. SpamCop requires a free registration, but the reporting service is also free.

❊ Report the cyberstalking or cyber harassment through the WiredSafety Web site (https://www.wiredsafety.org/forms/stalking.html). You must first report the abuse to local law enforcement agencies and then on the WiredSafety Web site. Once you report it, site volunteers will work to help you resolve the issue.

Spoofing, Phishing, and Other E-mail Scams

❊ Be skeptical of all incoming e-mail, but especially those e-mails that come from a person or company with which you're not familiar.

❊ Avoid click-through links that lead you to a Web site. Instead, type the URL for the main Web page directly into your browser's address bar.

❋ Don't fill out e-mail forms. E-mail forms that are controlled by a hacker or criminal could be harmful, and any information that you include in the form could be put at risk. Don't use e-mail forms unless you have no other choice.

❋ Check e-mail headers to ensure that the e-mail is arriving from the person who claims to be sending it, not from someone pretending to be that person or company.

❋ Check the security of any Web site that you're using, especially if you're using Web mail. A secure site usually has a small padlock icon in the bottom-right corner and https at the beginning of the URL.

❋ Disable JavaScript.

❋ Disable ActiveX controls.

❋ Report suspicious e-mail to the correct authorities.

Identity Theft

❋ Identity thieves don't care how they get your information, so they'll try anything once. From simple schemes to sophisticated schemes, if the reward is financial or personal information, an identity thief will try it. So, one of the best ways to protect yourself from identity theft is to view everything online with an extreme dose of skepticism, and when in doubt, double-check everything. For example, if you receive an e-mail that seems to be from your bank asking you to provide account information, call the bank and ask if they would send that type of communication, or why they need your information. If the e-mail was legitimate, your local branch will be able to verify it.

❋ Never download attached files from people you don't know. Attached files can be viruses, Trojans, keyloggers, or other types of malicious software. And they don't just come from strangers. Use caution when downloading any file, even from people you know. If you aren't expecting a file, don't open it until you verify that it really was meant for you and that it doesn't contain anything harmful.

❋ If an e-mail includes a link and instructions to click through the link, don't. Instead, type the main URL of the company that the e-mail was supposed to come from into the address bar on your Internet browser. Once you get to the Web site, sign into your account as you always would, and if there are issues of which you should be aware, there will probably be information about it on the Web site. If you don't find the answers you're looking for, you can always call the company directly.

❋ It seems to go without saying, but never post your username and password in a place where someone snooping around can find it. One of the biggest security risks on the Internet is someone else accessing your account. In today's busy world, keeping up with your username and password is the last thing you want to worry about. But writing your username and password down where other people can find them puts you unnecessarily at risk.

❊ Another username and password issue to avoid is using the same one for all of the services that you access online. Never use a single username or password for all of your Internet services. Instead, vary your username and passwords, and if possible, never use the same one twice. By varying these, you prevent a thief from having access to more than one of your accounts.

❊ Don't use passwords that are easy to figure out. It sounds like an old song and dance, but the truth is, the majority of people use a password that any experienced hacker could figure out in a matter of minutes. For example, do you use your anniversary or your spouse's birthdate as a password? Maybe it's a combination of your children's birthdates. The most effective and safest passwords are made up of random numbers and letters that have no meaning to you at all.

❊ Request that your name, address, e-mail address, and telephone number remain private when doing business with online merchants and service providers. Most merchants now give you the option to opt out of communications from their partners or affiliates. Opt out of those communications so that your personal information will not be shared with other merchants. Also, have your information removed from online directory services such as 411.com and Switchboard.com.

❊ Review the privacy policy of your ISP and any merchants with whom you do business. This document is long and boring, but it gives you information about how your personal information is handled. It also lets you know what recourses you have in the event that you think your privacy has been violated.

Credit Card Fraud

❊ One of the easiest ways to protect yourself from credit card fraud when shopping online is to have a single, low-balance account that you use only for shopping online. This account should be used only for online shopping and it should have a credit limit that's not over $500. A similar strategy is to have a pre-paid credit card that you use for shopping online. Pre-paid MasterCards and Visas work just like credit cards, but you add money to the card before you can make a purchase with it. The downfall with this type of card is that you have limited purchasing power. However, in the event that you fall victim to credit card fraud, a pre-paid card is an excellent way to limit your risk.

❊ Save every receipt and invoice for every credit card transaction in any given month and compare those receipts to the charges that appear on your monthly statement. If you find a charge to your account that you didn't authorize, immediately contact your credit card issuer to dispute the charge.

❋ Set up Internet billing and account access. One of the easiest ways for a thief to steal your credit card account is to take your bill out of the mailbox or to find a statement in the trash. Electronic account access, statements, and payment methods reduce your risk of credit card fraud as long as you keep your account number, username, and password safe.

❋ Immediately notify your credit card issuer if your bill doesn't arrive on time or if you expect to change your address in the near future. If your bill doesn't arrive on time, contacting the credit card issuer will help to ensure that there have been no changes to your account billing address. If you're changing your address, contact the company as soon as you know what your new address is to ensure that a credit card bill isn't left in the mailbox for the next people to move into the house or apartment that you're leaving behind.

❋ Never provide your credit card account number, username, or password to anyone via e-mail. If you receive an e-mail that requests you fill out a form with personal information and send it back, don't. If you're making a purchase online with a merchant who doesn't have a payment system set up online, don't send your credit card number to them through e-mail. Instead, opt to call the company directly and provide your credit card number that way.

❋ Mistrust any e-mail communication that you receive that states your account is in danger of being frozen or that tells you the credit card issuer suspects fraud and wants you to verify your account number, username, and password. Most companies will not contact you via e-mail for account verification. If you receive an e-mail from the company that you aren't sure is legitimate, either call the number listed on the back of your credit card or log on to the company's Web site by opening a new browser window and typing the direct Web address of the company into the address bar.

❋ Never enter your credit card information on a Web site that you aren't sure is secure. Secure Web sites usually have a small padlock icon in the bottom-right corner of the Web browser. The URL in the address bar may also have the prefix https, which means that the site was designed using a programming language specifically designed to promote Web security.

Investment Fraud

❋ Do your research. Don't invest in anything that you haven't taken the time to check out. For example, is the investment that you're considering audited by one of the large international accounting firms? Fraud investments are usually not audited at all, and if they are, they are audited by a small financial firm that might as well be the CPA down the street. It's someone you've never heard of, and often a criminal that's in on the fraud. Another sign to look for is whether or not the investment is registered with your state securities commission or the SEC. If it is not, the investment is a fraud, because investments must be registered with these agencies, even offshore investments. If an investment claims to be exempt from the required registration, take your money elsewhere, because it's a scam.

* Take your time investing. Many fraudulent investment schemes push investors to make snap decisions or to invest their money quickly without taking the time to check out the investment. They play on your emotions and try to cloud your judgment. Avoid any investment where you're pressured to make a fast decision. Legitimate investments and legitimate investment advisers won't push you to make a decision before you are ready.

* Know who you're dealing with. Even a flashy, well-designed Web site doesn't mean you're dealing with a legitimate investment company or adviser. Research the people you plan to invest with and in. It takes very little to create an eye-catching Web site and even less time to take it down once the criminal has your money. Refer back to rule number one: Always do your research *before* you make any investment.

* Be skeptical. It's an often-heard warning, but that's because it is so very valid. Be skeptical about any investment opportunity that comes to you through e-mail, especially if it's spam. Be skeptical of investments that promise guaranteed returns. Real investments can't guarantee a return. They may have a good chance of making a return, but they can't be guaranteed. Be skeptical of offshore investment opportunities. There are some valid investment opportunities in offshore companies, but those investment opportunities are regulated just like any other investment opportunity. If an investment scheme promises you that it's tax-free because it's an offshore investment or makes similar claims based on the fact that it's an offshore investment, don't risk your money.

* Understand what you're investing in. Take some time to learn about investing in general before you start looking at specific investments. If you don't know the difference between stocks and bonds or options and futures, you'll make an easy target for a criminal. Learn about the market before you even begin to look at investments.

* Get any and all investment details in writing. If you can't get the details about your investment in writing, before you make the investment, then don't! Getting the details in writing is a way to protect yourself. It's also a way to slow down the investment process so that you aren't taken by some scammer. And if they refuse to send you the details in writing, or if they push you to make the investment without the details, then you should walk away from the investment, no matter how good it seems.

Auction Fraud

❋ Pay by credit card. Federal law gives you some protection from fraudulent transactions. If you use your credit card to pay for an item that you win at auction and the item never arrives, you can report the fraudulent transaction to your credit card company. Many credit card companies have protection policies that allow you to get some, if not all, of your money back. Then the credit card company will pursue the fraudster through legal channels. If you pay by check or money order and don't receive the item, chances are your money is just lost.

❋ Check the feedback rating of anyone you do business with. This includes taking time to read through some of the feedback that other people have left. Usually, feedback ratings have space for some description of the transaction as well as a visual rating system (like a defined number of stars to represent how well you thought the transaction went). As you're looking at feedback, look too at how long the person has been active in the auction community. The newer the seller or buyer, the higher your chances of becoming a victim of auction fraud.

❋ Check auction listings for insurance and additional protections. Depending on what auction site you use and what payment method you use, sometimes your purchases are protected by insurance that those companies have in place. In other cases, you can pay a small fee to add insurance to your account to protect yourself in the event that a fraudster tries to take advantage of you. Be sure to read the fine print on the insurance, however. Most insurance policies have certain requirements that must be met before you can be reimbursed for losses.

❋ Never agree to participate in a transaction away from the protections of the auction Web site on which you choose to do business. Once you take a transaction to a private party, then you lose all of the protections that the auction site has put into place. In essence, you're taking your safety and the security of your transaction into your own hands. Not every private transaction is fraudulent, but why risk it when you can conduct business in a manner that ensures you're protected?

❋ Beware of auctions that seem too good to be true. If an item seems to be priced far below its actual value, or if the seller makes claims that seem unrealistic, avoid the auction. Your instincts will usually tell you when something sounds too good to be true. Listen to that instinct. In most cases, if it seems too good to be true, it is.

❋ Avoid making purchases on "second chance" offerings. In many cases, second chance offerings come to you because the seller or a friend of the seller has artificially inflated the price of the auction. When the auction ends, the seller will go back to the next highest bidder and offer the item to them at their highest bid. Choose a high price, a final bid that's your absolute best offer, and stick to it. Don't be goaded into bidding higher.

Viruses, Trojans, and Worms

❋ Your first step toward being protected is to ensure that all of your applications, including your browser and operating system, are currently updated and that all of the patches that have been issued for those programs have been installed. The greatest risk to your computer is through vulnerabilities in the software that operates the computer. Unfortunately, patches and updates can be a pain to download and install, and very often they're the last thing you think about when doing routine maintenance on your computer. However, a flaw found in an operating system or application is an immediate risk. Take the time to download and install all updates and patches. And if you're one of those people who's just too busy to think about it, consider enabling the automatic update function on your computer. Most computers and operating systems have this function.

❋ Never, ever open an attachment that arrives from someone you don't know. And it's even better if you only open attachments that you're expecting from the people that you do know. Too often, a virus is passed from friend to friend, because the assumption is that a file that comes from a friend is safe. If the friend doesn't know he is infected with a virus, however, the file might not be safe, and you take a risk when opening anything that comes from him. If you have a personal policy not to open anything that you aren't expecting, then you greatly reduce your chances of being infected with a piece of malicious software.

❋ If your e-mail program automatically downloads messages, change the setting so that it won't. It's inconvenient, but if you regulate the mail that is downloaded from your mail server, then you regulate your risk of infection. The same is true if your e-mail program has a preview pane that shows you a portion of the message without opening it. Often, this snippet of a preview is enough to activate the download and installation of the malicious code contained in the message. If you have a preview option in your e-mail program, especially if you're not using Web-based e-mail, change that setting so that you don't see a preview of the message.

❋ Use a firewall. There are many great firewalls available on the Internet for free, and some firewall is better than none at all. Of course, if you purchase the full version of one of the software firewalls that you can download online, you'll get better protection. There's more information about firewalls and what's available on the Web in Chapter 13.

❋ Install and subscribe to a good antivirus software program. It's not enough to install an antivirus and forget about it. You also need to have a subscription to the antivirus provider's virus definition service. New viruses appear on the Internet every day, making it necessary for the software to be updated every day. Without those updates, you may not be protected from some of the most recently released viruses. Get a good antivirus program (you learned what constitutes good in Chapter 14), and then make sure that you keep that program up-to-date, all the time.

Spyware

✳ Be sure all of your software is up-to-date. Spyware may exploit vulnerabilities in your operating system and other programs, so one of the best ways to protect yourself from spyware (and other threats) is to stay updated and patched. Use your operating system's automatic updates if necessary to stay current.

✳ Use the right protection technologies. Antivirus programs and firewalls are essential to protecting yourself from spyware. Although it's not technically a virus, some antivirus programs have anti-spyware capabilities, and firewalls will protect you from unwanted intruders that spyware might let into your system. Anti-spyware applications are also a requirement for protecting yourself. Find a good anti-spyware program and use it to scan your computer for spyware regularly. Once a month is good; once a week is better.

✳ Make sure your Web browser's security settings are adjusted to the right level to protect you. If you're using Microsoft's Internet Explorer, you can set your security settings to allow only the information that you want to accept. You can view your current Internet Explorer settings by going to the Tools menu in Internet Explorer and clicking on Internet Options. A dialog box appears. Select the Security tab, and your security settings will appear. From that window you can change them as you like.

✳ Use safe practices when surfing the Web and downloading programs. Most of those safe practices are ones that you've probably heard a dozen times: Don't download files from people you don't know or Web sites you don't trust; be wary of free programs; don't click Okay or Agree to close out of pop-up windows; and be sure to read all the documentation that comes with software *before* you download and install the software. It's also wise if you remind other computer users in your home of these basics frequently.

Index

❋ ❋ ❋